Educated REIT Investing

The Ultimate Guide to Understanding and Investing in Real Estate Investment Trusts

Educated REIT Investing

The Ultimate Guide to Understanding and Investing in Real Estate Investment Trusts

Stephanie Krewson-Kelly

Glenn R. Mueller, Ph.D.

WILEY

Published by John Wiley & Sons, Inc., Hoboken, New Jersey.
Published simultaneously in Canada.

Library of Congress Cataloging-in-Publication Data:

Names: Krewson-Kelly, Stephanie, author. | Mueller, Glenn R., author.
Title: Educated REIT investing : the ultimate guide to understanding and investing in real estate investment trusts / Stephanie Krewson-Kelly, Glenn R. Mueller, Ph.D.
Description: Hoboken, New Jersey : John Wiley & Sons, Inc., [2021] | Includes index.
Identifiers: LCCN 2020025486 (print) | LCCN 2020025487 (ebook) | ISBN 9781119708698 (cloth) | ISBN 9781119709046 (adobe pdf) | ISBN 9781119708711 (epub)
Subjects: LCSH: Real estate investment trusts. | Investments.
Classification: LCC HG5095 .K7378 2021 (print) | LCC HG5095 (ebook) |
DDC 332.63/247—dc23
LC record available at https://lccn.loc.gov/2020025486
LC ebook record available at https://lccn.loc.gov/2020025487

Cover Design: Wiley
Cover Images: 3d building © jl661227/Shutterstock, cycle chart curve graphic courtesy of Glenn Mueller

Printed in the United States of America

SKY10090299_110724

To my son, William, and my husband, Matthew. Thank you for indulging my passion for "The Three R's": reading, writing, and REITs!

To Jan for loving and living with your type A husband these last 44 years.

Contents

Foreword

Steven A. Wechsler
Nareit President & CEO

REITs were established by Congress in 1960 to make commercial real estate investment – once available only to the wealthy and large institutions – accessible to all investors. Today, more than 87 million Americans invest in REITs through their 401(k) or other retirement funds.

Even though REITs have grown to become an essential part of the investment universe with an equity market capitalization of approximately $1 trillion, there is room for greater understanding of all that REITs have to offer. Enter *Educated REIT Investing,* which makes the REIT approach to real estate investment easily understandable to investors of all sizes and experience levels.

Stephanie Krewson-Kelly, Glenn Mueller, and their contributors have written a book that delivers a comprehensive window into REIT investment, sharing their insights on everything from how REITs are formed to the fundamentals of REIT stock analysis.

Educated REIT Investing explains the benefits of investing in REITs, including the important roles REIT stocks can play in addressing volatility and boosting the performance of investment portfolios. Importantly, the book also introduces readers to the broad spectrum of REIT market segments, explains their business models, and sheds light on their performance in various market conditions.

I have known Stephanie and Glenn for many years, and they are both well equipped to make the case for REITs and REIT investment. Stephanie brings her experience heading investor relations at Corporate Office Properties Trust, a major NYSE-traded office REIT, coupled with her earlier roles as a well-regarded investment banker and REIT analyst.

Glenn is a longstanding member of Nareit's Real Estate Investment Advisory Council who has more than 40 years of real estate industry experience. He is internationally recognized for his Real Estate Market Cycle research and REIT research, his public and private market investment strategies, and his capital markets analysis.

I recommend this book to anyone looking to better understand REITs and real estate investment. Investors new to REITs can read it in its entirety and come away with a comprehensive introduction to REITs, while more experienced investors can also dive into the book for greater understanding of specific topics.

Preface

Many investors are unfamiliar with equity REITs – the world's largest real estate companies that own income producing properties, such as office, industrial warehouse, retail, apartment or hotel buildings – or with mortgage REITs, which invest in real estate-based (mortgage) loans.

The legislation that created the REIT structure was enacted by the US Congress in 1960 to allow small investors access to large multi-million-dollar and now even billion-dollar properties. In 2016, Standard & Poor's Dow Jones Indices (S&P) and MSCI Inc. (MSCI) created a new Global Industry Classification Standard (GICS) sector called *Real Estate*. Historically, REITs were classified in the Financials sector, but S&P and MSCI determined that real estate should be regarded as a distinct asset class – one that is different from banks and financial institutions. (Note mortgage REITs remained in S&P's *Financials* sector.) The Real Estate GICS sector elevated investor awareness of REITs, broadening their appeal to individuals and institutions.

Educated REIT Investing provides the essential information about REITs in an easy-to-understand format, using graphs, illustrations, and examples to make complex or unique concepts comprehensible. Even novice investors can gain a thorough understanding of the REIT market by reading the relevant industry background and simple examples presented in these pages. Part I, An Introduction to REITs, presents basic information that will help investors quickly gain an understanding of what REITs are in order to have more informed conversations with their financial advisors. Part II, Investing in REITs, is more technical in nature, with content geared for individuals who want to analyze and evaluate specific REITs before investing in them. The content in *Educated REIT Investing* is distinctly different from other REIT books – and may still be read cover-to-cover in a day.

Here are a few industry background facts to get started:

- The REIT industry's aggregate equity market capitalization has increased exponentially from a mere $8.7 billion at the beginning of 1990 to $1.3 trillion at the end of 2019 (see Table 1.1).

- Innovations to the REIT structure that eliminated conflicts of interest between management and shareholders helped fuel the industry's growth. Equity REITs were added into the S&P 500 Index in 2001. Since then, REIT shares have attracted an increasingly broader array of investors, including general money managers, pension funds, hedge funds, and individual investors. As a result, the average monthly dollar trading volume for REITs increased from approximately $350 million in 2000 to roughly $8 billion in 2019, providing good liquidity for all investors.
- Along with higher trading volume, REIT stock price volatility also has increased dramatically. While the stock market is emotional in the short run, it is normally logical in the long run. Thus, greater volatility creates greater risk short term, but also greater potential returns long term. Applying good fundamental analysis is very valuable and should be rewarded.
- Despite REITs' historical long-term outperformance over other stocks, most investor portfolios are underallocated to real estate securities. Institutional Investor Allocations to real estate range from 5% to 20% with an average close to 10% – even though the Real Estate asset class is 20% of their investible universe. Also know that home ownership is *not* income producing real estate; people live *in* their homes but must retire and live *on* their investments.

With REITs now in their 60th year and having grown rapidly over the past 30 years, it is surprising that basic information about REITs is not easy to find. Nareit® is a Washington, DC-based organization that represents and advocates for REITs globally. They provide a wealth of information on their website (www.reit.com) that is free, including the ability to receive daily emails and industry event information. They also show quarterly performance information with the Nareit T-Tracker, https://www.reit.com/data-research/reit-market-data/nareit-t-tracker-quarterly-operating-performance-series.

However, if investors don't know about Nareit and its online resources, information on individual REITs and the industry is difficult to obtain. If investors consult their financial advisors, they will still have incomplete information, as each brokerage firm typically has access only to information about the REITs actively covered by their research department. To remedy this information gap, the appendices of this book list the 219 REITs that comprise the FTSE Nareit All REITs Index at the end of 2019, as well as some basic information about each company. The following chapters present information in a progressive manner. Read as much or as little as you require, and welcome to the world of REITs.

Note: Unless noted otherwise, all prices, total returns, and data used in this book are as of December 31, 2019.

Acknowledgments

The following chapters reflect the experience and technical expertise of dozens of REIT industry professionals, whose contributions make this book a unique and invaluable resource for understanding and investing in real estate investment trusts.

Sincere thanks to the following individuals and organizations for their permission to reproduce select material and for the time they invested in editing this book's more technical content:

- John D. Worth, Ph.D., Calvin Schnure, John Barwick, and Christopher T. Drula at Nareit
- Keven Lindemann at S&P Global Market Intelligence
- Kevin T. Gannon and Nancy T. Schabel at Robert A. Stanger & Company, Inc.
- Green Street Advisors
- Michael Lewis, CFA, and Ki Bin Kim, CFA, at SunTrust Robinson Humphrey equity research

At the risk of omitting someone, we would like to thank numerous colleagues at Corporate Office Properties Trust (NYSE: OFC), especially Jack Lopez and Greg Thor for their technical edits to Chapters 8 and 11, respectively, and Michelle Layne, for her general edits to the entire manuscript and her mastery of PowerPoint. Sincere thanks also to the REIT equity research team at BTIG for their edits to Chapter 6. Kudos to Will Azar, Denver University Graduate Assistant, for his edits as "fresh eyes" while learning about REITs for the first time.

Special thanks to David M. Fick, CPA, for providing technical edits and guidance on the evolution, benefits, and risks of operating partnership units (Chapter 8).

Thank you to our family and friends for their love, patience, and support during the months it took to compose this work.

Last but never least, sincere thanks to Nareit's Calvin Schnure (Chapter 7) and Merrie Frankel (Chapter 9), not only for contributing content, but also for their generosity in providing comments and advice on the entire manuscript. It has been an absolute pleasure working with you both.

About the Authors

Stephanie Krewson-Kelly's 26 years of experience in the REIT industry began in 1994 and includes work in investment banking (1994–97) and as an equity research analyst (1997–2009) Since 2011, Ms. Krewson-Kelly has served as vice president of investor relations at Corporate Office Properties Trust (NYSE: OFC), a publicly traded office REIT. Prior to her career in REITs, Ms. Krewson-Kelly worked as an internal auditor for a global corporation headquartered in Paris, France.

Ms. Krewson-Kelly is on the Board of Advisors at the University of Wisconsin's James A. Graaskamp Center for Real Estate (Applied REIT program) and teaches as an adjunct professor of real estate at Franklin L. Burns School of Real Estate & Construction Management at Denver University.

In between retiring from Wall Street and joining her current firm, Ms. Krewson-Kelly wrote *REIT Roadmap: An Insiders Guide to Successful Investing in Real Estate Investment Trusts* (second edition published in 2012 under her maiden name, Krewson; now out of print). In 2016, Ms. Krewson-Kelly wrote *The Intelligent REIT Investor: How to Build Wealth with Real Estate Investment Trusts* (Wiley, 2016).

In 1992, Ms. Krewson-Kelly graduated from the University of Pennsylvania's College of Arts & Sciences and Wharton School of Business, where she earned her respective B.A. in English and B.S. in Economics.

Glenn R. Mueller, Ph.D. has 44 years of real estate industry experience, including 37 years of research. Mueller is internationally known for his market cycle research on income producing real estate, his real estate securities (REITs) research, and his public and private market investment strategies and capital markets analysis. Glenn is a professor at the University of Denver's F.L. Burns School of Real Estate & Construction Management, teaching and doing research in development, feasibility, investments, and real estate capital markets. DU's program started in 1938 and offers undergraduate (BS) and graduate (MS, MBA, & PhD) degrees in business RE&CM. He has published 100+ research articles and 110+ quarterly issues of his Real Estate

Market Cycle Reports. He held research positions at Legg Mason Inc., Price-WaterhouseCoopers, ABKB/ Jones Lange LaSalle Real Estate Investors, and Prudential Real Estate Investors.

He is also the Real Estate Investment Strategist at Black Creek Group, Advisory board member at Arden Group, former chairman of the board for European Investor's REIT fund, and a 20-year visiting professor at Harvard. He holds a B.S.B.A. from University of Denver, M.B.A. from Babson College, and Ph.D. in Real Estate from Georgia State University.

PART I

AN INTRODUCTION TO REITs

Part I of this book begins with very basic information that will be helpful to individuals who have little or no prior knowledge of REITs. Chapter 1 addresses industry size, the different ways REITs are classified, and online resources for learning more about the industry and individual companies. Chapter 2 provides an overview of the benefits of investing in REITs, followed by a discussion of real estate fundamentals in Chapter 3. Chapter 4 discusses REIT dividends in great detail, including how to calculate the current yield and the yield on cost, ways to quickly assess if a dividend is safe, and how dividends generally are taxed at the investor level. Chapter 5 provides an overview of different lease structures associated with various property types that REITs own, followed by a discussion in Chapter 6 of the property sectors and subsectors REITs own and that Nareit® tracks. Chapter 7 discusses mortgage REITs in detail.

These first seven chapters are designed to provide foundational information about real estate as an investment asset, REITs that own different types of real estate, and REIT dividends. The chapters that compose Part II of the book build upon this fundamental knowledge and address the more technical aspects of analyzing and investing in the common shares and fixed income securities that REITs issue.

CHAPTER 1

What Is a REIT?

A real estate investment trust (REIT, pronounced "reet") is an entity that receives revenue through owning or financing income-producing property. Similar to other industries, REITs can be private organizations, public but non-traded, or they can be publicly traded on a stock exchange. (Chapter 8 compares the benefits of publicly traded REITs versus private and public non-traded REITs.) By being publicly traded, REITs are similar to mutual funds that are accessible to all investors, who can benefit from receiving real estate income without purchasing, managing, or financing property directly.

Publicly traded REITs are bought and sold like the stock of any other public company. Unique to REITs, however, is their tax status. The *Real Estate Investment Trust Act of 1960* legislation that created the REIT structure exempts companies that qualify as REITs from paying corporate income tax (just like mutual funds), provided they distribute their taxable income as dividends. To qualify as a REIT in the eyes of the Internal Revenue Service (IRS), a company must meet many specific criteria. The most widely known provision is that a REIT must pay shareholders a dividend equal to at least 90% of what would otherwise be taxed as ordinary income. (Chapter 8 highlights the fundamental technical hurdles companies must clear to qualify for REIT tax status.)

Nareit® (formerly known as the National Association of Real Estate Investment Trusts) is the worldwide representative voice for REITs and publicly traded and non-traded real estate companies with an interest in US real estate and capital markets. Nareit's website, www.reit.com, provides investors with educational resources, research, and data and index information, as well as news and information about the industry.

SIZE OF THE REIT INDUSTRY

As of December 31, 2019, Nareit tracked information on 226 publicly traded REITs with a combined public equity market capitalization (or size) of $1.3 trillion. Table 1.1 presents year-end data on the REIT industry's capitalization going back to 1971. The market capitalization shown excludes operating partnership (OP) units, which are similar to shares of common stock in the REIT, but which are not publicly traded. (OP units are discussed in detail in Chapter 8.) The FTSE Nareit All REITs Index includes 219 of the total 226 REITs tracked; 184 REITs were listed on the New York Stock Exchange (NYSE) and the remaining 35 were listed on either the National Association of Securities Dealers Automated Quotation System (NASDAQ) or the NYSE American (NYSE MKT, and formerly known as the American Stock Exchange [AMEX]). Before delving into the benefits of investing in REITs, investors will find it instructive to understand a few more basics about how these companies are categorized and where information on each can be found.

CATEGORIES OF REITS

The two broadest categories for REITs – equity and mortgage – are based on the types of investments they make and the nature of their revenues. Equity REITs were included in S&P's *Real Estate* Global Industry Classifications Standart (GICS®) Sector Index when it was created in 2016; mortgage REITs (mREITs) remained in the *Financials* sector. REITs are also classified by the type of property they own, such as office or apartment buildings, and by other means discussed in the following pages. Before buying or selling any stock, investors should know whether the REIT is an equity REIT or a mortgage REIT, and what type(s) of property it owns. Nareit tracks equity REITs according to property type and mortgage REITs according to whether their investments are backed by residential or commercial real estate. Chapters 6 and 7 provide additional information to help investors identify REITs that fit their portfolio objectives.

Equity REITs

Equity REITs derive the majority of their revenue from rents paid by tenants according to the terms of leases that exist between the REIT (the landlord or lessor) and its tenants (the lessees). These REITs usually have *fee simple*

TABLE 1.1 Historical REIT Industry Market Capitalization and Total Returns*

	All REITs			All Equity REITs			All Mortgage REITs			Hybrid REITs		
Year Ended	# of REITs	EMC[a] ($MMs)	Total Return[b]	# of REITs	EMC[a] ($MMs)	Total Return[b]	# of REITs	EMC[a] ($MMs)	Total Return[b]	# of REITs	EMC[a] ($MMs)	Total Return
1971	34	$1,494	–	12	$332	–	12	$571	–	10	$592	–
1972	46	$1,881	11.2%	17	$377	8.0%	18	$775	12.2%	11	$729	11.4%
1973	53	$1,394	–27.2%	20	$336	–15.5%	22	$517	–36.3%	11	$540	–23.4%
1974	53	$712	–42.2%	19	$242	–21.4%	22	$239	–45.3%	12	$232	–52.2%
1975	46	$900	36.3%	12	$276	19.3%	22	$312	40.8%	12	$312	49.9%
1976	62	$1,308	49.0%	27	$410	47.6%	22	$416	51.7%	13	$483	48.2%
1977	69	$1,528	19.1%	32	$538	22.4%	19	$398	17.8%	18	$592	17.4%
1978	71	$1,412	–1.6%	33	$576	10.3%	19	$340	–10.0%	19	$496	–7.3%
1979	71	$1,754	30.5%	32	$744	35.9%	19	$377	16.6%	20	$633	33.8%
1980	75	$2,299	28.0%	35	$942	24.4%	21	$510	16.8%	19	$847	42.5%
1981	76	$2,439	8.6%	36	$978	6.0%	21	$541	7.1%	19	$920	12.2%
1982	66	$3,299	31.6%	30	$1,071	21.6%	20	$1,133	48.6%	16	$1,094	29.6%
1983	59	$4,257	25.5%	26	$1,469	30.6%	19	$1,460	16.9%	14	$1,329	29.9%
1984	59	$5,085	14.8%	25	$1,795	20.9%	20	$1,801	7.3%	14	$1,489	17.3%
1985	82	$7,674	5.9%	37	$3,270	19.1%	32	$3,162	–5.2%	13	$1,241	4.3%

(Continued)

TABLE 1.1 *(continued)*

Year	All REITs			All Equity REITs			All Mortgage REITs			Hybrid REITs		
Ended	# of REITs	EMC[a] ($MMs)	Total Return[b]	# of REITs	EMC[a] ($MMs)	Total Return[b]	# of REITs	EMC[a] ($MMs)	Total Return[b]	# of REITs	EMC[a] ($MMs)	Total Return
1986	96	$9,924	19.2%	45	$4,336	19.2%	35	$3,626	19.2%	16	$1,962	18.8%
1987	110	$9,702	−10.7%	53	$4,759	−3.6%	38	$3,161	−15.7%	19	$1,782	−17.6%
1988	117	$11,435	11.4%	56	$6,142	13.5%	40	$3,621	7.3%	21	$1,673	6.6%
1989	120	$11,662	−1.8%	56	$6,770	8.8%	43	$3,536	−15.9%	21	$1,356	−12.1%
1990	119	$8,737	−17.4%	58	$5,552	−15.4%	43	$2,549	−18.4%	18	$636	−28.2%
1991	138	$12,968	35.7%	86	$8,786	35.7%	28	$2,586	31.8%	24	$1,596	39.2%
1992	142	$15,912	12.2%	89	$11,171	14.6%	30	$2,773	1.9%	23	$1,968	16.6%
1993	189	$32,159	18.6%	135	$26,082	19.7%	32	$3,399	14.6%	22	$2,678	21.2%
1994	226	$44,306	0.8%	175	$38,812	3.2%	29	$2,503	−24.3%	22	$2,991	4.0%
1995	219	$57,541	18.3%	178	$49,913	15.3%	24	$3,395	63.4%	17	$4,233	23.0%
1996	199	$88,776	35.8%	166	$78,302	35.3%	20	$4,779	50.9%	13	$5,696	29.4%
1997	211	$140,534	18.9%	176	$127,825	20.3%	26	$7,370	3.8%	9	$5,338	10.8%
1998	210	$138,301	−18.8%	173	$126,905	−17.5%	28	$6,481	−29.2%	9	$4,916	−34.0%
1999	203	$124,262	−6.5%	167	$118,233	−4.6%	26	$4,442	−33.2%	10	$1,588	−35.9%
2000	189	$138,715	25.9%	158	$134,431	26.4%	22	$1,632	16.0%	9	$2,652	11.6%
2001	182	$154,899	15.5%	151	$147,092	13.9%	22	$3,991	77.3%	9	$3,816	50.8%
2002	176	$161,937	5.2%	149	$151,272	3.8%	20	$7,146	31.1%	7	$3,519	23.3%

2003	171	$224,212	38.5%	144	$204,800	37.1%	20	$14,187	57.4%	7	$5,225	56.2%
2004	193	$307,895	30.4%	153	$275,291	31.6%	33	$25,964	18.4%	7	$6,639	23.9%
2005	197	$330,691	8.3%	152	$301,491	12.2%	37	$23,394	−23.2%	8	$5,807	−10.8%
2006	183	$438,071	34.4%	138	$400,741	35.1%	38	$29,195	19.3%	7	$8,134	40.9%
2007	152	$312,009	−17.8%	118	$288,695	−15.7%	29	$19,054	−42.3%	5	$4,260	−34.8%
2008	136	$191,651	−37.3%	113	$176,238	−37.7%	20	$14,281	−31.3%	3	$1,133	−75.5%
2009	142	$271,199	27.5%	115	$248,355	28.0%	23	$22,103	24.6%	4	$741	41.3%
2010	153	$389,295	27.6%	126	$358,908	28.0%	27	$30,387	22.6%	§	–	–
2011	160	$450,501	7.3%	130	$407,529	8.3%	30	$42,972	−2.4%	§	–	–
2012	172	$603,415	20.1%	139	$544,415	19.7%	33	$59,000	19.9%	§	–	–
2013	202	$670,334	3.2%	161	$608,277	2.9%	41	$62,057	−2.0%	§	–	–
2014	216	$970,428	27.2%	177	$846,410	28.0%	39	$61,017	17.9%	§	–	–
2015	223	$938,852	2.3%	182	$886,488	2.8%	41	$52,365	−8.9%	§	–	–
2016	224	$1,018,730	9.3%	184	$960,193	8.6%	40	$58,537	22.9%	§	–	–
2017	222	$1,133,698	9.3%	181	$1,065,948	8.7%	41	$67,750	19.8%	§	–	–
2018	226	$1,047,641	−4.1%	186	$980,315	−4.0%	40	$67,326	−2.5%	§	–	–
2019	226	$1,328,806	28.1%	186	$1,245,878	28.7%	40	$82,928	21.3%	§	–	–

*Information prior to 1971 is not available.

§Nareit discontinued its FTSE Nareit Hybrid REIT Index in 2010.

[a]The equity market capitalization (EMC) numbers shown are based on year-end share prices and do not include operating partnership units (OP units), which are not publicly traded and which are discussed in Chapter 8.

[b]Total returns are from the FTSE Nareit All REITs Index, the FTSE Nareit All Equity REITs Index, and the FTSE Nareit Mortgage REITs Index. As of December 31, 2019, the FTSE Nareit All REITs and All Equity REITs indices excluded seven small cap equity REITs that trade less frequently.

Source: Reproduced by permission of Nareit® and is used subject to the Terms and Conditions of Use set forth on the Nareit website, including, but not limited to, Section 9 thereof.

interest in their properties and use debt to finance a percentage of the purchase price. This investment approach is similar to how individuals purchase homes in that the REIT generally uses some amount of debt and pays the remainder in cash (equity). Fee simple interest in real estate means the buyer receives title to the land and improvements, which include the building and any structures that exist on the land. The debt a REIT uses to finance a portion of a property ranges from a simple mortgage (which is also called *property-level* debt) to publicly traded, corporate-level bonds (also called *senior* or *unsecured* debt). Chapter 9 discusses real estate fixed income securities in greater detail.

Sometimes equity REITs own properties according to a leasehold interest, which is also called a *ground lease*. In this case, the REIT does not own the land on which the building(s) sits. The REIT pays the landowner (or *lessor*) a monthly fee for an agreed-upon time period – usually several decades – in exchange for the right to use the land as needed to support the building's operations.

REITs originally were externally advised like mutual funds, but later *The Tax Reform Act of 1986* allowed them to internalize management. Particularly since the *REIT Modernization Act of 1999*, equity REITs increasingly have operated as fully integrated real estate companies that also derive income from a range of real estate-related business activities. (See Chapter 10 for more information about legislative improvements to the REIT structure.) At December 31, 2019, Nareit tracked 186 equity REITs, 179 of which were included in the FTSE Nareit All REITs Index. These companies had an aggregate equity market capitalization of $1.2 trillion (excluding OP units), constituting the largest category of REITs in the United States. Chapter 6 provides more detail on equity REITs according to the different types of commercial properties they own.

Mortgage REITs

Mortgage REITs (mREITs) lend money to real estate owners directly by issuing mortgages, or indirectly by acquiring existing loans or mortgage-backed securities. mREITs derive the majority of their revenues from interest received on commercial mortgage loans or from investments in residential- or commercial-based real estate instruments.

mREITs are analogous to banks that lend almost exclusively to commercial real estate developers and landlords, except mREITs do not have customer deposits from which to lend. Instead, they raise capital by issuing debt and equity in private or public capital markets. Their revenue consists of the principal and interest payments received from their investments.

As of December 31, 2019, FTSE Nareit All REITs Index listed 40 mREITs with a combined equity market capitalization of $82.9 billion (excluding OP units). Since the *Dodd–Frank Wall Street Reform and Consumer Protection Act of 2010* (the Dodd–Frank Act) was signed into law in July 2010, the number of publicly traded mREITs tracked by Nareit has increased 48%, from 27 companies at the end of 2010 to 40 at the end of 2019; during the same time period, mREITs' equity market capitalization has more than doubled, from $30.4 billion to $83.0 billion. This renewed growth in mREITs is due in part to the tighter regulations the Dodd–Frank Act imposed on traditional banks and lenders. mREITs essentially stepped in to fill the credit void created by this and other legislation. Calvin Schnure, Nareit's Senior Vice President of Research & Economic Analysis, authored Chapter 7, which discusses mREITs in great detail and includes a list of mREITs that were publicly traded at the end of 2019.

Hybrid REITs

Prior to 2011, there was a third category of REITs, then called *hybrid REITs*. These companies combined the ownership strategies of equity and mREITs, depending on the investment opportunities available. Historically, hybrid REITs represented the smallest class of REITs in the industry and, in December 2010, Nareit reclassified the four remaining companies as mREITs.

Classification by Property Type

Most often, investors refer to REITs by the type of commercial property in which they invest, such as offices, apartments, retail, hotel, or warehouse buildings. A few years after the Great Recession of 2008–09, the IRS ruled that rental income from less traditional property types could also qualify as *good income* for REITs. (Chapter 8 addresses the concept of good or bad REIT income.) As a result, the industry now includes REITs that own billboards, cell phone towers – even gas and electric transmission lines – and other highly specialized real estate. Nareit classifies these new companies as *specialty* REITs. Many REITs used to own multiple property types, but have evolved to own only one property type; this change occurred largely because investors can diversify their portfolios by buying REITs that own different property types, and generally prefer management teams that have a clear investment focus and expertise. In addition to the information provided in Chapters 6 and 7, Appendix C provides additional summary information on all 219 REITs that were included in the FTSE Nareit All REITs Index at the end of 2019.

Size and Index Inclusion

In describing each classification of REIT, size is one important investment criterion, because companies that are large (as measured by their equity market capitalization) trade differently than small companies. Chapter 11 details how to calculate a REIT's equity market capitalization (also referred to as *equity market cap* or *EMC*) and other important metrics.

An important detail to keep in mind when looking at REIT data is that, in addition to the shares of common stock held by public shareholders, most REITs also have private, non-traded ownership units called *operating partnership (OP) units* outstanding. Specific to REITs, OP units are similar to shares of common stock in that they represent a percent ownership in a REIT (see Chapter 8). Generally, OP units can be exchanged on a one-for-one basis into common stock of the REIT and receive the same dividend. The main difference between OP units and common stock is that OP units are not publicly traded (also referred to as not being *liquid*). Unless expressly noted otherwise, market capitalizations for REITs that are available on financial service outlets, such as *Yahoo! Finance,* or Bloomberg, exclude OP units.

One of the reasons why large- and small-cap REITs trade differently is that larger REITs simply have a greater supply of common shares available to buy or sell on stock exchanges; the number of common shares outstanding is also referred to as a company's *float*. Larger-cap REITs with greater float tend to have higher average daily trading volumes, and institutional investors tend to prefer larger-cap REITs so that they do not have ownership concentration issues (see Chapter 8 for ownership limitations).

At the end of 2019, 118 REITs, or about 50% of public REITs, have market capitalizations and daily average trading volume levels that have qualified them for inclusion in major stock indexes. The 30 larger-cap REITs included in the S&P 500 Index at the end of 2019 are listed in Table 1.2.; REITs included in the S&P 400 Mid Cap and 600 Small Cap Indexes, respectively, are listed in Tables 1.3 and 1.4. Index inclusion is a significant factor in long-term REIT performance because money managers typically have to allocate money to invest in stocks that are part of the broader indexes against which they *benchmark*. Benchmarking is simply measuring the performance of an investment strategy against a standard, such as an index. Money managers who benchmark against the FTSE Nareit All Equity REITs Index,

TABLE 1.2 REIT Constituents of the S&P 500 Index

Company Name (Ticker)	Ticker	Property Focus	EMC*
American Tower Corporation	AMT	Infrastructure – Wireless	$101,586
Crown Castle International Corp.	CCI	Infrastructure – Wireless	59,098
Prologis, Inc.	PLD	Industrial	56,229
Equinix Inc.	EQIX	Data Centers	49,777
Simon Property Group	SPG	Retail – Malls	46,027
Public Storage	PSA	Self-Storage	37,166
Welltower, Inc.	WELL	Health Care	33,116
Equity Residential	EQR	Residential – Apartments	29,984
AvalonBay Communities	AVB	Residential – Apartments	29,233
SBA Communications - Class A	SBAC	Infrastructure – Wireless	27,292
Digital Realty Trust	DLR	Data Centers	24,940
Realty Income Corporation	O	Retail – Free Standing	23,997
Weyerhaeuser Company	WY	Timber	22,493
Ventas, Inc.	VTR	Health Care	21,513
Boston Properties	BXP	Office	21,302
Essex Property Trust	ESS	Residential – Apartments	19,772
Alexandria Real Estate Equities	ARE	Office	18,606
Healthpeak Properties, Inc.[a]	PEAK	Health Care	16,929
Mid-America Apartment Communities	MAA	Residential – Apartments	15,032
Extra Space Storage Inc.	EXR	Self-Storage	13,679
UDR, Inc.	UDR	Residential – Apartments	13,676
Host Hotels & Resorts	HST	Lodging / Resorts	13,304
Duke Realty Corporation	DRE	Industrial	12,744
Vornado Realty Trust	VNO	Diversified	12,686
Regency Centers Corporation	REG	Retail – Shopping Centers	10,569
Federal Realty Investment Trust	FRT	Retail – Shopping Centers	9,643
Iron Mountain, Inc.	IRM	Specialty	9,143
Kimco Realty Corporation	KIM	Retail – Shopping Centers	8,741
Aimco	AIV	Residential – Apartments	7,687
SL Green Realty Corp.	SLG	Office	7,361
Total for all 30 REITs in the S&P 500 Index			$773,319

*Equity market caps are in millions of dollars and as of December 31, 2019.

[a]Formerly known as HCP, Inc. (NYSE: HCP).

Source: Reproduced by permission of Nareit® and is used subject to the Terms and Conditions of Use set forth on the Nareit website, but not limited to, Section 9 thereof.

TABLE 1.3 REIT Constituents of the S&P 400 Mid Cap Index

Company Name (Ticker)	Ticker	Property Focus	EMC*
Medical Properties Trust	MPW	Health Care	$10,923
Camden Property Trust	CPT	Residential – Apartments	10,258
Liberty Property Trust[a]	LPT	Industrial	9,384
Omega Healthcare Investors, Inc.	OHI	Health Care	9,254
National Retail Properties, Inc.	NNN	Retail – Free Standing	9,203
Kilroy Realty Corporation	KRC	Office	8,894
Douglas Emmett, Inc.	DEI	Office	7,694
Lamar AdvertisingCo. (REIT)	LAMR	Specialty – Billboards	7,638
CyrusOne, Inc.	CONE	Data Centers	7,405
American Campus Communities, Inc.	ACC	Residential – Apartments	6,455
Brixmor Property Group	BRX	Retail – Shopping Centers	6,440
Park Hotels & Resorts	PK	Lodging / Resorts	6,202
Cousins Properties Inc.	CUZ	Office	6,036
EPR Properties	EPR	Specialty – Cineplex	5,542
JBG SMITH Properties	JBGS	Diversified	5,349
First Industrial Realty Trust	FR	Industrial	5,251
EastGroup Properties, Inc.	EGP	Industrial	5,096
Highwoods Properties	HIW	Office	5,072
Life Storage	LSI	Self-Storage	5,049
Spirit Realty Capital Inc.	SRC	Retail – Free Standing	4,905
PS Business Parks	PSB	Industrial	4,520
Healthcare Realty Trust Inc.	HR	Health Care	4,463
Rayonier Inc.	RYN	Timber	4,247
CoreSite Realty Corporation	COR	Data Centers	4,226
Sabra Health Care REIT, Inc.	SBRA	Health Care	4,134
Weingarten Realty Investors	WRI	Retail – Shopping Centers	4,019
Service Properties Trust[b]	SVC	Lodging / Resorts	4,001
Macerich Company	MAC	Retail – Malls	3,802
Pebblebrook Hotel Trust	PEB	Lodging / Resorts	3,502
Corporate Office Properties Trust	OFC	Office	3,288

TABLE 1.3 (*continued*)

Company Name (Ticker)	Ticker	Property Focus	EMC*
PotlatchDeltic Corporation	PCH	Timber	$2,925
Urban Edge Properties	UE	Retail – Shopping Centers	2,309
Mack-Cali Realty Corporation	CLI	Office	2,090
CoreCivic[c]	CXW	Specialty – Prisons	2,069
GEO Group Inc.	GEO	Prisons	2,013
Diversified Health-care Trust[d]	DHC	Health Care	2,006
Taubman Centers, Inc.	TCO	Retail – Malls	1,902
Alexander & Baldwin	ALEX	Diversified	1,512
Tanger Factory Outlet Centers, Inc.	SKT	Retail – Shopping Centers	1,368
Total for all 39 REITs			$200,445

*Equity market caps are in millions of dollars and as of December 31, 2019.
[a]Prologis (NYSE: PLD) acquired Liberty Property Trust (NYSE: LPT) in January 2020.
[b]Formerly known as Hospitality Properties Trust (NASDAQ: HPT).
[c]Name changed from Corrections Corporation of America; same ticker symbol.
[d]During 2019, changed its name and ticker symbol from Senior Housing Properties Trust (NASDAQ: SNH).
Source: Reproduced by permission of Nareit® and is used subject to the Terms and Conditions of Use set forth on the Nareit website, including, but not limited to, Section 9 thereof.

TABLE 1.4 REIT Constituents of the S&P 600 Small Cap Index

Company Name (Ticker)	Ticker	Property Focus	EMC*
Agree Realty Corporation	ADC	Retail – Free Standing	$2,976
Apollo Commercial Real Estate Finance	ARI	mREIT – Commercial	2,808
American Assets Trust Inc.	AAT	Diversified	2,741
Lexington Realty Trust	LXP	Diversified	2,632
Xenia Hotels & Resorts Inc.	XHR	Lodging / Resorts	2,434
Invesco Mortgage Capital	IVR	mREIT – Residential	2,378
Washington REIT	WRE	Diversified	2,335
Acadia Realty Trust	AKR	Retail – Shopping Centers	2,255
DiamondRock Hospitality Company	DRH	Lodging / Resorts	2,232
Retail Opportunities Investments Corp.	ROIC	Retail – Shopping Centers	2,049

(*continued*)

TABLE 1.4 *(continued)*

Company Name (Ticker)	Ticker	Property Focus	EMC*
PennyMac Mortgage Investment Tr	PMT	mREIT – Residential	$2,028
Essential Properties Realty Trust	EPRT	Retail – Free Standing	2,010
National Storage Affiliates Trust	NSA	Self-Storage	1,994
CareTrust REIT Inc.	CTRE	Health Care	1,972
Four Corners Property Trust	FCPT	Retail – Free Standing	1,928
Redwood Trust	RWT	mREIT – Residential	1,864
Global Net Lease	GNL	Diversified	1,814
LTC Properties, Inc.	LTC	Health Care	1,779
Easterly Government Properties	DEA	Office	1,760
Kite Realty Group Trust	KRG	Retail – Shopping Centers	1,639
New York Mortgage Trust	NYMT	mREIT – Residential	1,636
Safehold, Inc.	SAFE	Specialty	1,630
Universal Health Realty Income Trust	UHT	Health Care	1,613
Uniti Group Inc.	UNIT	Infrastructure – Wireless	1,586
Office Properties Income Trust	OPI	Office	1,546
Industrial Logistics Properties Trust	ILPT	Industrial	1,459
Getty Realty Corp.	GTY	Retail – Free Standing	1,348
Summit Hotel Properties, Inc.	INN	Lodging / Resorts	1,297
Independence Realty Trust Inc.	IRT	Residential – Apartments	1,280
Saul Centers, Inc.	BFS	Retail – Shopping Centers	1,219
RPT Realty	RPT	Retail – Shopping Centers	1,209
KKR Real Estate Finance Trust	KREF	mREIT – Commercial	1,172
ARMOUR Residential REIT	ARR	mREIT – Residential	1,058
Armada Hoffler Properties Inc.	AHH	Diversified	1,017
Granite Point Mortgage Trust	GPMT	mREIT – Commercial	1,008
Franklin Street Properties Corp.	FSP	Office	918
iStar Inc.	STAR	mREIT – Commercial	902
Innovative Industrial Properties Inc.	IIPR	Industrial	899
Community Healthcare Trust Inc.	CHCT	Health Care	865

TABLE 1.4 (*continued*)

Company Name (Ticker)	Ticker	Property Focus	EMC*
Chatham Lodging Trust	CLDT	Lodging / Resorts	$854
Capstead Mortgage Corporation	CMO	Mortgage – Residential	749
Urstadt Biddle Properties	UBA	Retail – Shopping Centers	743
Ready Capital Corp.	RC	mREIT – Residential	695
Washington Prime Group Inc.	WPG	Retail – Malls	679
Hersha Hospitality Trust	HT	Lodging / Resorts	562
Whitestone REIT	WSR	Diversified	548
Pennsylvania REIT	PEI	Retail – Malls	413
Cedar Realty Trust, Inc.	CDR	Retail – Shopping Centers	263
CBL & Associates Properties	CBL	Retail – Malls	182
Total for all 49 REITs			$72,977

*Equity market caps are in millions of dollars and as of December 31, 2019.

Source: Reproduced by permission of Nareit® and is used subject to the Terms and Conditions of Use set forth on the Nareit website, including, but not limited to, Section 9 thereof.

for example, will manage investors' money with the objective of exceeding that index fund's annual returns.

REITs that are included in the S&P 500, 400, or 600 Indexes are more visible to investors and money managers and, accordingly, tend to outperform non-index companies when REITs are in favor as an investment class. In contrast, when investors do not want to own REITs, the index companies often experience disproportionate declines (albeit, temporary) compared to non-index REITs. (Chapter 10 discusses how REITs, as an industry, have performed in different market conditions, and some of the factors that drove those performances.)

Geographic Focus

REITs typically own and operate regional or national portfolios of properties. Investors interested in investing in "the US office market" could invest in a REIT, such as Boston Properties, Inc. (NYSE: BXP), which owns office buildings in five major US cities, namely Boston, Los Angeles, New York, San Francisco, and Washington, DC. By contrast, an investor who wants to capitalize on a rise in demand for office space in West Coast markets, could focus on a stock such as Kilroy Realty Corporation (NYSE: KRC).

Certain larger-cap US REITs have expanded their real estate holdings outside the United States. Stocks like Prologis, Inc. (NYSE: PLD) provide a way for investors to participate in the economics of owning warehouse/distribution space in the global marketplace. Similarly, Simon Property Group, Inc. (NYSE: SPG) affords individuals the opportunity to invest in the company's globally diversified portfolio of high-end shopping malls.

Risks and Rewards of Geographic Concentration

There are risks and rewards associated with each REIT's degree of geographic concentration and the supply-and-demand characteristics associated with their property markets. (Chapter 11 demonstrates how to assess a REIT's geographic concentration.) Landlords that own apartment buildings in New York City's Manhattan market will likely generate different levels of rent growth, occupancy, and shareholder returns than apartment landlords in Dallas, Texas. In all cases, the decisions, competency, and discipline of a company's senior management and property management teams are key determinants of a REIT's ability to increase shareholder value, regardless of geography or property focus. That said, investors who strongly believe one property type, region, or market in the country will experience disproportionately better – or worse – economic times than the rest of the country can capitalize on their conviction by investing in (or selling out of) REITs based on their property and geographic focus.

Earnings Growth Strategy

A less common but nonetheless important way of classifying REITs (at least for investment purposes) is according to the tactics they use to grow earnings. (Note that REITs measure their "earnings" with an industry-specific metric, *Funds from Operations[FFO]*, which is discussed in Chapter 11.) Every REIT can be broken down into three activities that support their financial results:

1. **Internal growth** generated by managing assets the REIT already owns by increasing occupancy and/or rents, and also by reducing operating costs; internal growth is sometimes called *organic growth*
2. **External growth** generated by acquiring or developing additional properties
3. **Financing** internal and external growth through issuing new debt or equity, and/or by selling properties; this includes lowering debt costs and risks (also known as *positive leverage*)

There is no one "right way" for REITs to grow earnings, though each company's cost of capital affects the opportunities on which a management team can capitalize. Cost of capital, also referred to as a company's *weighted average cost of capital* (WACC), equals the blended cost of a company's common equity (including OP units), preferred equity, and debt. Generally, a management team will only pursue new development or acquisition opportunities if the expected return exceeds the company's cost of capital. Chapters 10 and 11 discuss cost of capital in more detail, but for purposes of this chapter, the following rule is sufficient.

Companies with lower costs of capital are able to grow faster and with higher quality investments than companies with higher, less competitive costs of capital.

Each REIT's management team pursues the strategy they deem to be optimal for that company's chosen property type, real estate markets, opportunities, and cost of capital. The following truisms should assist investors in evaluating individual companies before making an investment:

Risk Axioms for Growth Strategies

Developing = More Risk Than Acquiring Properties
Acquiring = More Risk Than Actively Managing Existing Properties
More Debt* = More Risk

*This tactic may produce higher returns to equity holders, but only for a short period of time.

- **Development:** Growing earnings by developing properties tends to be riskier than acquiring assets that already exist, especially in property types that take more than a year to construct. This is because market demand for new property may erode during construction, causing the developer to deliver a building that is substantially (or completely) vacant. The added risk associated with development is why companies expect to earn a higher yield, or return, on monies they invest in development. (Typically at least 100 basis points – or an additional 1% – of extra return is needed on development projects relative to the cap rates at which a REIT could acquire similar assets.) The higher returns compensate for the higher risk of potential failure, where the latter is measured by how well leased the new development is upon delivery or shortly thereafter.

Many REITs have been able to execute successful development strategies, however, by being extremely careful in their selection of location, by achieving some level of pre-leasing prior to commencing construction (including build-to-suits that are 100% pre-leased to the future tenant), producing higher efficiency buildings with lower operating costs, and/or by operating their business with lower levels of debt. Development has less risk in times of economic expansion, but higher risk of loss during economic downturns and recessions.

- **Acquisitions:** Acquiring assets bears more risk than managing properties a REIT already owns. When a REIT buys a property, management underwrites the local trade area and real estate market surrounding that asset. If management overestimates the demand for space, the acquired property may underperform expectations. By the same token, if management underestimates the supply of new space, and other landlords develop too many competing buildings, then the acquired property may underperform expectations due to the REIT's difficulty in growing occupancy and raising rents. Managing existing assets can include redeveloping buildings to reposition them in their markets, which generally is less risky than acquiring properties, especially if the acquisitions are in a new geographic area for the acquiring REIT.
- **Financing:** Regarding how a REIT sources capital for existing operations and any level of external growth, it is hard to find a REIT – or any company – that went bankrupt because it had *too little* debt. REITs are like any company in that more debt, which also is referred to as *leverage,* equates to higher returns on equity, *but also* higher risk and lower certainty of future earnings and cash flow.

No REIT ever went bankrupt from having *too little* debt.

Positive Leverage. The math behind returns on equity when leverage is used is straightforward: if a landlord buys a property that earns a 6% cash-on-cash return and uses debt with an annual interest rate of 4% to finance half of the investment, the return to equity is 8%, calculated as follows:

- 6% cash return × $1 invested = 6 cents unlevered return

- Half the $1 was financed with debt, so there are 2 cents of interest expense to be paid on the 50 cents (50% debt × $1 invested × 4% interest rate = 2 cents of interest expense)
- 6 cent cash return, less 2 cents of interest expense = a 4 cent return to the 50 cents of equity, which equals an 8% return on equity (4 cent levered return ÷ 50 cents of equity invested)

The ability to achieve higher returns on equity by using debt to partially finance an investment is also called *positive leverage,* but leverage carries risk: at a minimum, the amount of debt a REIT carries can affect its ability to take advantage of market opportunities. For example, a REIT that has a debt-to-gross book value ratio of 40% has greater financial flexibility than a REIT with a 60% ratio. (Please refer to Chapters 4 and 11 for a definition of gross book value.) The REIT with lower leverage should be able to successfully navigate adverse economic times without lowering its common dividend or selling assets at fire-sale prices. Low-leveraged companies should also be able to purchase strategic, premium-quality assets that distressed sellers may bring to market during times of economic adversity, such as during the Great Recession of 2008–09. Last but definitely not least, companies with low levels of debt typically can raise debt and equity capital at lower prices than more highly leveraged companies, thereby achieving a lower WACC.

WHERE TO FIND INFORMATION ON REITS

Nareit's website, www.reit.com, contains a broad array of industry and company-specific information. Once on the Nareit site, the Nareit T-Tracker® contains broad aggregate data on REIT operating performance, including many of the metrics discussed in these chapters, including operating data such as NOI, occupancy rates, dividends paid, earnings (FFO) data, information about leverage (debt to total assets, measured at both book and market value; debt-to-EBITDA), and the average maturity of debt – to name a few data points. (Note: the data in the T-Tracker either are sums of dollar amounts or are weighted by book assets, rather than weighted by market capitalizations.) Also, investors can download spreadsheets with data dating back to 2000 for free using this link: https://www.reit.com/data-research/reit-market-data/nareit-t-tracker-quarterly-operating-performance-series.

In addition to Nareit's website, there are several resources to consult for additional information on the industry and individual REITs. The resources detailed below should provide sufficient information for analyzing the majority of REITs that were publicly traded at the end of 2019.

Company-Specific Websites

Each REIT's website will provide the most complete and timely information for investors, including press releases, annual reports, quarterly statements filed with the Securities and Exchange Commission (SEC), and other useful information.

In December 2015, the Internet Corporation for Assigned Names and Numbers (or ICANN) designated Nareit to operate a dot-REIT (.REIT) top-level domain registry. As more REITs adopt the .REIT identifier for their websites, searching for companies that are REITs by using the Internet will become faster and easier. See Appendix C for the website addresses of the REITs in the FTSE Nareit All REITs Index.

Indexes for Tracking REIT Performance

FTSE Nareit Indexes. The FTSE Group is a joint venture between the *Financial Times* of London and the London Stock Exchange and is the largest provider of financial indices in the United Kingdom. The acronym *FTSE* is pronounced "footsie" and stands for Financial Times Stock Exchange.

In conjunction with the FTSE, Nareit publishes several indexes to track US REIT performance; the three most popular indexes, and the number of companies that comprised each one at December 31, 2019, are as follows:

1. FTSE Nareit All REITs Index – tracks publicly traded equity and mortgage REITs (219 companies)
2. FTSE Nareit All Equity REITs Index – tracks publicly traded equity REITs (179 companies)
3. FTSE Nareit Mortgage REITs Index – tracks publicly traded mortgage REITs (40 companies)

Appendix A and B provide listings of REITs that comprised the FTSE Nareit All REITs Index at December 31, 2019. Companies are listed alphabetically by their name in Appendix A and by their stock exchange (or *ticker*) symbol in Appendix B. Chapters 6 and 7 and Appendix C of this book also list each REIT according to property focus and present summary information on each company, including website addresses.

S&P Dow Jones Indices. S&P Dow Jones Indices (S&P DJI) (us.spindices.com) is the world's largest global resource for index-based concepts, data, and research. Home to iconic financial market indicators such as the S&P 500® and the Dow Jones Industrial Average®, the organization's founder, Charles Dow, invented the first index in 1884, making it the most experienced firm at constructing innovative and transparent solutions to fulfill investors' needs. Using its Global Industry Classifications Standard (GICS®), the organization classifies all companies in their S&P 500 index into one of eleven Sector Indices. In 2016, S&P DJI created the eleventh Sector, Real Estate (Ticker: IXRE); it includes equity REITs and other public real estate operating companies, and excludes mREITs, which remain in the Financials Sector.

S&P Dow Jones Indices publishes many indices that track the performance of real estate companies and equity REITs, including the Dow Jones Composite All REIT Index (RCI and, for total returns, RCIT). The RCI is a unique census of all REITs versus a sample like most indexes. At the end of 2019, it tracked 217 publicly traded US equity REITs.

MSCI Indexes. Nareit and MSCI, a leading provider of investment-decision-support tools, provide indices that track REIT performance:

- MSCI US REIT Index, ticker symbol RMZ on the NYSE American, is a real-time, price-only index that tracks approximately 99% of the publicly traded US equity REITs; it excludes mREITs and certain equity REITs. At the end of 2019, 151 equity REITs composed the RMZ. Investors can obtain real-time quotes for the RMZ on financial websites, such as *Google Finance* and *Yahoo! Finance*, and can learn more about the index by going to www.msci.com.
- MSCI also publishes the RMS, a daily total return version of the RMZ, which encompasses the companies' dividend yields. The RMS is not a real-time index; the total return of the REITs that compose the index is published at the end of the day.

Cohen & Steers Indexes. In 1985, Cohen & Steers, Inc. (NYSE: CNS) created the first real estate mutual fund and, today, is a global investment manager specializing in liquid real estate assets, including real estate securities, listed infrastructure, commodities, and natural resource equities, as well as preferred securities and other income solutions. Two of the real estate indexes they offer for tracking REIT performance are:

- Cohen & Steers Realty Majors Portfolio Index (RMP), which tracks the largest, most liquid US REITs
- Cohen & Steers Global Realty Majors Index (GRM), which tracks global real estate securities that stand to lead or benefit most from the securitization of commercial real estate worldwide

MUTUAL FUNDS THAT INVEST IN REITS

There are about 40 actively managed mutual funds that focus on REITs as their investment target. They all have different strategies and investment styles. Investors can find a list of REIT and real estate focused mutual funds on Nareit's website, www.reit.com, and should discuss different funds with their financial advisors before investing.

EXCHANGE-TRADED FUNDS FOR INVESTING IN REITS

The indexes in the preceding paragraphs only track and report REIT performance. Several ETFs exist that enable investors to purchase an index (or bundle) of REITs – similar to buying a mutual fund that approximates the returns of the S&P 500 Index or other broad-based stock market indexes. In 1993, the NYSE American introduced the first ETF. Today, there is an ETF to suit nearly every investment preference – even ETFs that allow investors to *short* (that is, *bet against*) a rise in REIT share prices. Three of the most well-known REIT ETFs are listed below:

1. **VNQ** – The Vanguard Group's REIT exchange-traded fund that trades under the ticker symbol VNQ is the largest REIT ETF available and is designed to track the performance of the MSCI US REIT Index (see RMZ discussion earlier in this chapter)
2. **SCHH** – The Schwab US REIT ETF invested in 116 US equity REITs at year-end 2019 and charges an even lower fee than the VNQ
3. **REET** – iShares Global REIT ETF managed by BlackRock® invests in REITs based in the United States and around the world. At the end of 2019, REET had approximately 65% invested in US REITs and 35% in REITs in other countries

For a more complete listing and discussion of real estate ETFs, investors should consult with their financial advisors.

CONCLUSION

REITs are like mutual funds in that by paying their shareholders a dividend equal to at least 90% of what would otherwise be taxed as ordinary income, they avoid paying federal taxes on that income. Instead, the shareholders pay individual taxes on the dividends received.

There are many resources where investors can obtain information on REITs and the REIT industry, including S&P Global Market Intelligence, and free resources such as Nareit (www.reit.com) and each individual REIT's websites (see Appendix C for a list of publicly traded REITs and their websites).

CHAPTER 2

Benefits of Investing in REITs

Many investors buy REITs solely for the attractive dividend yields they offer relative to government bonds and other investments. However, there are many more, equally compelling reasons to include REITs as part of a well-balanced portfolio. Two such reasons are that for investment periods of 20, 25, and 30 years, the compound annual returns from equity REITs have exceeded those of the S&P 500 Index, and that REIT dividends generally increase faster than inflation (as measured by increases in the Consumer Price Index [CPI]), making REITs an effective hedge against inflation. REITs are also an effective diversification tool; a wealth of research has shown that investing in REITs helps lower risk and increase returns on a portfolio of stocks and bonds. Last but not least, investing in REITs provides investors with a way to add real estate returns to their portfolios without the liquidity risk associated with direct real estate investments.

DIVIDENDS

Dividend income is one of the primary reasons to invest in REITs, in large part because their yields represent an attractive premium to yields offered by other investments. As of December 31, 2019, the FTSE Nareit All REITs Index yielded 4.06%, which compares to a 1.92% yield on 10-year US Treasury notes and a 1.85% yield from the S&P 500 Index. (A basis point [bp] is equal to 1/100th of a percentage point; for example, 1% equals 100 bps.)

REITs are an attractive investment for people seeking current income, provided that the REIT has a conservatively leveraged balance sheet and well-located assets that are competitively managed. When a REIT possesses these qualities, it generally can sustain – and preferably grow – the dividend it pays to shareholders. Chapter 4 discusses the characteristics of REIT dividends and dividend yield, and also provides quick calculations for investors to assess the sustainability of a REIT's dividend.

DOUBLE-DIGIT TOTAL RETURNS

Investor total returns on stock investments are calculated as the sum of dividends received plus any appreciation (or less any decline) in stock price during the time the stock is owned. Due in part to their attractive current yields, REITs have tended to deliver long-term annualized total returns of 8–12% over time. As shown in Table 2.1, since inception equity REITs delivered

TABLE 2.1 Comparative Compounded Total Annual Returns

Timeframe*	All REITs	All Equity REITs	S&P 500	NASDAQ†	DJIA
2019	28.1%	28.7%	31.5%	36.7%	25.3%
3-Year	10.3%	10.3%	15.3%	19.9%	15.7%
5-Year	8.5%	8.4%	11.7%	14.9%	12.6%
10-Year	12.5%	12.6%	13.6%	16.1%	13.4%
15-Year	7.8%	8.4%	9.0%	9.9%	9.5%
20-Year	11.3%	11.6%	6.1%	4.0%	7.2%
25-Year	10.6%	10.9%	10.2%	10.4%	8.4%
30-Year	10.2%	10.8%	10.0%	10.5%	8.1%
1972–2019	9.8%	11.8%	10.7%	8.9%	7.5%

*Compounded annual total returns for the number of years ended December 31, 2019. Shaded areas represent time periods when equity REITs and the NASDAQ outperformed other major indexes shown.

†Price appreciation only. Compounded annual returns from 1972 to 2019 are calculated from the NASDAQ Composite's inception date of December 31, 1973.

Source: Reproduced by permission of Nareit® and is used subject to the Terms and Conditions of Use set forth on the Nareit website, including, but not limited to, Section 9 thereof.

long-term average total annual returns of 11.8% from 1972 to 2019 – or 110 basis points more than the 10.7% annual total return achieved by stocks in the S&P 500 Index and 290 basis points higher than the NASDAQ's 8.9% annual return during the same period.

More scientifically, CEM Benchmarking (CEM), an independent provider of benchmarking information for institutional investors, updated their groundbreaking 2016 study for Nareit in 2019 (CEM 2019 Study), highlighting the advantages of owning publicly traded REITs versus private real estate and other investments. For the 20-year period from 1998 to 2017, the CEM 2019 Study tracked returns from over 200 public and private pension plans (institutional investors) with combined assets of nearly $3.8 trillion and, across 12 asset classes, compared gross and net average annual total returns (where net means the returns were adjusted for fees or expenses born by the investor). The results, which are summarized in Figure 2.1, demonstrated that listed equity REITs provided the second highest returns (net of expenses), with average total returns of 10.9%.

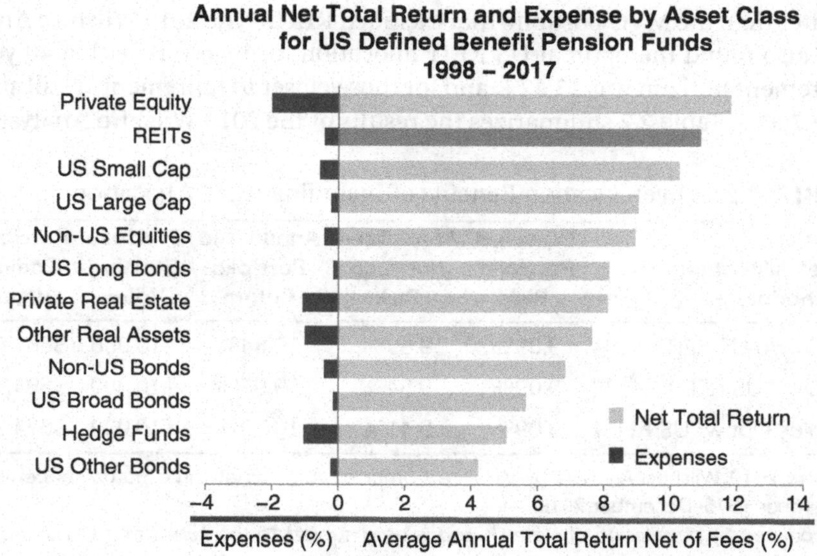

FIGURE 2.1 CEM Benchmarking Study: US Defined Benefit Pension Plan Performance

Source: CEM Benchmarking, 2019. *Reproduced by permission of Nareit® and is used subject to the Terms and Conditions of Use set forth on the Nareit website, including, but not limited to, Section 9 thereof.*

PORTFOLIO DIVERSIFICATION

REITs are a proven diversification tool for portfolio management, a fact that has been demonstrated in multiple studies by various prominent investment advisory firms using different techniques, data sources, and time periods. In simplistic terms, diversification means that adding a particular investment to a portfolio increases the overall expected returns of that pool of investments while also reducing risk. Note that risk is also referred to as *volatility*. An analysis performed by Wilshire Associates in 2019 (the 2019 Wilshire Analysis), for example, demonstrates how a REIT allocation in a portfolio increased returns and reduced risk. The study analyzed three portfolios constructed using mean variance optimization (MVO) to allocate assets to maximize portfolio returns and control risk. The second portfolio included an allocation to Global REITs, as did the third. However, the third portfolio also was constructed with surplus optimization (SO), wherein risk (as measured by volatility) is tracked and controlled more closely than in an MVO portfolio. The SO portfolio that included REITs resulted in a portfolio value at the end of 2018 that was 13.4% higher than the MVO portfolio with REITs, and 19.2% greater than the MVO portfolio that excluded REITs. The 2019 Wilshire Analysis also found the optimal US REIT allocation for investors with a 40-year retirement horizon was 13.42%, and for those closer to retirement, a still sizeable 7.91%. Table 2.2 summarizes the results of the 2019 Wilshire Analysis:

TABLE 2.2 Diversification Benefits of Including REIT Allocation

Asset Allocation Methodology	Expected Portfolio Risk	Annualized Portfolio Risk	Annualized Portfolio Return	Portfolio Starting Value	Portfolio Ending Value
MVO w/o US REITs	9.09%	9.59%	9.84%	$10,000	$565,805
MVO w/ US REITs	9.09%	9.54%	9.97%	$10,000	$594,576
Surplus Opt w/ US REITs	9.09%	9.41%	10.29%	$10,000	$674,162

Source: 2019 Wilshire Analysis by Wilshire Compass. Analysis of three portfolios between December 1975–December 2018.

Reproduced by permission of Nareit® and is used subject to the Terms and Conditions of Use set forth on the Nareit website, including, but not limited to, Section 9 thereof.

Fact

A portfolio invested in a combination of equities, bonds, and equity REIT shares produces greater returns and exhibits less risk than the same-sized portfolio that does not include an allocation to equity REITs.

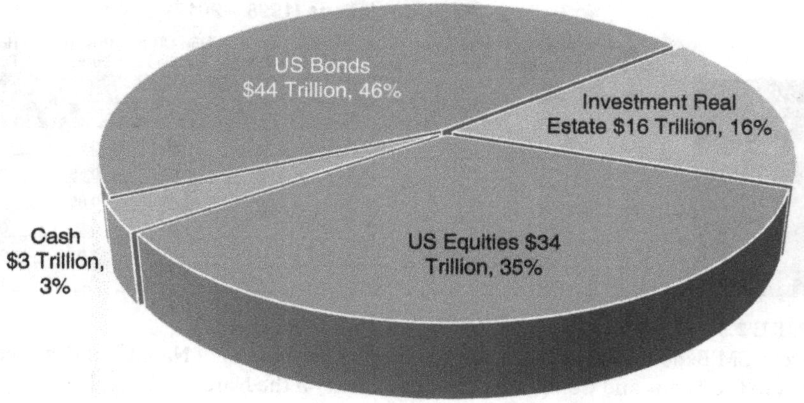

FIGURE 2.2 Investment Real Estate Is the Third Largest Asset Class in the US
Source: Stocks and bond data from Board of Governors of the Federal Reserve, Financial Accounts of the United States, 2018Q4; commercial real estate market size data based on Nareit analysis of CoStar property data and CoStar estimates of Commercial Real Estate Market Size, 2018Q4. Reproduced by permission of Nareit® and is used subject to the Terms and Conditions of Use set forth on the Nareit website, including, but not limited to, Section 9 thereof.

REITs provide diversification to a portfolio because commercial real estate (including REITs) represents the third largest of four fundamental types of investment assets; the largest is bonds, followed by stocks (also called *equities*), then real estate, and cash. Figure 2.2 summarizes the relative sizes of these investment asset classes. At the end of 2018, US investment real estate (which excludes single-family homes owned by individuals) is estimated to represent $16 trillion, or 16% of the $97 trillion investable assets in the United States. Because real estate has its own unique drivers and cycle, real estate investments behave differently than bonds, other equities, or cash; said more concisely, REITs have a relatively low correlation with other asset classes. (Chapter 3, Real Estate Fundamentals, discusses the real estate cycle in detail.)

Correlation describes the linear relationship that may or may not exist between the performances of two or more investments, as measured on a scale of positive one to negative one (+1 to −1). A correlation of +1 means the investments trade in lockstep, implying their performance is contingent upon the same macroeconomic and other factors. Conversely, when investments trade inversely with one another, they have a negative correlation as low as −1. The CEM 2019 Study referenced earlier also calculated correlations among the 12 asset classes it analyzed. As Figure 2.3 demonstrates, REIT and unlisted (private) real estate returns had a high positive correlation

Key Correlations (1998 – 2017)

	REITs	Private Real Estate	US Long Bonds	US Large Cap	US Small Cap	Non-US Equities	Private Equity	Hedge Funds
REITs	1.00	0.91	−0.03	0.53	0.62	0.56	0.49	0.50
Private Real Estate		1.00	−0.06	0.47	0.57	0.54	0.53	0.43
US Long Bonds			1.00	−0.41	−0.51	−0.50	−0.61	−0.30
US Large Cap				1.00	0.92	0.89	0.85	0.92
US Small Cap					1.00	0.88	0.89	0.79
Non-US Equities						1.00	0.89	0.85
Private Equity							1.00	0.79
Hedge Funds								1.00

FIGURE 2.3 Key Correlations of REITs vs. Other Investments
Source: CEM Benchmarking, 2019. Reproduced by permission of Nareit® and is used subject to the Terms and Conditions of Use set forth on the Nareit website, including, but not limited to, Section 9 thereof.

of 0.91, whereas REIT returns had relatively low correlations as compared to returns generated by US Long Bonds (negative correlation of 0.03), Private Equity (positive 0.49), and other US equities (positive correlations ranging from 0.53 to 0.62).

SUPERIOR RISK-ADJUSTED RETURNS

An investment's risk-adjusted return is its total return adjusted to reflect the risk, as measured by volatility, associated with earning that return. In 1966, William F. Sharpe developed the Sharpe Ratio to quantify how much return an investor earns for each unit of risk taken. In its original form, it is calculated as the difference between the expected return of an investment and a risk-free asset of similar duration (which for REITs is usually the yield on 10-Year US Treasury notes), divided by the investment's standard deviation. The higher the Sharpe Ratio, the higher (i.e., better) the risk-adjusted return.

The CEM 2019 Study also compared risk-adjusted returns across the 12 asset classes and found that, except for US bonds, REITs had the highest Sharpe Ratio, reflecting their above-average returns and moderate volatility. In this study, only two investments – both long duration, fixed income investments – achieved higher risk-adjusted returns than REITs. The bonds' higher Sharpe Ratios were due to their combination of modest returns and extremely low volatilities. Figure 2.4 summarizes the report's findings:

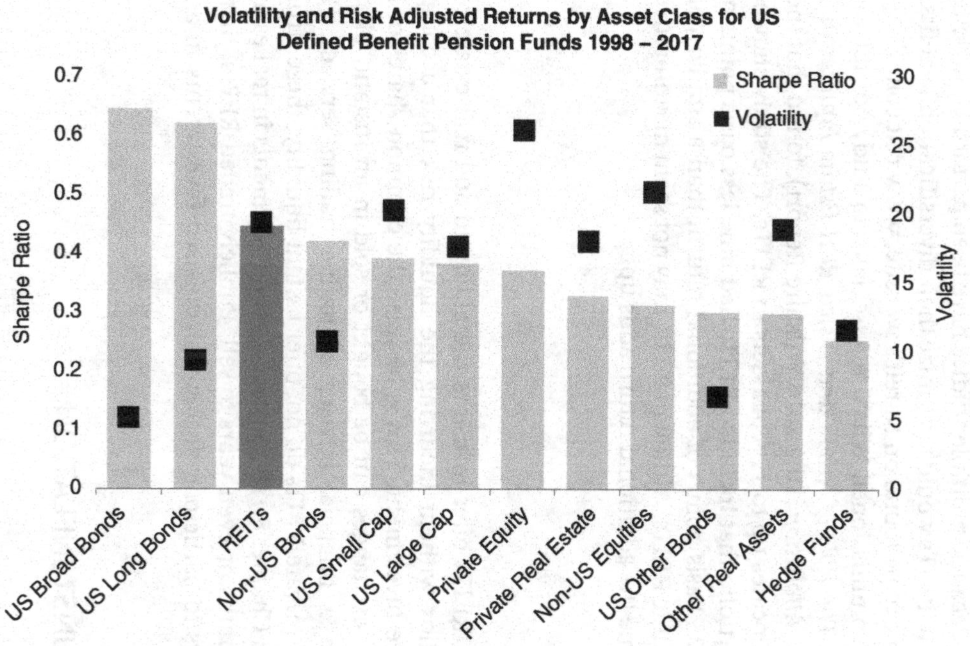

FIGURE 2.4 Risk-Adjusted Returns and Volatilities by Asset Class
Source: CEM Benchmarking, 2019. *Reproduced by permission of Nareit® and is used subject to the Terms and Conditions of Use set forth on the Nareit website, including, but not limited to, Section 9 thereof.*

Owing to the attractive risk-adjusted returns REITs typically generate, investors should consider allocating a portion of their investment portfolios to the sector. *Allocation* speaks to what percent of the total portfolio amount is invested in an asset class. For example, individuals may allocate (invest) 20% of their portfolio in REITs, 40% in equities, and 40% in bonds. During the past several decades, multiple studies have been performed to determine what allocation to REITs would maximize their diversification benefits, summaries of which can be found on Nareit's website, www.reit.com.

Nareit also commissioned Wilshire Associates to study portfolio allocations to REITs. *The Role of REITs and Listed Real Estate Equities in Target Date Fund Asset Allocations* (the 2016 Wilshire Report), found that the optimal portfolio allocates up to 17% of assets to REITs. The study showed that a diversified portfolio that included REITs had nine less basis points of risk, and generated 33 basis points of additional return, than a similar portfolio that did not include REITs. Although 0.33% may not seem meaningful on the surface, over time the additional return adds up.

LIQUIDITY

Publicly traded REITs offer investors the ability to add real estate returns to their portfolios without incurring the liquidity risk that accompanies direct real estate investment. This is because the common shares of REITs traded on stock exchanges can be bought or sold in an instant, like other stocks, through a financial advisor or online trading services. (Public non-traded and private REITs do not offer instant liquidity; these structures are discussed in Chapter 8.) In contrast, direct investments in real estate can take several months or even years to sell. Publicly traded REITs, therefore, enable investors to participate in real estate-based investments in a liquid manner.

HEDGE AGAINST INFLATION

Equity REITs rent their properties to tenants using leases and lease terms that tend to protect the REITs' operating margins from the effects of inflation. A REIT's operating margin is similar to a manufacturing company's gross margin, where real estate revenues are the sales, and property operating expenses (including property management fees or salaries, utilities, taxes, and insurance) are the cost of goods sold. As discussed in Chapter 5, most leases provide that landlords will bill tenants for various property operating costs after they have been incurred. The tenant reimbursements of operating expenses above a base year level (also discussed in Chapter 5) enable the landlord to pass the risks of inflation in operating costs through to the tenant. In the case of triple-net leases, the landlord does not pay any operational costs; instead, tenants pay the costs directly. Apartment landlords typically have one-year leases, and generally can increase their rents (also called *marking-to-market*) to keep pace with inflating costs. The ability to pass along increases in operating costs to tenants enables REIT revenues to keep pace with or exceed inflation – albeit with some lag. The result is that REITs generate inflation-adjusted earnings, making their stocks attractive investments during times of inflation.

Table 2.3 is excerpted from the 2019 Wilshire Analysis referenced earlier in this chapter, and shows how often different investments – namely REITs, commodities (as represented by the S&P GSCI Total Index), the S&P 500 Index, and Treasury Inflation Protected Securities (TIPS) – generated total returns that exceeded inflation. The higher the percentage shown, the more effective the investment was at protecting (or hedging) against inflation. From 1975 through 2018, REIT total returns exceeded inflation 73% of the time on a rolling 6-month basis, and 76% of the time on a rolling 12-month basis. REITs' ability to produce total returns that were greater than inflation was comparable to owning the S&P 500 Index, which exceeded inflation 70% of the time over a 6-month period and 76% of the time over a 12-month period. It may surprise investors to learn that REITs were a much more effective hedge against inflation than commodities, where commodity

TABLE 2.3 Percent of Rolling Periods in Which Total Returns Met or Exceeded Inflation: 1975–2018

	FTSE Nareit All Equity REITs Index	S&P GSCI Total Index	S&P 500 Index	Barclays Capital U.S. TIPS Index*
6-month rolling returns	73%	56%	70%	65%
12-month rolling returns	76%	56%	76%	70%

*Barclays Capital US TIPS Index inception was October 1, 1997.

Reproduced from the 2019 Wilshire Analysis and by permission of Nareit® and is used subject to the Terms and Conditions of Use set forth on the Nareit website, including, but not limited to, Section 9 thereof.

Source: Wilshire Compass.

returns exceeded inflation only 56% of the time on a rolling 6-month basis and on a 12-month basis.

TRANSPARENT CORPORATE STRUCTURES

REIT industry results are highly transparent in part because real estate and the leases that generate rental revenues are tangible, and also because publicly traded REITs face a high degree of analyst and investor scrutiny each quarter. There are dozens of firms in the United States that employ at least one equity analyst to provide equity research on REITs. Additionally, based on data provided by S&P Global Market Intelligence, 66 of the 219 REITs in the FTSE Nareit All REITs Index at the end of 2019 were able to issue public fixed income securities that were rated by the top credit ratings organizations in the United States. Chapter 9 discusses investment-grade and non-investment-grade-rated REIT securities in further detail. These companies represent approximately 74% of the industry's equity market capitalization and have at least one fixed income analyst also scrutinizing their quarterly results. If a management team pursues a questionable business practice, such as using short-term variable rate debt to finance growth, one of these analysts is bound to report on it, alerting investors and likely causing that REIT's stock price to suffer. Against the backdrop of accounting scandals like the Enron Corporation (former NYSE: ENE) in 2001 and Ponzi schemes like that of Bernie Madoff, which was revealed in 2008, investors historically have taken comfort in the tangibility of REIT cash flows, and the daily scrutiny REITs endure from the equity and fixed income analyst communities.

Secondly, REITs are compelled to pay out at least 90% of their otherwise taxable income, and many pay out 100% or more. REITs also pay their dividends in cash (though the IRS has, in the past, allowed REITs to issue new stock to pay their dividends) and, therefore, operate with limited retained earnings. As a result, they generally issue new public equity every other year in order to finance growth. REITs are unique as publicly traded stocks in that they issue additional equity to grow, whereas most publicly traded non-REIT corporations only raise equity once, through an initial public offering (IPO). This means that REITs *must* perform well to get investors interested in purchasing new shares to help the REIT execute its growth strategy.

Whichever group or Wall Street firm a management team selects to underwrite a stock issuance will subject the REIT to yet another level of scrutiny as part of the investment bank's due diligence. As the accounting irregularities discovered at American Realty Capital Properties (formerly NYSE: ARCP) in 2014 proved, the REIT industry is not immune to scandal. However, incidents of fraud are few and far between in the REIT world. The difficulty REIT management teams would have in hiding accounting irregularities for any extended period of time without disrupting their ability to pay dividends and/or without being found out by the analyst community or underwriters, minimizes the risk of fraud. The heavy scrutiny under which REITs operate, as well as the discipline the dividend payout requirement imposes on management, combine to make REITs a highly transparent investment class that delivers attractive risk-adjusted returns.

CONCLUSION

Investors are attracted to REITs for many reasons, including attractive dividend income and superior long-term total returns, immediate liquidity, and better portfolio diversification. Investing in REITs increases an investment portfolio's returns while reducing risk because investment real estate is its own asset class with its own unique drivers that differentiate it from other equities and bonds. Investing in REIT common shares enables investors to enjoy the benefits of investing in investment real estate, without the liquidity risk associated with direct property ownership.

CHAPTER 3

Real Estate Fundamentals

COMMERCIAL REAL ESTATE AND HOME OWNERSHIP ARE COMPLETELY DIFFERENT

The US economy goes through cycles and so does real estate. Commercial and residential real estate cycles are completely different, because commercial income-producing real estate is an investment process that generates income, while owner-occupied residential real estate (homes, townhomes, and condominiums) is a use asset for the owner – just like a car. The only way to invest in residential real estate for a return is to buy the securities of publicly traded home builders who, like automotive manufacturers that produce cars, follow a production process to build homes. In contrast, commercial income-producing real estate is driven by two separate cycles: physical and financial. The "Physical Market Cycle" is the interaction between users (demand for space) and developers and owners (supply of space) in each individual market and property type. Income growth comes from a combination of higher occupancy which also drives rents higher. The "Financial Market Cycle" concerns the price of commercial real estate, which is driven by the capital markets (the interaction of buyers and sellers of properties) that have evolved from local in the 1970s, to national in the 1980s, to public company (REITs) in the 1990s, to global in scope since the beginning of the 2000s.

THE PHYSICAL MARKET CYCLE

Many observers consider real estate cycles to be a delayed mirror of the US economic cycle. As one of the four factors of production (land, labor, capital, and raw materials), demand for real estate is a necessary and important part of an economy's growth. As the population of the world grows, additional people need a place to work, shop, eat, play, sleep, pray, and store things, which constantly increases the amount of space needed (demand). The main reason that real estate is a cyclical industry comes from the fact that demand for space is affected by economic cycles, particularly employment growth. The next factor is the supply response to demand growth, which is not immediate or efficient. Part of this lag comes from the long time it takes to develop and build certain types of properties. The lag between demand growth and the supply of space response is the second major cause of volatility in physical real estate cycles, after the effect of economic employment cycles on demand growth.

Estimating the physical market cycle is relatively straightforward with much data available in the US for both the demand variables (via employment and population growth) and supply variables (via estimates of real estate projects in planning, being permitted, started construction, and completed).

Greater Transparency

The US real estate markets and their cycles are much more transparent than they were in the 1990s. There are many sources of US data for purchase, such as CoStar, REIS, CB Commercial, Jones Lange LaSalle, and others that cover many of the 366 Metropolitan Statistical Areas (MSAs) in the US. If an investor is looking for information on a single city, they can usually obtain this information from a local real estate broker who specializes in the property type they are interested in – and this data is usually shared for free when working with the broker. The key variables that should be available are space absorption (rent up), occupancy/vacancy rates, and rental rates.

The occupancy rate is the inverse of the vacancy rate: take 100% minus the vacancy rate to get the occupancy rate. This allows the investor to visualize the relationship between occupancies and rents more clearly. Figure 3.1 shows the historic US relationship between office occupancies and rent growth. Peak office occupancies occurred in 1982, 1999, 2006, and 2019. The historic correlation between occupancies and rent growth was 76%. Rent growth was also at its highest levels at or near each of the occupancy cycle peaks. When the national office average was above its long-term average of 88% occupancy, rental growth was always positive and above the rate of inflation. During a down cycle in occupancies and at the bottom of the occupancy cycles in 1991, 2002, and 2009 rental growth was negative as owners dropped their rents to attract tenants.

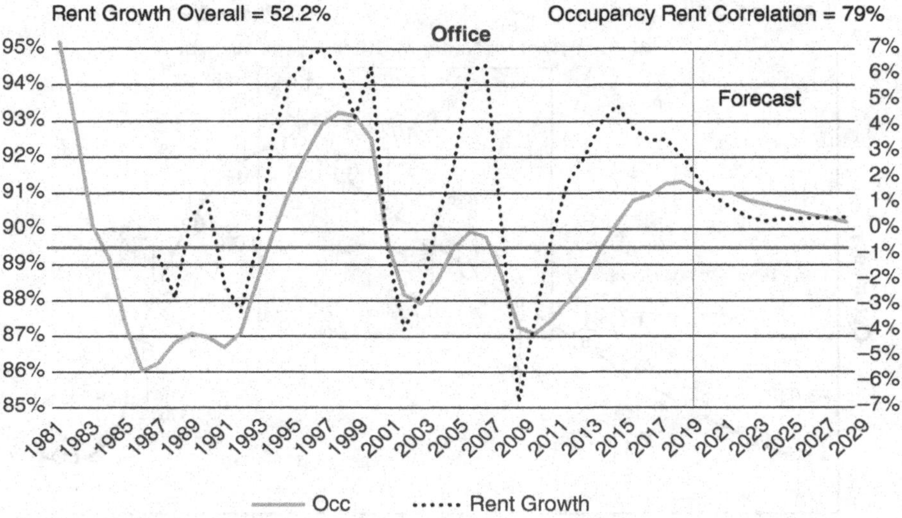

FIGURE 3.1 Office Occupancy and Rent Growth
Source: CoStar 4Q2019 and Mueller.

The Mueller Real Estate Market Cycle paper (*Real Estate Finance,* 1995) of historic occupancy cycles put 16 points on the cycle graph representing a historical 16-year office occupancy cycle. Figure 3.2 shows 30-year historical average office rental growth rates at different points in the cycle. Commercial real estate markets are cyclical due to the economic cycle and the lagged relationship between demand and supply for physical space. The long-term occupancy average is different for each market and each property type. Long-term occupancy average (points # 6 and #14 on Figure 3.2) is a key factor in determining rental growth rates. Occupancy increase plus rent increase equals the income growth for each real estate property.

Supply and demand interaction is important to understand. Starting in Recovery Phase I at the bottom of a cycle (see Figure 3.2), the marketplace is in a state of oversupply from either previous new construction supply or negative demand growth. At this bottom point, occupancy is at its trough (vacancy at its peak). Typically, the market bottom occurs when the excess construction from the previous cycle stops. As the cycle bottom is passed, demand growth begins to slowly absorb the existing oversupply and new supply growth is nonexistent or very low. As excess space is absorbed, occupancy rates rise, allowing rental rates in the market to stabilize and even begin to increase. As this recovery phase continues, positive expectations about the market allow landlords to increase rents at a slow pace (typically at or below

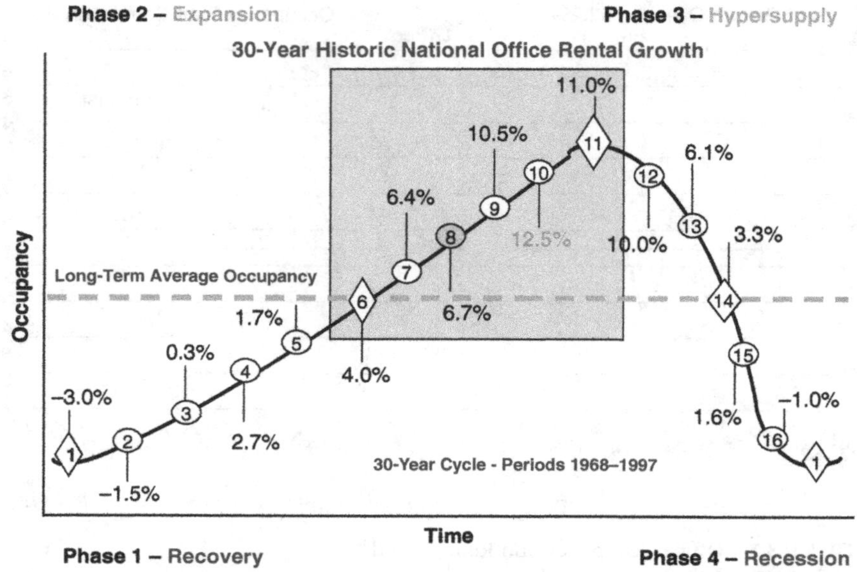

FIGURE 3.2 Rent Growth Rates at Different Cycle Points
Source: Mueller, Real Estate Finance, 1995.

inflation). Eventually, each local market reaches its ***long-term occupancy average,*** whereby ***rental growth is equal to inflation***.

In Expansion Phase II, demand growth continues at increasing levels, creating a need for additional space. As occupancy levels rise above the ***long-term occupancy average,*** signaling that supply is tightening in the marketplace, rents begin to rise rapidly until they reach a ***cost-feasible rent level*** (see point #8 on Figure 3.2) that justifies new construction to commence. In this period of tight supply, rapid rental growth has been experienced, which some observers call "rent spikes." (Some developers may also begin speculative construction in anticipation of cost-feasible rents if they are able to obtain financing). Once cost-feasible rents are achieved in the marketplace (point #8 on the cycle graph), demand growth is still higher than supply growth – a lag in providing new space due to the time to construct. Long expansionary periods are possible and many historic real estate cycles show that the overall up-cycle is a slow, long-term, uphill climb. As long as demand growth rates are higher than supply growth rates, vacancy rates should continue to fall. The cycle peak point is where demand and supply are growing at the same rate or ***equilibrium***. Before equilibrium, demand grows faster than supply; after equilibrium, supply grows faster than demand.

Hypersupply Phase III of the real estate cycle commences after the peak / equilibrium point #11 – where demand growth equals supply growth. Most real estate participants do not recognize this peak/equilibrium's passing, as occupancy rates are at their highest and well above long-term averages – a strong and tight market. During Phase III, supply growth is higher than demand growth (hypersupply), causing occupancy rates to decline back toward the long-term occupancy average. While there is no painful oversupply during this period, new supply completions compete for tenants in the marketplace. As more space is delivered to the market, rental growth decelerates. Eventually, market participants realize that the market has turned down and commitments to new construction should slow or stop. If new supply grows faster than demand once the long-term occupancy average is passed, the market falls into Phase IV.

Recession – Phase IV begins as the market moves past the long-term occupancy average with high supply growth and low or negative demand growth. The extent of the market down-cycle is determined by the difference (excess) between the market supply growth and demand growth. Massive oversupply, coupled with negative demand growth (that started when the market passed through long-term occupancy average in 1984), sent most US office markets into the largest down-cycle ever experienced. During Phase IV, landlords realize that they could quickly lose market share if their rental rates are not competitive. As a result, they then lower rents to capture tenants, even if only to cover their buildings' fixed expenses. Market liquidity is also low or nonexistent in this phase, as the bid–ask spread in property prices is too wide. The cycle eventually reaches bottom as new construction and completions cease, or as demand growth turns up and begins to grow at rates higher than that of new supply added to the marketplace.

It is important for investors to know where markets are in their physical cycle. Remember that demand and supply is *very* local in nature – so office demand, supply, occupancies. and rents in New York can be very different from the office fundamentals in Boston. Figure 3.3 shows the 54 largest cities in the United States and their cycle points at the fourth quarter of 2019. Thus, above-inflation rental growth should happen in all markets in the growth and hypersupply phase of the cycle. The numbers after some cities show their movement from the previous quarter (note that markets can move both forward and back in cycle position). Also, the largest markets are in bold and italics. It takes only 11 office markets to make up 50% of all 54 markets listed on the cycle graph. The most current cycle report can be found at www.du.edu/burnschool.

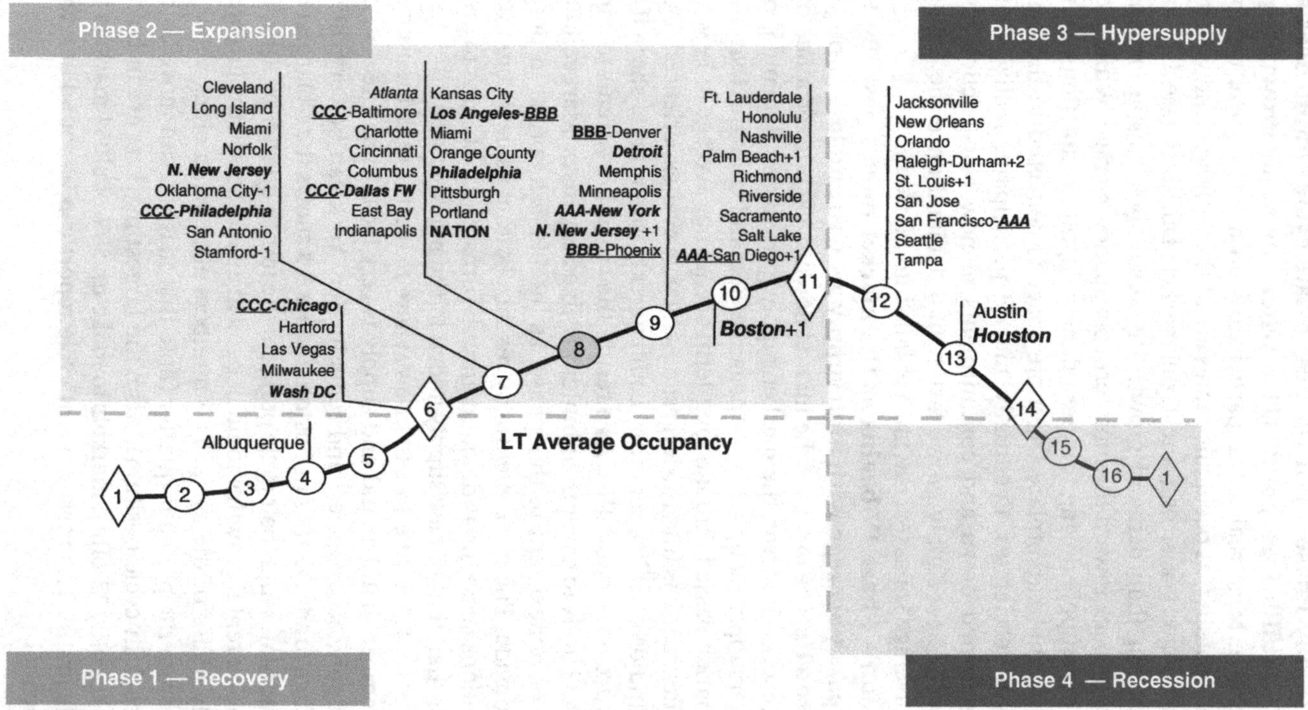

FIGURE 3.3 Office Market Cycle Forecast
Source: Glenn Mueller, Ph.D.

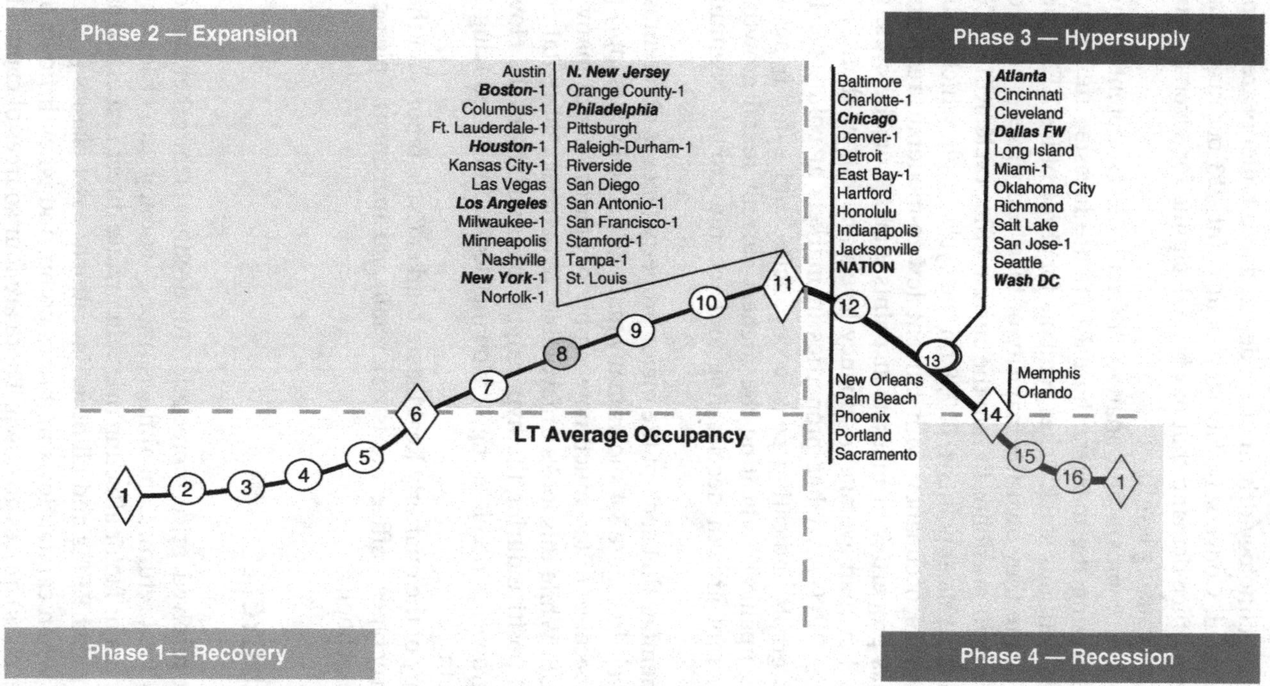

FIGURE 3.4 Apartment Market Cycle Forecast
Source: Glenn Mueller, Ph.D.

Note that Austin is in Hypersupply (point #13 on the graph) due to oversupply – it has technology-driven office demand and builders are supplying more than needed. Conversely, Houston is at point #13 because it has oil industry driven office demand that has been declining for several years due to low oil prices causing layoffs.

Investors can compare and analyze different REITs' potential income growth by analyzing the markets those REITs are invested in. Figure 3.3 also has three fictitious stock ticker symbols for three office REITs next to the markets where they own the majority of their properties – so investors can see where their portfolios fit into the current office cycle. REIT CCC has properties in markets at points 4, 6, 7, 8 on the cycle graph, which indicates long-term average occupancy with current low-to-moderate rent growth. REIT BBB has properties in markets at points 8 and 9 on the cycle graph indicating higher than average occupancy levels and higher than inflation rental growth. REIT AAA has properties in markets at points 10, 11, 12 on the cycle graph, indicating peak occupancies, and some hypersupply (declining occupancy), indicating the highest current rental growth with some risk of rent growth decelerating and income growth beginning to slow down.

Also remember that each of the major property types is different, so the apartment cycle in Figure 3.4 shows many markets in the hypersupply phase of the cycle because of too much new supply of apartments in many cities around the US. While this looks unfavorable, remember that rental growth rates are still positive during the hypersupply phase of the cycle. However, the rate of growth is decelerating or slowing down, thus producing lower income growth.

For a copy of the quarterly Real Estate Market Cycle reports on the four major property types – office, industrial, retail, and apartment – please go to du.edu/burnsschool.

FINANCIAL CYCLES

After income received, price appreciation (or decline) is the other part of any investment's total return. Capital flows (money coming into or leaving real estate) is the major factor affecting prices in private direct real estate as well as publicly traded REITs and all other investment asset classes (i.e., stocks and bonds). When capital flows in, prices go up, and when it flows out (to another asset class), prices go down. There are four sources of capital flows: private equity, public equity, private debt, and public debt.

Capital flows are difficult to follow and even more difficult to predict as the emotion and outlook of investors has not been captured in any known statistics. One major source of real estate transaction data is Real Capital Analytics, Inc. (www.rcanalytics.com), which in 2001 started tracking every commercial real estate transaction over $2.5 million in size in the United States. CoStar Group (NASDAQ: CSGP) (www.costar.com) also tracks capital flows. Both organizations provide data on price, capitalization rates, buyer, seller, and other important information. Figure 3.5 shows that the Commercial Property Price Index (CPPI) has followed the volume of capital flows very closely over the past 14 years.

But all property types do not move together, as shown in Figure 3.6. Notice that office and apartment prices were well above their 2007 peak prices in 2019, but the other property types were not. Investors should review all local market transaction reports (such as ones from Real Capital Analytics) so they can analyze the price trends and differentiate between the different property types and different property classes (such as A, B, or C level properties).

During positive economic times, like those present at the beginning of 2020, many industry analysts forecast that continued economic growth and the positive physical fundamentals of good occupancy and rental growth should continue to attract a large array of investors to real estate, thus keeping capitalization rates low and prices high. However, if prices

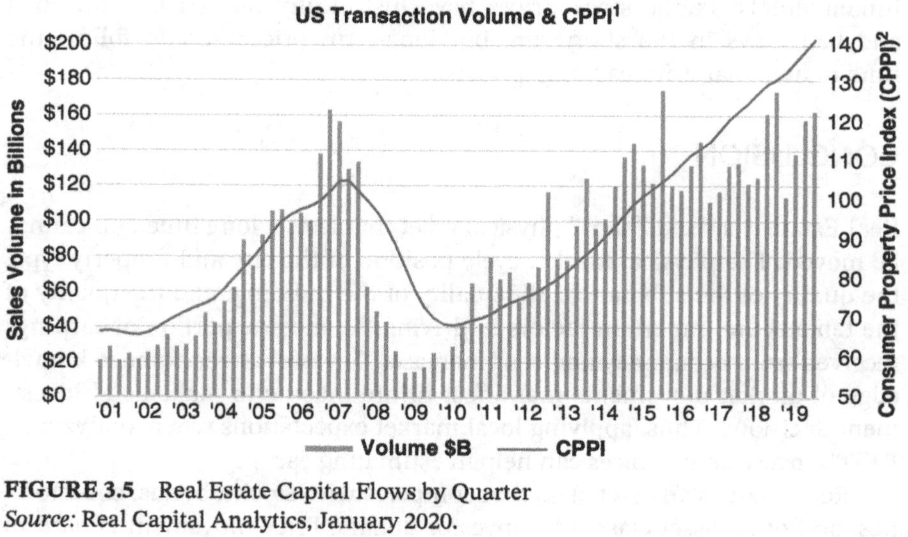

FIGURE 3.5 Real Estate Capital Flows by Quarter
Source: Real Capital Analytics, January 2020.

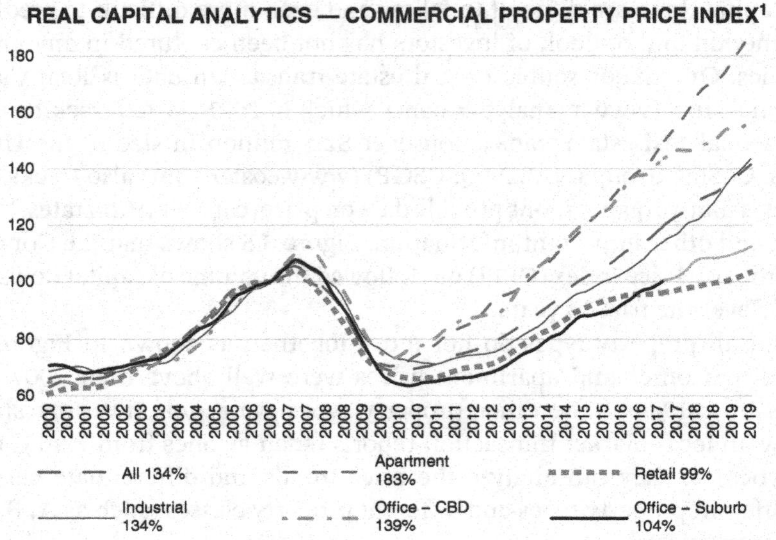

FIGURE 3.6 Commercial Real Estate Property Prices.
[1] CPPI represents the Commercial Property Price Index of all major properties on a national level.
Source: Real Capital Analytics, Inc., February 2019.

appreciate too far ahead of occupancy and rent fundamentals, it could lead to a price correction even with stable economic and physical market cycle fundamentals. Public stock prices have historically reacted to both good and bad news in the short run, but long-term prices should follow the fundaments that drive earnings growth.

CONCLUSION

Real Estate is a fixed "hard" physical asset that lasts a long time and cannot be moved. The physical market cycle position of the city and property type, the quality of the submarket, the quality of the building, and the quality of the tenants are important factors in driving the income portion of earnings received from occupancy and rent increases. Investors need to have knowledge of market movements that affect future income to make good investment decisions. Thus, applying local market expectations when analyzing a REIT's investment choices can help in estimating earnings.

Real estate is an asset class that competes with stocks, bonds, commodities, and other asset classes for investor dollars. Price movement is hard to predict, and it is important to know what current transaction prices in the markets are, and who the buyers and sellers may be. Many foreign investors see the United States as a safe haven for investing due to the strong legal ownership laws, stable government, and large, broad economy. When real estate investments are held long enough (through at least one full cycle) they have done well historically. However, if an investor is forced to sell at a specific point in time, they could lose money if the market is in the wrong part of the physical or financial cycle. In the public REIT market, short-term price swings from emotional reactions to current events can be an issue, but using a long-term perspective REITs have produced long-term returns that follow direct real estate return patterns with the added benefit of positive leverage and management's ability to improve property operations and portfolio property mix.

Websites for Data Sources:

CoStar: www.costar.com.

CBRE Econometric Advisors: https://www.cbre-ea.com/.

REIS Reports: www.reis.com.

Dodge Global Network: http://programs.construction.com/dodge-global-network-sem/?utm_term=fw%20dodge&utm_campaign=PMC_Brand_DGN&utm_source=bing&utm_medium=paid%20search&msclkid=5c2b3d4ad2581e8bff2a679c65555e32.

Homer Hoyt Institute: www.Hoyt.org.

Real Capital Analytics: www.rcanalytics.com.

CRE Finance Council: https://www.crefc.org/.

Situs RERC: http://www.situs.com/services-2/situs-rerc/.

CHAPTER 4

REIT Dividends

As Chapter 2 highlighted, many investors are drawn to REITs first and foremost because of the attractive current income they offer relative to bonds or stocks. A REIT's dividend yield is only attractive, however, if it is sustainable and able to be increased over time. This chapter discusses how to calculate the dividend yield on a REIT's shares, as well as how to assess the safety and sustainability of a REIT's dividend. Additionally, because investors pay the taxes on the dividend income they receive, this chapter addresses how REIT dividends are taxed. Last, this chapter highlights a few basics regarding preferred stock dividends, which typically offer a higher yield than common stock dividends. Chapter 9, Real Estate Debt and Fixed Income Securities, discusses the risks and rewards of investing in preferred shares of REITs in greater detail.

KKM REIT

Krewson–Kelly Mueller REIT, or KKM REIT (ticker symbol: KKM), is a fictional company used to illustrate concepts discussed in this and the remaining chapters.

REIT YIELDS

To qualify each year under the US Tax Code as a REIT, a REIT must distribute at least 90% of its otherwise taxable income to shareholders by paying investors in its common and, if applicable, preferred shares a dividend. Because of this distribution requirement, the current income – or *current yield* – on REIT shares tends to be higher than the yields on other income investments, such as US Treasuries and corporate bonds. Figure 4.1 illustrates the average yield REITs have offered investors over time, versus the yield on the S&P 500 Index and on 10-year US Treasuries. Between 1977 and 2019, the 7.1% average yield offered by REITs is 110 basis points higher than the average yield on 10-year US Treasuries and 440 basis points more than the S&P 500 Index during the same period. More recently, at the end of 2019, the FTSE Nareit All REITs Index offered a 4.06% yield, or 214 basis points higher than the 1.92% yield on 10-year US Treasuries and 221 basis points higher than the 1.85% dividend yield from the S&P 500 Index.

As with any stock, a REIT's current yield equals its most recently paid, regular dividend, annualized (multiplied by four if they pay a quarterly dividend, and by 12 if they pay monthly), then divided by its current stock price. REITs sometimes pay special dividends near the end of the year to comply with the 90% payout rule, usually in association with realizing large gains on properties sold. It is important to exclude special dividends from the above yield calculations, as these cash payouts are non-recurring.

Because many investors hold investments for several years, it is also important to understand the concept of *yield on cost,* which is calculated by dividing the current, annualized common dividend by the investor's cost

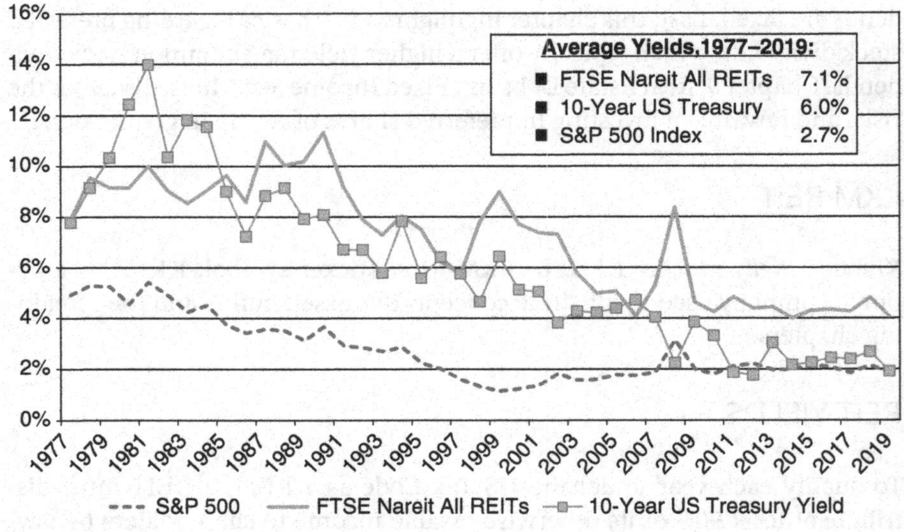

FIGURE 4.1 REIT Yields versus Yields on Other Investments
Sources: Nareit; Yahoo! Finance.

basis (i.e., original purchase price) in the REIT's common stock:

$$\text{Yield on Cost} = \frac{\text{Current quarterly dividend} \times 4}{\text{Shareholder's per share cost basis}}$$

For example, assume an investor paid $10 per share two years ago for common stock of KKM REIT (KKM). Today, KKM's stock price is $15 per share and it pays a quarterly dividend of $0.25, which annualizes to $1. KKM's current yield is 6.7% (or $1 ÷ $15), but the investor's yield on cost is 10%, calculated as the $1 annualized dividend divided by their $10 cost basis. When evaluating whether to sell these REIT shares to invest in something else, the investor will need to compare the 10% yield on cost to the current yields of competing investments. An increasing dividend is more attractive than a fixed bond yield for the life of the bond.

A few REITs pay dividends on a monthly, instead of quarterly basis. In such cases, their current dividend needs to be multiplied by 12, rather than 4, to calculate their yield. Table 4.1 lists those REITs at the end of 2019 that were paying monthly dividends.

TABLE 4.1 US REITs That Pay Monthly Dividends

AGNC Investment Corp. (AGNC)
American Finance Trust, Inc. (AFIN)
Apple Hospitality REIT, Inc. (APLE)
ARMOUR Residential REIT, Inc. (ARR)
Chatham Lodging Trust (CLDT)
Colony Credit Real Estate, Inc. (CLNC)
Dynex Capital, Inc. (DX)
Ellington Financial Inc. (EFC)
EPR Properties (ERP)
Gladstone Commercial Corporation (GOOD)
Gladstone Land Corporation (LAND)
KBS Real Estate Investment Trust II, Inc. (KBRS)
LTC Properties, Inc. (LTC)
Orchid Island Capital, Inc. (ORC)
Realty Income Corporation (O)
STAG Industrial, Inc. (STAG)
Whitestone REIT (WSR)

As of December 31, 2019.
Source: S&P Global Market Intelligence.

ARE REIT YIELDS SAFE?

REIT yields may be attractive, but they are meaningless if the dividend behind them is not sustainable. Historically, the contractual nature of rental revenue from leases has enabled REITs to pay dividends that have proved to be secure, even during most economic recessions. Equity REITs derive the majority of their income from leases that, depending on their duration and the credit of the tenant, provide REITs with recurring, more bond-like cash flows than most non-REIT companies can offer. Provided a REIT management team does not operate its business with excessive levels of debt (or *leverage*), the preferred and common dividends of that company should be safe. Many people look at the dividend paid versus the REIT's FFO per share.

That said, the 2007–08 global financial crisis (GFC) that precipitated the Great Recession of 2008–09 (Great Recession) served as a grim reminder about economic and market forces that can jeopardize REIT dividends. According to S&P Global Market Intelligence, in 2008–09 over two-thirds of all REITs cut or suspended their common dividends in response to the GFC in order to conserve cash. Equity REITs produced a dismal total return of negative 37.7% in 2008, before rebounding in 2009 and achieving a positive total return of 28.0%. (Please refer to Table 1.1 in Chapter 1 for annual REIT returns.) Despite widespread dividend cuts, in 2008 REITs underperformed the S&P 500 Index by only 73 basis points and then actually outperformed that index by 153 basis points in 2009.

Rule of Thumb

During an economic crisis or "Black Swan" event, such as the GFC of 2007–08 and the dramatic economic disruption associated with combatting the Coronavirus (COVID-19) pandemic of 2020, many REIT boards of directors may elect to cut or temporarily suspend dividend payments to preserve capital. To mitigate the risk of a dividend cut, invest in REITs that operate with lower leverage levels than their peers and/or REITs that invest in more essential property types (such as industrial, office, apartments, or grocery-anchored shopping centers).

The rash of dividend cuts by REITs during the Great Recession was similar to the percentage of REITs that slashed their dividends in the wake of the savings and loan crisis (S&L Crisis) of the late 1980s. In both instances, a broad liquidity crisis translated into dividend cuts for the majority of REITs. More recently, the Coronavirus (COVID-19) pandemic in early 2020 precipitated rapid business closures, stay-at-home quarantines, and mandatory social-distancing practices across the US. With travel abruptly grinding to a halt, non-essential retail stores and businesses being forced to close for months, and tens of millions of American workers suddenly unemployed, every hotel REIT and 18 – or nearly half – of the 37 retail REITs (including freestanding retail) either suspended or dramatically reduced their common dividends to preserve capital. During each of these three crises, the REITs that maintained or increased their dividends were those that were operating with lower levels of debt and owned commercial property types for which demand remains steady during adverse or uncertain economic conditions. Demand elasticity for different property types is discussed in greater detail in Chapters 6 and 10.

QUANTIFYING DIVIDEND SAFETY

Investors can use two approaches to quantify dividend safety, the first of which focuses on near-term expected earnings growth and the second of which measures a REIT's balance sheet leverage. Chapter 11 reiterates the metrics that follow and also provides additional insight as to their relative utility for analyzing dividend safety.

Dividend/FFO Payout Ratio

A payout ratio is defined as the percent of net income a company pays out to its common shareholders as a dividend. For example, a company that generates net income per share (or *earnings per share*) of $1 and pays out a 10 cent dividend per share has a payout ratio of 10%. As discussed in Chapter 11, REITs use a metric called *funds from operations* (FFO) to measure profitability instead of earnings per share (EPS). A REIT's expected dividend payout ratio is calculated as its current annualized dividend, divided by an estimate of next year's expected FFO per share. Estimates of FFO per share may be obtained from individual company reports generated by investment banks' research departments and from data service providers, such as S&P Global Market Intelligence and Thomson Reuter's First Call. The resulting dividend/FFO payout ratio (which is also referred to as an *FFO payout ratio*) gives a quick indication of a REIT's ability to pay its current dividend. An FFO payout ratio below 100% indicates that Wall Street expects that REIT to generate FFO sufficient to cover its current annualized dividend. By contrast, an FFO payout ratio above 100% should generate immediate concern and cause potential investors to dig deeper into a REIT's expected earnings ability.

Investor Tip

If the Dividend/FFO payout ratio for a REIT is greater than 100%, the dividend may be at risk.

Financial Leverage Determines Dividend Safety

Higher leverage equals higher risk. REITs can enhance the safety of their dividend by running their operations with lower amounts of debt. A company is obligated to pay interest and principal due to lenders and dividends associated with preferred stock before paying the dividend due to common shareholders. Accordingly, the less debt a company has, the more likely it will be able to pay its common dividend. Investors can calculate two leverage metrics – debt-to-total market capitalization and debt-to-tangible book value – to determine if a REIT potentially has too much debt. There is a third metric, debt-to-adjusted earnings before interest, taxes, depreciation and amortization (or *debt-to-EBITDA* for short), that also quantifies a REIT's leverage, but investors generally will not have enough information to calculate this for themselves. Rather, many REITs, especially those that issue investment grade rated fixed income securities, provide their debt-to-EBITDA ratios in their supplemental information packages. Chapter 11 provides more detail on all three metrics, so this chapter focuses on providing historical data and examples.

Debt-to-Total Market Capitalization Ratio

At September 30, 2019, and according to Nareit, equity REITs' average debt-to-total market capitalization ratio was 27.5% and mortgage REITs' (mREITs) average debt ratio was 39.8%. Because the debt-to-total capitalization ratio changes depending on a REIT's current stock price, this ratio can over- or understate a company's leverage, depending on market conditions. For example, if KKM REIT has $100 million of debt and 10 million common shares that trade at $15 a share, it has a debt-to-total market capitalization ratio of 40%:

$100 of debt ÷ ($100 of debt + [$15 × 10 shares of KKM]) = 40%

If KKM's stock price declines to $10 per share, however, its debt-to-total market capitalization ratio increases to 50%:

$100 of debt ÷ ($100 of debt + [$10 × 10 shares of KKM]) = 50%

Because a variety of events influence a company's stock price, not all of which are within a management team's control, another way of gauging a REIT's leverage is to use its debt-to-tangible book value ratio.

Debt-to-Tangible Book Value Ratio

Tangible book value is calculated by taking total assets listed on a REIT's balance sheet, less any goodwill or intangibles, plus any accumulated depreciation and amortization (generally listed in the footnotes of the financial statements). As of September 30, 2019, the average debt-to-tangible book ratio of equity REITs was 44%. Putting this industry statistic into context, private landlords, including private equity firms that took publicly traded REITs private in 2005–07, had employed an average 75% debt and as much as 90% leverage to finance their real estate purchases. At the end of 2006, which was the last year before the 2007–08 GFC, equity REITs had an average debt-to-tangible book value of 57%. Although some REITs exceeded what, in hindsight, were prudent levels of leverage, REITs nonetheless were more conservative in their use of leverage than the average private real estate investor.

Leverage: Less Is More

To minimize the risk of investing in REITs with at-risk dividends, investors should focus on REITs with debt-to-tangible book values below 50%.

In fact, out of the 130 REITs that comprise the FTSE Nareit All REITs Index at the end of 2006 and before the global financial crisis, only one REIT, General Growth Properties (formerly NYSE: GGP), filed for protection from its creditors under Chapter 11 bankruptcy. Before the crisis, General Growth Properties' debt-to-tangible book value ratio was 74%, or 17 percentage points higher than the industry average. The company restructured its debt in the bankruptcy courts, emerged from bankruptcy in November 2010, and ultimately was taken private by Brookfield Property Partners in 2018. (Note that most of the debt-to-tangible book value ratios cited in the section were provided by S&P Global Market Intelligence.)

Debt-to-EBITDA

Debt-to-EBITDA measures how long it would take a company to pay off its debt, assuming it only sustains (rather than grows or shrinks) its most recent quarterly income. As mentioned earlier, investors generally do not have enough information to calculate this metric themselves. Since the GFC of 2007–08, most REITs that issue investment grade rated securities now provide their debt-to-EBITDA ratio in their quarterly supplemental information packages. In principle, the calculation takes total debt outstanding, less unencumbered cash, and divides it by the most recent quarter's real estate EBITDA, annualized.

There is not a source for tracking property sector level or industry level debt/EBITDA ratios. Nareit's T-Tracker® used S&P Global Market Intelligence data to create the data shown in Table 4.2, which provides a perspective on the different debt/EBITDA ratios among REIT property

TABLE 4.2 Debt/EBITDA Ratios by Property Sector for US Equity REITs

Property Sector	2010	2011	2012	2013	2014	2015	2016	2017	2018	2019*
Office	8.1 x	7.5 x	7.4 x	7.4 x	7.0 x	6.8 x	6.2 x	6.2 x	5.9 x	6.1 x
Industrial	12.8 x	16.1 x	7.8 x	6.6 x	6.2 x	5.2 x	4.7 x	3.9 x	3.8 x	4.1 x
Retail	7.8 x	7.1 x	7.2 x	7.1 x	6.9 x	5.6 x	5.5 x	6.0 x	5.8 x	6.1 x
Residential	9.0 x	8.2 x	7.1 x	7.5 x	6.7 x	5.8 x	4.1 x	5.4 x	5.9 x	5.6 x
Health Care	5.7 x	7.0 x	5.8 x	5.9 x	5.9 x	6.9 x	6.0 x	5.6 x	5.5 x	5.6 x
Lodging/Resorts	9.0 x	7.6 x	6.3 x	5.7 x	4.5 x	4.3 x	4.0 x	4.2 x	4.2 x	5.0 x
Data Centers	5.8 x	4.7 x	4.7 x	4.8 x	4.6 x	5.0 x	5.5 x	5.8 x	5.6 x	5.7 x
Other	5.8 x	4.0 x	4.5 x	4.9 x	4.8 x	5.0 x	5.7 x	5.1 x	5.2 x	6.5 x
All Equity REITs	7.7 x	7.2 x	6.6 x	6.4 x	6.1 x	5.8 x	5.4 x	5.5 x	5.5 x	5.8 x

*As of September 30, 2019.
Source: S&P Global Market Intelligence, Nareit T-Tracker®.

sectors, and how those ratios have changed since 2010. On average, REIT debt-to-EBITDA ratios have declined by 25% since the end of 2010.

Legal Standing of Leases Supports Dividend Safety

As is discussed in Chapter 5, leases are a contract between the landlord (REIT) and the tenant, and bankruptcy courts view them as operating expenses, which are legally senior to non-operating expenses – meaning the tenant is obligated to pay their rent before paying any interest or principal on outstanding debt, or any dividends on preferred or common stock. Therefore, even if a REIT's tenant goes bankrupt, the tenant must continue paying the REIT its contractual rent until the bankruptcy court judge allows the tenant to reject the lease. As a result, REITs generally do not go bankrupt from lost income, even when some of their tenants do. The relative stability and visibility of these underlying cash flows are a primary reason that investors view real estate and REITs as defensive investments that pay reasonably safe dividends.

REIT DIVIDENDS AND TAXATION

The two most widely known features of REITs are that they pay relatively high dividends and that they generally do not pay corporate income taxes. As discussed at the beginning of this chapter, to qualify each year as a REIT for IRS purposes, REITs must pay their common and preferred shareholders dividends that equal at least 90% of what would otherwise be taxed as ordinary income. If a REIT pays out only 90% of its taxable income, it will owe corporate taxes on the 10% it retains. By paying a dividend equal to 100% of taxable income (including capital gains) and satisfying other REIT requirements, REITs can avoid paying corporate income taxes. REIT shareholders pay their appropriate taxes on dividend income received. Thinking about this from a debits and credits perspective, when a partnership makes a distribution to its partners, the entity credits cash and debits equity to report the reduction in cash and the reduction in partner's capital account balance; when a REIT distributes earnings by paying dividends, it also credits cash but then it debits the income statement, reducing its corporate taxable income by the amount distributed.

Because of their 90% minimum distribution requirement, REITs have higher dividend payout ratios than non-REIT C-corporations (C-corps).

In fact, non-REIT C-corps may elect to pay *no* dividends to shareholders. Because REITs must comply with their minimum distribution requirement, REIT management teams tend to manage their portfolios (what they own, and where) and balance sheets conservatively so that they can maintain and/or grow the dividend. REITs can elect to reduce or cut their common dividends, but not without severely damaging short-term stock price performance in the process.

Changes to the tax laws since 2000 have affected how dividends are taxed at the investor level. The *Jobs and Growth Tax Relief Reconciliation Act of 2003* (also known as the *Bush Tax Cuts*) lowered the individual's tax rate on previously taxed earnings of C-corps paid out to shareholders as qualified dividends to a maximum of 15%. (Note that *The American Taxpayer Relief Act of 2012* added a 20% rate on the highest tax bracket.) Dividends paid by non-REIT C-corps are taxed at both the corporate and investor levels, and, per the Bush Tax Cuts and IRS, *qualify* to be taxed at the investor's capital gains rate. REIT dividends avoid the "double taxation" to which other C-corps dividends are subject. Because they are not taxed at the corporate level, the portion of a REIT's dividend that is characterized as ordinary taxable income does not qualify for the lower tax rate; that is, REIT dividends are *non-qualified dividends* under this law.

Pursuant to changes enacted by the *Tax Cuts and Jobs Act of 2017* (or *Trump Tax Cuts of 2017*), the portion of REIT dividends that is characterized as ordinary taxable income continues to be non-qualified and taxed at an investor's ordinary income tax rate. However, under the Trump Tax Cuts of 2017, Section 199A allows investors to deduct up to 20% of their combined qualified REIT dividends, defined in Section 199A(e)(3) as any dividend from a REIT that is not a capital gain dividend or qualified dividend income. Said more simply, the first 20% of the portion of a REIT's dividend that is classified as ordinary income is not taxed. Table 4.3 shows a simple example of how a REIT's dividend is taxed at the investor level.

REITs not only pay out higher dividends than non-REIT C-corps, they also provide higher after-tax returns. As Figure 4.2 demonstrates, the Trump Tax Cuts of 2017 provided a similar reduction in effective tax rates for REITs and non-REIT C-corps. Figure 4.2 also shows that a dollar paid out by a REIT is taxed 33.4% on average, whereas every dollar a non-REIT C-corp pays out has already been taxed 21% at the corporate (entity) level, and then another 18.8%, on average, at the individual shareholder level, for a total of 39.8% in taxes paid.

TABLE 4.3 Example of How US REIT Dividends Are Taxed

Assumptions:

- The REIT has a 100% payout ratio
- The investors pay the highest possible marginal tax rate on the non-qualified REIT dividend

	REIT
Earnings before taxes	$100.00
– Dividends (100% payout)	(100.00)
Net Income	0.00
– Federal Corporate Taxes (21%)	N/A
– Blended State Corporate Taxes (6%)	N/A
Retained earnings	$0.00

	Investor
Dividend income	$100.00
– Business income deduction (20%)	(20.00)
Net Income	$80.00
– Non-qualified dividend maximum tax rate: 37%	(29.60)
+ Business income deduction	20.00
After-tax cash to investor	$70.40

REITs Do Not Pay Out All of Their Cash in Dividends

Investors often make the mistake of thinking REITs pay out all of their free cash flow in the form of dividends. In fact, the cash REITs generate from their properties typically is greater than the dividends they pay to shareholders. From an accounting perspective, taxable income for IRS purposes is often less than the dividend paid to shareholders, resulting in no tax obligation to the REIT. Taxable income is calculated according to rules set by the IRS, whereas net income for public reporting purposes to the SEC is determined by GAAP. In calculating both types of income, REITs are permitted to deduct

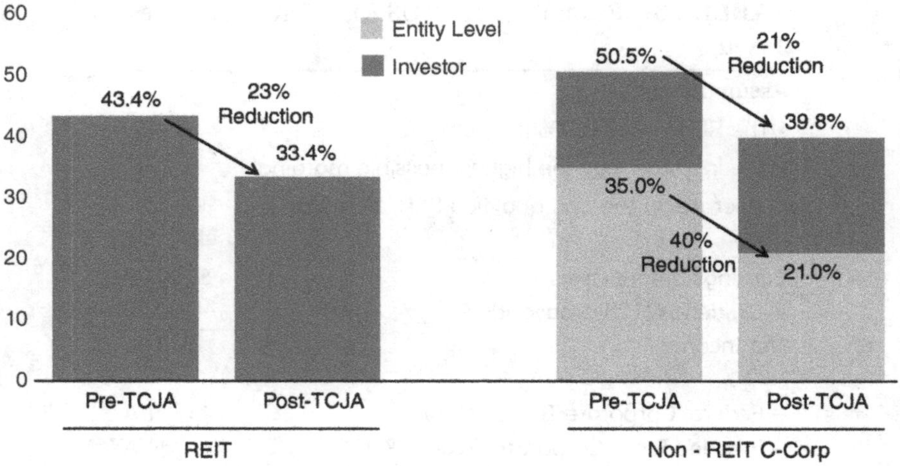

FIGURE 4.2 Effective Tax Rate for REITs and Non-REIT C-Corps
Source: Reproduced by permission of Nareit® and is used subject to the Terms and Conditions of Use set forth on the Nareit website, including, but not limited to, Section 9 thereof.

many non-cash expenses, such as the annual depreciation of their buildings and amortization of fixed costs. Note that only the buildings, improvements, and personal property, and not the land on which buildings are constructed, are depreciable.

For example, if KKM REIT buys a building for $11 million, and the land under it is worth $1 million, it will depreciate the $10 million building over a 40-year period. This annual $250,000 depreciation expense (equal to $10 million divided by 40 years) reduces KKM REIT's income for IRS, GAAP, and tax purposes; it is not a cash expenditure. Instead, KKM REIT reduces its basis in that building by $250,000 each year. Continuing the example, after four years, KKM REIT's basis in the property would be $9 million, calculated as the building's initial $10 million cost, less four years of $250,000 depreciation expense (i.e., $10 million less [4 years × $250,000 annual depreciation expense]). Connecting the dots between taxable income, depreciation expense, and cash flow (where FFO is a proxy for cash flow), if KKM REIT's net income is $750,000, its FFO would be $1 million ($750,000 of net income + $250,000 of depreciation expense = $1 million of FFO). This simple example illustrates how REIT cash flow is nearly always higher than after-tax income.

The Components of a REIT's Common Dividend

The example in Table 4.3 was an oversimplified illustration of how REIT common dividends are taxed at the individual investor level. Rarely is a REIT's dividend taxed entirely as ordinary income. Instead, a REIT dividend generally consists of a combination of three types of income, which are taxed at different levels. These three income classifications are:

1. ordinary dividends (individual shareholders' tax rates apply);
2. capital gains (generally 0%, 15%, or 20% at December 31, 2019, for most assets held for more than one year); and
3. return of capital (non-taxable).

REITs typically disclose the tax treatment of each year's dividends in a press release issued in late January or early February. (Refer to each REIT's website for current and past press releases. Website addresses for the REITs in the FTSE All REITs Index at the end of 2019 are provided in Appendix C.) The "dividend treatment" press release typically contains a table that clearly states how much of the common dividend should be taxed as ordinary dividend income, how much is a classified as capital gains, and how much, if any, is a non-taxable return of capital.

Ordinary Dividend Income

Generally, the majority of REIT common dividends are characterized and taxed as ordinary income, meaning that the business activities that generated the cash flow being paid out as dividends to shareholders were "ordinary," such as from collecting rents. So, if investors receive $1 per share in dividends and are in the 37% ordinary income tax bracket, they will owe $0.30 of federal taxes on every dollar of REIT dividends they receive (80% of $1 times 37% tax rate rounds up to 30 cents). (Please also refer to Example A in Table 4.4.) However, if a REIT engages in transactions during its fiscal year that are not ordinary, such as selling a building at a gain or loss relative to its investment basis, the REIT may recognize long-term capital gains and/or a return of capital, both of which are discussed next.

Capital Gains

If a REIT sells a business asset (i.e., depreciable asset or real property held in trade or business for more than one year) for more money than its depreciated

TABLE 4.4 Sample Calculations of Taxes on KKM REIT's Dividend

Assumptions:

- KKM REIT pays a dividend of $1.00 per share
- The shareholder paid $20.00 for each share of KKM REIT original basis
- The maximum individual ordinary income tax rate is 37%
- The maximum individual long-term capital gains tax rate is 20%
- **Example A** – KKM REIT classifies 100% of its dividend as ordinary income
- **Example B** – KKM REIT classifies 60% of its dividend as ordinary income, 25% as a long-term capital gain, and 15% as a return of capital

	Example A	Example B
Shareholder's dividend received from KKM REIT	$1.00	$1.00
x Percent of dividend classified as Ordinary Income	x 100%	x 60%
Income taxable at ordinary rate	$1.00	$0.60
– Business income deduction (20%)	($0.20)	($0.12)
Taxable ordinary income	$0.80	$0.48
x Federal tax rate on ordinary income	x 37%	x 37%
(A) Income tax due on ordinary income	**$0.30**	**$0.18**
Shareholder's dividend received from KKM REIT	–	$1.00
x Percent of dividend classified as long-term capital gains	–	x 25%
Income taxable at capital gains rate	–	$0.25
x Federal tax rate on long-term capital gains	–	x 20%
(B) Income tax due on long-term capital gains	–	**$0.05**
Shareholder's dividend received from KKM REIT	–	$1.00
x Percent of dividend classified as return of capital	–	x 15%
Income taxable as return of capital	–	$0.15
x Federal tax rate on capital gains	–	–
(C) Income tax due on return of capital	–	**$0.00**
(D) Shareholder's total tax liability (A + B + C)	**$0.30**	**$0.23**
Effective tax rate for shareholder	30%	23%
Shareholder's original basis in KKM shares	$20.00	$20.00
– Return of capital received	–	($0.15)
(E) New basis in KKM	$20.00	$19.85
After-tax income to shareholder of KKM ($1.00 - D)	**$0.70**	**$0.77**
After-tax yield on KKM REIT shares [($1.00 - D) / E]	**3.5%**	**3.9%**

basis (also referred to as its *adjusted tax basis* in the property), the REIT will recognize a capital gain on the sale. The REIT can then pass the capital gains through to shareholders by classifying part of the common dividend as capital gains. Capital losses are not passed through to investors, however, because REITs are taxed as corporations for income tax purposes. Shareholders pay taxes on this portion of the dividend, but at the then-current capital gains rate.

Return of Capital

Assuming E&P (earnings and profits) equal taxable income, if a REIT distributes more than its taxable income for IRS purposes, the amount paid to shareholders that exceeds 100% of taxable income is classified as a return of capital, which is not taxed. Rather, it lowers an investor's basis in a common stock and eventually may be taxed in the form of capital gains when the investor sells his or her shares. A return of capital, therefore, increases both an investor's tax-adjusted current yield, as well as the after-tax total return he or she realizes upon selling the shares.

By way of a simple example, if KKM REIT generates taxable income of $1.25 per share in year 1 and pays an annualized, regular dividend of $1.50 per share in that same year, then 25 cents will be classified as a return of capital. From the investors' perspective, they will not pay taxes on the 25 cents and their basis in shares of KKM will be reduced by the same amount.

Examples A and B in Table 4.4 illustrate how individual investors in the 37% income tax bracket would calculate their tax liability on KKM REIT's common dividend using 2019 tax rates, comparing the taxation of a dividend that is all ordinary taxable income versus one that is partially classified as ordinary income, capital gains, and return of capital.

Example A in Table 4.4 illustrates the investor's tax liability assuming the entire dividend is ordinary income. **Example B** illustrates how having some of the dividend classified as long-term capital gains or a return of capital lowers an investor's effective tax rate on dividends, thereby increasing the after-tax yield.

In summary, a REIT's common dividend generally consists of one or more types of income for taxation purposes: ordinary income, which is taxed at the highest individual or "ordinary" rate; capital gains, which are taxed at the long-term capital gains tax rate; and a return of capital, which is not taxed and which lowers a shareholder's cost basis in each share. When a REIT classifies portions of its dividend as long-term capital gains or a return of capital, the shareholder's effective tax rate is lower than if the dividend were classified entirely as ordinary income. Many investors have chosen to hold REITs in their retirement accounts (IRA or 401(k)) to avoid or defer paying taxes on dividends received.

Preferred Stock Dividends

As mentioned earlier, REITs can satisfy their 90% payout requirement by paying dividends to both its common *and* preferred shareholders. At the end of 2019 and according to S&P Global Market Intelligence, the liquidation value of REIT preferred shares outstanding totaled $29.2 billion, whereas the market value of common equity for REITs in the FTSE Nareit All REITs Index was $1.3 trillion. Though the market for REIT preferred stock is small, it nonetheless is worth knowing a few basic facts associated with its attractive yield.

> Yield × liquidation value of preferred stock = the annual dividend payable to preferred shareholders

Preferred shares are sold according to a liquidation (or *par*) value, typically equal to $25 per share. When a REIT wants to raise $100 million by issuing preferred equity, it would issue 4 million shares ($100 million gross proceeds, divided by $25 per share par value). The yield associated with the issuance is established as a spread (or *risk premium*) to long-term US Treasury rates, and the risk premium is a function of the issuing the REIT's investment-grade qualifications. For example, if the underlying US Treasury rate is yielding 2.5%, a REIT that is BBB– and Baa3 rated by S&P and Moody's, respectively, may issue preferred shares at a 300-basis point premium, or at 5.5%. That 5.5% yield on the par value translates into a dividend of $1.375 per share, calculated as 5.5% times the $25 par value.

CONCLUSION

The income that investors can access by investing in REITs is a powerful wealth-building tool, but only if the REITs can sustain and preferably grow their dividends over time. The risk of wealth destruction and underperformance associated with REITs that have cut their common dividends in the past is examined more thoroughly in Chapter 10.

CHAPTER 5

Leases

Prior to exploring the different types of commercial properties that REITs own, it is instructive to understand the different types of leases that REITs, as landlords, use. A lease is a legal contract between a landlord (the *lessor,* which is the REIT) and a tenant (the *lessee*) whereby the tenant agrees to pay rent for a defined period of time in exchange for the right to occupy/use the landlord's space. Most leases require monthly payments of rent, but other intervals – for example, annual payments – can also exist. It depends on the terms to which the landlord and tenant agree. The terms of the lease discussed in this chapter are standard items negotiated between a landlord and a tenant, which are spelled out in the resulting lease agreement.

Along with the length of each lease, which is usually expressed in months or years, different lease structures translate into different cash flow streams to a landlord. Tenants and landlords negotiate all aspects of a lease, including the length of time a property will be leased (lease *length, term,* or *duration*), who will pay for certain operating expenses, and who will pay for improvements (tenant finish) to the tenant's space. Each type of lease allocates different costs to the landlord or tenant and determines which party bears the risk of paying higher costs if utility or other expenses increase. Lease length and structure, therefore, are fundamental predictors of REIT income and stock price performance, examples of which are discussed in Chapter 10. The content of this chapter provides an overview of the four major types of leases, including which structures are most commonly used among different property types.

LEASE TERMINOLOGY

Most people are familiar with the concept of paying rent, but many are not aware of the different types of rent they will pay under different scenarios. An asking rent of $15 per square foot listed on a building's "for rent" sign means something very different under a gross lease than under a full-service lease, both of which are addressed in the following pages. Before discussing the four basic types of leases, it is helpful to become familiar with some basic terminology:

- **Base year** is the first 12 months of a lease or the period that ends with the first full calendar year of a lease. In the latter instance, the base year can be more than 12 months. It is often used to set the expense stop (defined below) in a full-service or modified gross lease.
- **Common area maintenance (CAM)** are charges the landlord incurs to maintain areas of a multi-tenanted property (which simply is a building that has more than one tenant) that are accessible to all tenants. CAM fees cover expenses the landlord incurs for services, including property management, labor costs associated with the building's engineering team, lobby maintenance, shared restrooms, and parking area. In a multi-building office park or campus, CAM fees can also include costs associated with a fitness center or foodservice area that are accessible by tenants throughout the campus. CAM fees are in addition to a tenant's base rent, and the landlord typically bills tenants according to the percentage of the building they rent. For example, if a tenant's space represents one-third of the building's rentable square footage, then that tenant would be billed for one-third of the CAM associated with the building's upkeep.
- **Escalation clauses**, or escalators, are future increases in rent that the tenant agrees to pay during the course of a lease. Escalations can be expressed in dollar amounts or as a percent, and typically occur on an annual basis. Rent escalations tend to be tied to increases in the Consumer Price Index (CPI) or expressed as fixed periodic increases. As an example, a tenant may agree to pay a monthly base rent of $1,000 in the first year of a lease, and then an additional $100 per month each subsequent year for the duration of the lease. In Year 5, therefore, the tenant's monthly rent would have escalated to $1,400 (Year 1 = $1,000; Year 2 = $1,100; Year 3 = $1,200; Year 4 = $1,300; Year 5 = $1,400).

- **Expense stops** are most common in full-service and modified gross leases. The landlord will bear the operating expenses and CAM associated with the tenant's space up to the expense stop amount; the tenant will bear any expense overage. For example, operating expenses and CAM on Tenant A's space in Year 1 are $4.50 per square foot, so the expense stop is set for the duration of the lease at that level. For the remainder of the lease, the landlord will use $4.50 of the base rent received to pay the tenant's operating expenses and will bill the tenant for any amounts that exceed this expense stop.
- **Capped expenses** are similar to expense stops and, in some areas of the country, are referred to as expense stops. However, instead of being a fixed dollar amount, expense stops are a maximum percentage increase in expenses.
- **Leasing commissions (LCs)** are paid to real estate brokers who represent the tenant and/or landlord. (Tenants' brokers are often referred to as *tenant representatives* or simply *tenant reps*.) Typically the brokers are paid 50% of their LC upon lease execution and 50% upon lease commencement. The LC generally is calculated as 2–8% of the total rent payable for the initial term of the lease. For example, if a tenant will pay a landlord annual rent of $10,000 for three years, and the leasing commission rate in that market is 4% , then the landlord will need to pay the leasing agent $1,200 ($10,000 × 3 years × 4%). If there is a broker representing the landlord, then an additional LC would be owed following a similar schedule.
- **Operating expenses** are costs associated with operating and maintaining the rented area of a building. Such costs include real estate taxes, property insurance, utilities, and janitorial services for tenant-specific areas (as opposed to common areas shared with other tenants). Operating expenses do not include capital expenditures for structural maintenance of the building, and they do not include interest payments on any mortgage associated with the property being leased. Each lease specifically identifies what can and cannot be included as part of the operating expenses.
- **Rent** – The different types of rental revenue, including escalations, are summarized in Table 5.1:
  - **Total, base, gross, or contract rent** are all ways of describing the amount of money a tenant must pay the landlord each period, as defined in the lease. It includes agreed-upon expense stops and reflects any rent escalations that have become effective.

TABLE 5.1 Comparison of Different Components of Rent

Assumptions:

- 15,000 SF rentable area
- 5-year lease term
- $25.00 base rent per SF
- $4.50 expense stop & CAM
- 3% annual escalations on base rent
- 4% leasing commission
- 4 months of rent (after concessions)
- TI allowance of $15 per SF

	Year 1	Year 2	Year 3	Year 4	Year 5
Total rent per SF	$25.00	$25.00	$25.75	$26.52	$27.32
+ Escalation	–	$0.75	$0.77	$0.80	$0.82
New total rent per SF	$25.00	$25.75	$26.52	$27.32	$28.14
x Rentable SF	15,000	15,000	15,000	15,000	15,000
Total rent	$375,000	$386,250	$397,838	$409,773	$422,066
– Expense stop & CAM[a]	–67,500	–67,500	–67,500	–67,500	–67,500
Net rent before concessions	307,500	318,750	330,338	342,273	354,566
– 4 months of free base rent	–125,000	–	–	–	–
Effective rent landlord realizes	182,500	318,750	330,338	342,273	354,566
Less:					
Tenant Improvement Allowance[b]	–225,000	–	–	–	–
Leasing Commission[c]	–61,137	–	–	–	–
Net effective rent received by landlord	–$103,637	$318,750	$330,338	$342,273	$354,566
Aggregate net effective rent received	$1,242,289				
Net effective rent per SF[d]	$16.56				

[a]"Expense stop & CAM" amount is calculated as $4.50 x 15,000 rentable square feet (RSF).
[b]"Tenant Improvement Allowance" is calculated by multiplying the $15 TI allowance times the rentable square feet, or $15 x 15,000 RSF.
[c]"Leasing Commission" is calculated by adding the "Effective rent landlord realizes" in all five years, then multiplying that sum by 4%.
[d]"Net effective rent per square foot" equals the "Aggregate net effective rent received," divided by the RSF, divided by the lease term ($1,242,289 ÷ 15,000 RSF ÷ 5 years).

  - **Net rent** is the amount of rent a landlord retains each period, after paying (that is, *net of*) expenses associated with property operations and maintenance.
  - **Effective rent** is net rent, adjusted to reflect the cost of any concessions and leasing commissions the landlord has agreed to as part of the lease agreement. The most common concessions are tenant improvements and free rent, both of which are discussed later in this chapter.
  - **Free rent** is a period of time (usually a few months but sometimes a year or more) during which time a landlord grants the tenant occupancy rights to the rental space without requiring contract rent be paid. Free rent is a concession a landlord is willing to pay to entice a tenant to lease a space.
  - **Market rent** is the prevailing rental rate associated with comparable spaces in similar buildings and locations.
- **Square feet:** There also are different ways of measuring the same building, depending on the information needed:
  - **Gross square feet (or gross building area)** measures a building's total constructed area to the middle of the exterior walls. Landlords typically do not use gross square feet for leasing purposes unless the tenant leases the entire building. A building's gross square feet do not change with leasing and configuration changes, which do affect the rentable square feet (discussed below).
  - **Useable square feet (or useable area)** measures the space a tenant occupies. According to Barron's *Dictionary of Real Estate Terms* (7th edition), a tenant's useable area is measured "from paint to paint inside the permanent walls and to the middle of partitions separating one tenant's space from that of other tenants on the same floor," within the walls defining the space they have rented. Note that if a building is leased entirely to one tenant, then useable square feet equals rentable square feet.
  - **Rentable square feet** equals the sum of a tenant's useable area, plus the tenant's pro rata share of a core factor, usually as defined by Building Owners and Managers Association (BOMA). A core factor represents, the difference between rentable and useable square footage, and includes common areas such as lobbies, atriums, and restrooms, as well as the mechanical core, which includes elevators, janitorial closets, and phone/electric closets. In some areas, landlords use a fixed core factor, rather than BOMA's calculation, in

which case they apply a flat percentage to calculate a building's useable area. In some markets, the core factor is referred to as the *load factor*.

For example, a building contains 50,000 rentable square feet and has a core factor of 10%, indicating that common areas take up 5,000 square feet (50,000 × 10%). One tenant occupies 15,000 useable square feet, and a second tenant occupies the remaining 30,000 useable square feet. The first tenant pays rent on its 15,000 useable square feet plus on one-third (15,000 ÷ 45,000 useable square feet) of the 5,000 square feet of common areas, for total rentable square feet of 16,650 (15,000 SF + [33% × 5,000 SF]). Similarly, the second tenant occupies 30,000 square feet and pays rent on 33,350 square feet.

> To summarize the square footage measurements:
> - Multi-tenanted building: Gross > Rentable > Useable
> - Single-tenant building: Gross > Rentable = Useable

- **Tenant improvement (TI) allowance** is an amount of money the landlord is willing to spend on a space to either retain an existing tenant or entice a new tenant to lease a space. Note that TIs paid by a landlord that improve its ability to lease the space in the future – such as lobby and bathroom renovations – are depreciated on a different schedule than the building itself. Tenant improvements typically are depreciated over a 7-year life, versus a 15-year life for leasehold improvements, and 40 years for the base building.
  - **TIs for first-generation space:** When space is newly constructed, the landlord typically budgets for a higher TI allowance because the tenant will need to build out space from a building shell condition (also referred to as *unimproved*), which means there are no tenant suite partitions, drywall, finished floors and ceilings, or other improvements that office tenants require. Because of the greater expense associated with building out new space, tenants that lease first-generation space typically sign longer-term leases of five or more years. Tenants often exceed the landlord's TI allowance and invest additional money into their space. The more a tenant invests its own money into rental space, the more likely that tenant is to renew the lease at the end of the lease term.

- **TIs for second-generation space:** When a space has been occupied previously, it is called second-generation space. The TI dollars a landlord pays to retain the existing tenant tend to be for cosmetic improvements, such as new carpet and painting the walls. If the lease length being negotiated is long enough, or if the landlord is trying to re-tenant the space with a new tenant (perhaps one with better credit), then TIs are likely to be higher and include some modest structural improvements, such as updating the tenant's bathroom(s).

THE FOUR MAJOR TYPES OF LEASES

There are four broadly defined types of operating lease agreements: gross, net, modified gross, and full service. (Equity REITs generally do not use capital leases, wherein the landlord finances the leased asset, but the tenant ends up with ownership at the end of the lease term.) **The name of each lease structure is *not* universal in nature; each region of the country tends to have its own nomenclature and lease standards**. Putting precise terminology aside, any lease that results from landlord–tenant negotiations reflects risks and rewards that both parties agree upon and are willing to bear. Table 5.2 summarizes the major types of leases, including a simplified example of the different payments made by a tenant to the landlord according to the general terms associated with each type of lease, which are described as follows:

1. **Gross lease:** A lease in which the tenant pays the landlord a fixed monthly rent and the landlord assumes responsibility for paying all operating expenses, taxes, and insurance associated with the property. If costs rise, the landlord absorbs them, which is another way of saying a gross lease shifts all the risks onto the landlord during the term of the lease. The tenant's rent does not change. Apartments operate on gross leases. For commercial space, the gross lease is rarely (if ever) used, and often only for short periods of time and/or at lower-quality properties.
2. **Net lease:** A lease in which the tenant pays the landlord a fixed monthly rent and is also responsible for paying all or some of the expenses associated with operating, maintaining, and using the property. There are three levels of "net" that express which expenses the tenant pays in addition to rent:

- Maintenance, which includes items like utilities, water, janitorial, trash collection, snow plowing, and landscaping.
- Taxes.
- Insurance.

A **single-net lease** generally implies the tenant pays rent and property taxes. In a **double-net lease** the tenant pays rent, property taxes, and insurance; the landlord bears the other costs (though often with an expense stop). A double-net lease more often is referred to as a "modified gross" or "gross industrial" lease, which is described in the following paragraph. In a **triple-net lease**, in addition to the monthly rent the tenant pays all costs associated with property operations and maintenance, insurance, and taxes. The landlord essentially collects monthly "coupon" payments from the tenant, similar to receiving monthly interest income from fixed income (bond) investments.

Triple-net leases are used most often by landlords leasing a freestanding building to a single tenant, where that tenant wants the operating flexibility associated with the triple-net structure. Examples of the types of buildings REITs own that generally are leased using the triple-net structure include fast-food restaurants, industrial warehouses, health-care facilities, or office buildings that serve as corporate headquarters.

3. **Modified gross lease:** A lease that is similar to the double-net lease described in the preceding discussion on net leases. Often called a gross industrial lease, the modified gross lease is one in which the tenant pays the rent plus the property taxes and insurance, and any increases in these items over the base year. The landlord pays the operating expenses and sometimes the maintenance associated with the property. In the case in which a landlord uses modified gross leases and has multiple tenants in one building, the landlord will charge the tenants a common area maintenance or CAM fee. As described at the beginning of this chapter, CAM charges are additional rent charged for maintenance that benefits all tenants, such as landscaping, snow removal, and outdoor lighting. Tenants generally will be charged a dollar amount representing their proportionate share of expenses, based on the square feet they lease. Modified gross leases most often are used with multitenant office, industrial, and retail properties.
4. **Full-service lease:** A lease in which the tenant pays the landlord a fixed monthly rent that includes an expense stop calculated off the

TABLE 5.2 Comparison of Major Lease Types

			Modified	
	Gross	Net*	Gross	Full-Service
Contractual rent per square foot paid to landlord	$15.00	$15.00	$19.00	$23.00
— Base-year expense stop & CAM†	n/a	n/a	−4.00	−8.00
Net rent to landlord	15.00	15.00	15.00	15.00
+ Reimbursement for expense overage‡	n/a	n/a	2.00	2.00
Total rent per square foot paid to landlord	$15.00	$15.00	$17.00	$17.00
Risk of cost increase borne by:	Landlord	Tenant	Tenant†	Tenant†
Who pays what:				
• Non-structural repair & maintenance	Landlord	Tenant	**	Tenant
• Operating expenses (utilities, janitorial, etc.)	Landlord	Tenant	**	Tenant
• Property taxes	Landlord	Tenant	**	Tenant
• Insurance	Landlord	Tenant	**	Tenant
• CAM	Landlord	Tenant	**	Tenant
Property type(s) most associated with this lease structure:	Lower-priced, lower-quality properties	Retail Industrial Single-Tenant	Industrial Office	Office

*Example illustrates a triple-net lease.

†With a base-year expense stop, the tenant reimburses the landlord for any cost overages. The only risk the landlord bears is during the first (or *base*) year of the lease: if actual expenses per square foot end up being higher than the amount forecasted in lease negotiations, then the landlord will have to absorb the cost difference. Also, if the lease is a full-service lease without a base-year expense stop, the landlord would have to absorb any increases in costs.

‡This example assumes operating and CAM costs exceed the established expense stops in the modified gross and full-service leases by $2.00; the tenant will need to reimburse the landlord for this overage.

**Depends on the terms of the lease. Generally, in a modified gross lease the tenant pays taxes and insurance.

base year. The landlord pays all the monthly expenses associated with operating the property, including utilities, water, taxes, janitorial, trash collection, and landscaping and charges the tenant in subsequent years to the extent operating expenses exceed the expense stop. The tenant gets full service in exchange for the monthly rent and does not have to contract with service providers directly. Full-service leases most often are associated with office buildings.

LEASES AND TENANT BANKRUPTCIES

As discussed in Chapter 4, if a REIT's tenant goes into bankruptcy, that tenant still has to pay the rent due under its lease(s) with the REIT. This is because the leases are legal contracts and are viewed by bankruptcy courts as operating expenses, which have a senior claim over that of creditors or investors on the cash flows of the company reorganizing under bankruptcy laws.

Fact

Bankruptcy courts view a lease between a landlord and tenant as an operating expense of the tenant's business, which is senior to the bankrupt tenant's debt obligations to its lenders. Accordingly, a tenant must continue to pay rent to its landlord (the REIT), even while going through bankruptcy.

The tenant must continue to pay the REIT its contractual rent until the bankruptcy court judge allows the tenant to "reject" the lease. The fact that leases are legal, senior claims on the cash flows of tenants is a major reason that REITs do not go bankrupt, even when some of their tenants do.

GAAP Accounting for Operating Leases and the New ASC 842 Standard

Straight-Line Rent Adjustment. In compliance with GAAP, REITs report rental income using the accrual method, not the cash flow method. Rents must be *straight-lined,* meaning a REIT reports the average rental income it expects to receive over the term of the lease, rather than the contractual cash rent received (or to be received) each period. A 10-year lease at $10 per square foot with one year of free rent would generate $90 per square foot of total rent over the 10 years; the straight-lined revenue recognized would be $9 per square foot in each of the 10 years. The concept is similar to depreciating an asset, in that straight-lining rental revenues assumes a tenant uses its space consistently over the term of the lease. If there are any set escalations in a lease, the average rent a REIT recognizes during the first half of a lease will be greater than the cash rent collected and, by the same convention, the cash rent received during the latter half of a lease term will exceed the average rental revenues reflected in the REIT's income statement. In order to calculate a REIT's adjusted funds from operation (AFFO) and net asset value (NAV), both of which are covered in Chapter 11, the effect of straight-line rents needs to be adjusted out to arrive at true cash rents received (or receivable). Table 5.3 demonstrates the straight-lining of rents.

Changes in Accounting for Operating Leases under the New Lease Accounting Rule (ASU 2016-02; ASC Topic 842). In February 2016, the Financial Accounting Standards Board (FASB) issued significant and final changes to the accounting treatment of operating leases (ASC 842), which became effective for REITs on January 1, 2019. FASB is the organization that establishes standards of financial accounting for US companies, and the SEC recognizes those standards as being appropriate.

TABLE 5.3 Example for Straight-Lining of Rents

	Year 1	Year 2	Year 3	Year 4
Contractual rent per SF	$15.00	$16.50	$18.00	$19.50
x Square feet leased	5,000	5,000	5,000	5,000
Cash rent to be received ("A")	$75,000	$82,500	$90,000	$97,500
Cumulative cash rent to be received	$345,000			
÷ Lease length (in years)	4			
Average rent reported annually for GAAP ("B")	$86,250			
Therefore:				
GAAP rent reported on financial statements	$86,250	$86,250	$86,250	$86,250
–Straight-lined rent adjustment (A – B)*	–11,250	–3,750	3,750	11,250
Cash rent received	$75,000	$82,500	$90,000	$97,500

*Note that after the halfway point in the lease, the straight-lined rent adjustment becomes positive, meaning that the rental revenue or NOI calculated from the REIT's income statement will need to be increased by the straight-line adjustment amount to reflect cash rent collected by or due to the REIT.

From a tenant perspective, lessors historically did not capitalize operating leases on their balance sheets and, instead, treated rent payments as expenses that were accounted for in their income statements. The biggest change for tenants under ACS 842 is that they now have to create an asset equal to the present value of lease payments agreed to in their leases (representing their "right of use" on leased space), and a matching liability on their balance sheets. As a result, tenants may prefer to lease space for shorter durations in order to minimize the lease payments-related liability on their balance sheets.

The greater impact of ACS 842 fell upon landlords (REITs), which had to change their accounting treatment for certain internal leasing and legal costs. In July 2016, the equity REIT analysts at SunTrust Robinson Humphrey, Michael Lewis, CFA, and Ki Bin Kim, CFA, published a useful guide that summarized the impact of ASC 842 on REITs relative to prior accounting rules. According to this report, "Only costs that are direct results of the specific lease being executed can be capitalized, while all others [must] be expensed as incurred. This means that internal leasing costs, such as non-commission-based leasing personnel compensation (e.g., employees paid base salary and 'bonus'), will now have to be fully expensed." The report also provided a summary table of direct costs that can still be capitalized versus indirect costs that are now expensed; Table 5.4 reproduces this information. Although REIT cash flows were not affected by ASC 842, because certain internal leasing and legal costs had to be expensed rather than capitalized, starting in 2019 REITs generally reported modestly lower funds from operations (FFO) and net asset values (NAVs) than they would have without the accounting rules change.

ASC 842 also requires a landlord to separate the lease components from non-lease components when reporting rental revenue. Most REITs elected to adopt the "practical expedient" allowed by the new rule, and collapsed variable rental revenue items, such as tenant reimbursements, into a single line called "lease revenue" or something similar. REITs that previously reported tenant reimbursements as part of their rental revenues generally now disclose that detail in their supplemental information packages, though they may have renamed them to comply with the rule.

The third change related to ASC 842 relates to when and how landlords account for the collectability of rents. Before ASC 842, a landlord would create an asset called a *reserve,* representing the at-risk rent; the offsetting account goes against retained earnings (since the landlord is not sure it will have earnings from the at-risk rents). According to ASC 842, a landlord now

TABLE 5.4 Direct vs. Indirect Leasing Costs per ASC 842

Direct Costs (Capitalized)	Excluded from Direct Costs (Expensed)
• Broker commissions • Legal fees resulting from the execution of the lease • Lease document preparation costs incurred after the execution of the lease • Certain payments to existing tenants to move out • Consideration paid for a guarantee of a residual asset by an unrelated third party	• Leasing employee salaries • Legal fees for services rendered before the execution of the lease • Advertising used to generate leasing deal • Other origination efforts • Costs related to an idle asset

Reproduced with permission from SunTrust Robinson Humphrey.

measures collectability against an 80% factor. If the landlord is less than 80% certain it will collect rents related to a lease, the landlord must write-off all the straight-lined rent associated with that lease and then account for that lease on a cash (rather than an accrued) basis. Writing-off the straight-lined rents will negatively affect a REIT's EBITDA and FFO but has no effect on cash flow (AFFO).

Conclusion

On a fundamental level, a REIT's cash flow is the sum of all cash received from tenant leases, less any overhead costs for paying management, interest payments on any debt outstanding, and dividends payable on outstanding shares of preferred and common equity. Supply and-demand fundamentals differ widely among the various types of commercial properties and ultimately are the largest governors of REIT returns. However, tenant quality and the length and structure of a lease also dictate how stable (or volatile) a landlord's cash flows are over time.

Knowing the average lease length and the type of lease structure a REIT uses helps predict how its shares may trade during times of economic expansion and contraction.

Chapter 10 demonstrates how the different lease durations associated with each property type have affected stock price performance in the past. In general, shorter leases translate into more volatile future earnings and, by extension, wider daily price swings for those REITs' shares. Longer leases generate steady income that is similar to receiving interest payments from a bond. This consistent income stream tends to translate into stock price movements that reflect the underlying stability in rents. Both extremes – short-term leases (hotels) and long-term leases (triple-net or specialty REITs) – have their respective opportunities and risks. Understanding the type of lease a REIT uses with tenants can help predict how its income may grow and how common shares may trade during different economic scenarios.

CHAPTER 6

REITs by Property Type

As discussed in the first chapter, one of the primary ways to classify REITs is by the type of property in which they invest. This chapter provides a basic overview of the major property types that equity REITs own, as well as basic information on mortgage REITs, which are the subject of Chapter 7. This chapter also provides sublists of the 179 equity REITs and 40 mortgage REITs that composed the FTSE Nareit All REITs Index at the end of 2019, categorized according to Nareit's property sector and subsector classifications, and sorted by total assets owned as of September 30, 2019. (Appendix C presents additional information on each company, including headquarters location and website addresses.) Go to Nareit's website, www.reit.com, for a current list of REITs.

Each type of real estate is associated with distinct supply-and-demand fundamentals that in turn assign certain risks and rewards to the owner's expected income. Although these risks and rewards become most apparent during times of economic boom or bust, they constantly govern the profitability of different property types and by extension affect stock-price performance. This chapter also highlights economic factors that influence demand for each property type; Chapter 3, Real Estate Fundamentals, provides an in-depth discussion of the links between current economic news, such as changes in interest rates or employment trends, and their effects on the stock prices of different types of REITs.

DIVERSIFIED AND SPECIALTY REITS

Diversified REITs are equity REITs that invest in two or more types of commercial property (see Table 6.1); on the opposite end of the property spectrum are specialty REITs (Table 6.2), which own only one type of highly specialized real estate, such as billboards, correctional facilities, or farmland. Many of the specialty REITs are new to the industry, though other specialized

TABLE 6.1 Diversified REITs

Company Name	Ticker Symbol	Total Assets*
Colony Capital Inc.	CLNY	$22,124
Vornado Realty Trust	VNO	18,216
VEREIT Inc.[a]	VER	14,456
W. P. Carey Inc.	WPC	14,084
JBG SMITH Properties	JBGS	6,022
Mack-Cali Realty Corp.	CLI	5,721
Global Net Lease	GNL	3,609
Lexington Realty Trust	LXP	3,035
American Assets Trust Inc.	AAT	2,789
Washington REIT	WRE	2,675
Alexander & Baldwin Inc.	ALEX	2,122
Armada Hoffler Properties Inc.	AHH	1,761
Alexander's Inc.	ALX	1,283
Whitestone REIT	WSR	1,012
Gladstone Commercial Corp.	GOOD	978
One Liberty Properties Inc.	OLP	785
Medalist Diversified REIT	MDRR	79
HMG/Courtland Properties Inc.	HMG	33
Total for 18 REITs:		$100,783

*Total Assets are as of September 30, 2019, in millions of dollars.

[a]Former name: American Realty Capital Properties (NYSE: ARCP).

Sources: Nareit, S&P Global Market Intelligence. Many of these REITs employ long-term triple-net leases.

TABLE 6.2 Specialty REITs

Company Name	Ticker Symbol	Total Assets*	NAREIT Sub-Property Type
Iron Mountain Inc.	IRM	$13,577	Specialty
VICI Properties Inc.	VICI	12,581	Casino
Gaming and Leisure Properties	GLPI	8,505	Casino
EPR Properties	EPR	6,633	Diversified
Lamar Advertising Co. (REIT)	LAMR.REIT	5,932	Advertising
OUTFRONT Media Inc. (REIT)	OUT.REIT	5,321	Advertising
GEO Group Inc.	GEO	4,283	Prison
CoreCivic Inc.	CXW	3,749	Prison
Safehold Inc.	SAFE	1,637	Diversified
Farmland Partners Inc.	FPI	1,097	Land
Gladstone Land Corp.	LAND	757	Land
Total for 11 REITs:		$64,072	

*Total Assets are as of September 30, 2019, in millions of dollars.
Sources: Nareit, S&P Global Market Intelligence. These REITs generally use long-term triple-net leases and/or ground leases.

property types, such as Data Center REITs (Table 6.3), Infrastructure REITs (Table 6.4), and Timber REITs (Table 6.5), are more established and now have their own Nareit classification. As of September 30, 2019, there were 44 REITs in these combined categories with total assets of $337 billion.

Data Center REITs own, develop, and manage wholesale data center properties and, to a lesser degree, data center shells. Ever increasing consumer use of cell phones and wireless devices for communications and entertainment-based activity, such as video streaming and social media, has driven robust demand for data center space during the first two decades of the twenty-first century. Additionally, a wide array of organizations – including social media companies like Facebook Inc. (NASDAQ: FB), the US and other governments, and firms that analyze demographic data for political and consumer marketing purposes – need data center capacity (measured in megawatts and kilowatts, rather than in square feet) to analyze user data. Knowing who-is-buying-what, and who-is-communicating-to-whom is big business, whether its consumer goods driven, political, or for reasons of national security.

TABLE 6.3 Data Center REITs

Company Name	Ticker Symbol	Total Assets*
Digital Realty Trust Inc.	DLR	$23,173
Equinix Inc. (REIT)	EQIX.REIT	22,842
CyrusOne Inc.	CONE	5,893
QTS Realty Trust Inc.	QTS	3,123
CoreSite Realty Corp.	COR	2,047
Total for 5 REITs:		$57,078

*Total Assets are as of September 30, 2019, in millions of dollars.
Sources: Nareit, S&P Global Market Intelligence. These REITs may employ some long-term triple-net leases.

The risks Data Center REITs face depend on the type of data centers they own. The least risky are data center shells where the tenants invest in all the mechanical equipment and cooling (i.e., *infrastructure*) they require for their operations. On the other end of the risk spectrum, wholesale data centers require the owner (REIT) to invest in all the infrastructure, which tenants then lease as part of their rent. Because technology, industry standards, and service requirements for wholesale data centers are rapidly evolving, they carry the highest risk of obsolescence among data centers. Such costs are part of doing business in this space. Long-term, the demand for more and more efficient data centers, and incremental demand from users moving to *the cloud* (especially as 5G connectivity rolls out), artificial intelligence, and self-driving vehicles should continue to drive data center demand for the foreseeable future.

REITS THAT USE TRIPLE-NET LEASES

Recall from Chapter 5 that a triple-net lease is one in which the landlord collects a base rent that excludes (or is *net of*) taxes, insurance, and maintenance expenses associated with occupying the property. These and other operating expenses are paid directly by the tenant to the various service providers. REITs that use triple-net leases typically lease their properties to a single tenant for ten or more years. The majority of these properties are standalone office, industrial, or retail buildings. Nareit no longer includes

TABLE 6.4 Infrastructure REITs

Company Name	Ticker Symbol	Total Assets*
American Tower Corp. (REIT)	AMT.REIT	$39,307
Crown Castle Intl. (REIT)	CCI.REIT	38,344
SBA Communications Corp. (REIT)	SBAC.REIT	9,201
Uniti Group Inc.	UNIT	5,031
CorEnergy Infrastructure Trust	CORR	656
Power REIT	PW	22
Total for 6 REITs:		$92,561

*Total Assets are as of September 30, 2019, in millions of dollars.
Sources: Nareit, S&P Global Market Intelligence. These REITs generally use long-term triple-net leases and/or ground leases.

a ***triple-net*** property category. However, several companies categorized by Nareit as Specialty, Infrastructure, and Timber REITs use triple-net leases (including ground leases), as do some of the diversified REITs.

Infrastructure REITs (Table 6.4) invest in communications (including cellular towers), energy, and transportation projects. The technology behind driverless vehicles depends on low-latency wireless connections, which should translate into increased demand for some of the Infrastructure REITs. Timber REITs (Table 6.5) own acres of forest, the trees on which are harvested for paper and wood products.

TABLE 6.5 Timber REITs

Company Name	Ticker Symbol	Total Assets*
Weyerhaeuser Co.	WY	$16,832
Rayonier Inc.	RYN	2,767
PotlatchDeltic Corp.	PCH	2,257
CatchMark Timber Trust Inc.	CTT	684
Total for 4 REITs:		$22,540

*Total Assets are as of September 30, 2019, in millions of dollars.
Sources: Nareit, S&P Global Market Intelligence . These REITs generally use long-term triple-net leases and/or ground leases.

Risks and Rewards of REITs That Use Triple-Net Leases

During times of economic expansion, landlords that use long-term, triple-net leases do not profit as much as other landlords that use shorter-term, gross, or full-service leases because they cannot capture rising market rents. However, triple-net landlords do benefit from steady, bond-like cash flows generated by their leases. As a result, triple-net REITs are viewed as more defensive, less volatile REITs and tend to outperform other REITs during times of economic uncertainty.

One source of risk in the triple-net REIT model relates to how these companies grow. Few if any of the triple-net REITs grow through development, and their internal growth is embedded in the long-term nature of their leases (often indexed to inflation). For these REITs, acquisitions are the primary source of external growth. As such, it is imperative that these companies attain *and then maintain* a low cost of capital. (See Chapter 11 for a discussion of REITs' cost of capital, also referred to as *weighted average cost of capital, or WACC*.) By way of a simple example, if the investment yield on a property leased pursuant to a long-term triple-net lease is 5%, then the triple-net REIT needs to have a cost of capital that is less than 5% in order for the acquisition to be additive to its future cash flow. Note that the difference between the yield on the investment opportunity and the REIT's cost of capital is also called its *spread*. (So, debt at 4% and equity dividend at 4.5% would accomplish the lower cost of capital.)

Since the Great Financial Crisis of 2007–08, the number of income-oriented investors competing to buy buildings that are triple-net leased to creditworthy tenants has increased dramatically. The very-low interest rate environment in the United States that followed in the wake of the Great Recession of 2008–09 was a primary cause of the increase in demand for many high-yield investments, including triple-net properties that generate yields of 5% or more. Although higher interest rates in the future may cause a marginal decline in property values, implying higher yields from real estate than today, management teams of triple-net REITs – or any REIT that relies on acquisitions to grow – need to remain vigilant about their costs of capital.

HEALTH-CARE REITS

Nareit lists 17 Health-Care REITs with combined assets of $129 billion (Table 6.6). Health-Care REITs receive their income primarily from leasing facilities to health-care providers, usually on a triple-net or modified-gross

TABLE 6.6 Health-Care REITs

Company Name	Ticker Symbol	Total Assets*
Welltower Inc.	WELL	$31,864
Ventas Inc.	VTR	24,804
Healthpeak Properties[a]	PEAK	14,010
Medical Properties Trust Inc.	MPW	12,452
Omega Healthcare Investors	OHI	8,996
Diversified Healthcare[b]	DHC	6,917
Healthcare Trust of America	HTA	6,323
Sabra Health Care REIT	SBRA	6,068
Physicians Realty Trust	DOC	4,248
Healthcare Realty Trust Inc.	HR	3,491
National Health Investors Inc.	NHI	3,019
New Senior Investment Group	SNR	2,204
CareTrust REIT Inc.	CTRE	1,525
LTC Properties Inc.	LTC	1,512
Global Medical REIT	GMRE	812
Community Healthcare Trust Inc.	CHCT	533
Universal Health Realty Trust	UHT	484
Total for 17 REITs:		$129,262

*Total Assets are as of September 30, 2019, in millions of dollars.

[a]During 2019, Healthpeak Properties (NYSE: PEAK) changed its name and ticker symbol from HCP, Inc. (NYSE: HCP).

[b]During 2019, Diversified Health-care Trust (NASDAQ: DHC) changed its name and ticker symbol from Senior Housing Properties Trust (NASDAQ: SNH).

Sources: Nareit, S&P Global Market Intelligence. These REITs generally use long-term triple-net leases.

basis. (Please refer to Chapter 5 for detail on lease structures.) Property types include senior and assisted living/rehabilitation facilities, medical clinics, medical office buildings (also referred to as *MOBs*), health-care laboratories, and hospitals.

Population growth, aging demographics, shifts in consumer preference (away from hospitals and toward more convenient medical office buildings), and cost savings have all fueled the growth in non-hospital health-care locations and, in turn, Health-Care REITs.

Risks and Rewards of Health-Care REITs

In general, Health-Care REITs should continue to benefit from robust demand for an increased number of health-care facilities required to support the expanding and aging US population in as cost-efficient a manner as possible. Where there is growth in demand, there is also the possibility for too much new supply being built. Investors should be aware of this potential risk when evaluating where different Health-Care REITs are building and buying facilities.

Health-Care REITs' tenants are doctors and health-care service providers, who in turn have varying degrees of exposure to government policy vis-à-vis reimbursement levels for Medicare and Medicaid. Most REITs have minimized their exposure to potential changes in Medicare and Medicaid reimbursement levels by leasing to tenants that emphasize private-pay care. Even so, Health-Care REIT total returns remain subject to risk associated with potential reductions to government Medicare and Medicaid reimbursement rates. Even if no changes are made, if investors believe reimbursement rate cuts are possible, most Health-Care REITs are likely to underperform other property types. Additionally, advances in "aging-in-place" technologies that help elderly people to stay in their own homes longer than in the past may decrease demand, at least on the margin, for senior care facilities in the future.

The COVID-19 pandemic of 2020 demonstrated how different health-care facilities were able to operate and pay rent to their REIT landlords during a crisis. Life science facility operators, hospitals, and medical office buildings (MOBs) were able to operate reasonably unaffected by the pandemic. Life science operators are likely to benefit from streamlined Food and Drug Administration (FDA) approvals and increased funding for research and development to combat viruses and other medical conditions. Hospitals and MOBs faced lower revenues for several weeks as higher-margin elective surgeries were delayed to ensure that enough beds and equipment were available for possible COVID-19 patients; they also had to absorb higher operating costs for labor and equipment, the effects of which are longer lasting as new protocols for social distancing and patient care are established. In addition to rising labor and equipment costs, skilled nursing facility (SNF) and seniors housing facility (SHF) operators incurred steep initial declines in occupancy during the pandemic related to greater mortality rates among residents and, for the SNFs, the deferral of elective procedures. While SNF occupancies will likely rise as elective procedures recommence, SHF occupancies may take longer to rebuild due to heightened concerns that possible residents and their families may have about enrolling, especially at facilities that reported high COVID-19 contagion and death rates during the pandemic.

The final risk to consider when reviewing Health-Care REITs is their use of long-term triple-net leases with the tenants who use their facilities. In a rising interest rate environment, REITs that use triple-net leases tend to be valued like long-term bonds, in that their stock prices typically underperform other types of REITs that use shorter-term leases. (See Chapter 10 for more information about the exogenous factors that influence REIT share price performance.)

INDUSTRIAL REITS

Nareit lists 14 Industrial REITs with combined assets of $82 billion at September 30, 2019 (Table 6.7). Industrial properties are leased to businesses for a variety of purposes, including distribution warehousing, light manufacturing, and research and development (R&D).

Industrial property is among the most stable, least volatile property types in the United States. National warehouse/industrial occupancy in the United States typically ranges between 89% and 95%, evidencing the steady demand-and-supply fundamentals associated with warehousing and distribution facilities. Easy and quick to build, the fact that supply of newly constructed industrial property tends to track demand closely is one of the primary reasons behind the sector's stability.

Demand for industrial property is correlated to consumer spending and growth in the country's gross domestic product (GDP). The more demand for all goods – whether they are purchased at traditional brick-and-mortar locations like malls, or online through the Internet (a.k.a., *e-commerce*) – the greater the need for warehouses to store and distribute goods to consumers. Supply increases through new development. Industrial properties are fairly simple to build, consisting essentially of four concrete walls tilted up on a six-inch slab of concrete, with a roof that holds it all together. As such, it typically takes only six to nine months to construct an industrial property after breaking ground. Due to the relatively short development time, industrial property markets tend not to get overbuilt.

TABLE 6.7 Industrial REITs

Company Name	Ticker Symbol	Total Assets*
Prologis Inc.	PLD	$39,448
Duke Realty Corp.	DRE	8,263
Liberty Property Trust[a]	LPT	7,339
Americold Realty Trust	COLD	4,142
STAG Industrial Inc.	STAG	3,745
Rexford Industrial Realty Inc.	REXR	3,502
First Industrial Realty Trust	FR	3,377
Industrial Logistics Ppts	ILPT	2,468
EastGroup Properties Inc.	EGP	2,400
PS Business Parks Inc.	PSB	2,118
Terreno Realty Corp.	TRNO	2,045
Monmouth Real Estate	MNR	1,872
Innovative Industrial Ppts Inc.	IIPR	623
Plymouth Industrial REIT Inc.	PLYM	602
Total for 14 REITs:		$81,945

*Total Assets are as of September 30, 2019, in millions of dollars.
[a]In the first quarter of 2020, ProLogis, Inc. acquired Liberty Property Trust.
Sources: Nareit, S&P Global Market Intelligence.

Risks and Rewards of Industrial REITs

Property size (many warehouses are now over one million feet in size), number of truck dock doors, truck parking and turning radius, and ease of access are some of the key metrics for good properties. Historically, the trade-off for the industrial sector's stability was that these REITs did not enjoy the rapid price appreciation associated with other, more volatile property sectors, especially during periods of robust economic growth. Since 2010, e-commerce – or buying and selling consumer goods online – has accelerated and, according to Statista, represented 14.1% of all retail sales worldwide. Known as the "Amazon Effect," all retailers must deliver quickly, thus they need more warehouses. Moreover, Statista forecasts that online shopping could account for 17% to 18% of worldwide retail sales by 2021.

The COVID-19 pandemic and related shelter-in-place and work-from-home (WFH) protocols enacted by most of the United States greatly accelerated e-commerce, both within companies already employing it as a sales channel and by those that had not adopted it before the pandemic. From a retailer and consumer perspective, the COVID-19 shutdowns caused e-commerce to rapidly evolve from a "want" to a "need." This secular change in consumer buying habits and retailer distribution has fueled sustained, strong demand for warehousing and logistics, which has translated into equally strong stock price appreciation for the Industrial REITs. Long before the COVID-19 pandemic, industrial space proved to be a useful tool for distributing goods to end consumers. Post-pandemic, it is essential.

Lease Terms

Industrial property landlords employ triple-net or modified-gross leases. As explained in Chapter 5, the tenant is responsible for all of a property's maintenance, taxes, and insurance in the former case; in the latter, the landlord/REIT typically pays basic property taxes and insurance. Lease lengths range from one to three years for small-space users with local distribution needs, and five, seven, or ten-plus years for larger tenants distributing goods regionally or nationally. At either end of the spectrum, tenant renewal rates tend to be high (roughly 65% or more) since distribution space is a critical component of a tenant's supply chain. (Tenants cannot get their goods to end users without warehousing and distribution space.) Industrial rents tend to escalate annually, or every two or three years; these contractual rent bumps typically are indexed to increase with inflation.

LODGING/RESORT REITS

There were 19 Lodging/Resort (Hotel) REITs in the FTSE Nareit All REITs Index with $81 billion of total assets at September 30, 2019 (Table 6.8). The majority of US hotels are affiliated with national or international franchises or brands. REITs generally own hotels branded under the most widely recognized flags and tend to focus on the urban markets or destination locations where demand remains high year-round. Popular brands (and their respective *flags*) include Marriott International (Courtyard, Residence Inn), Hilton (Hilton Garden Inn, Hampton Inn), Hyatt (Grand Hyatt, Andaz), and InterContinental Hotels Group (Intercontinental, Holiday Inn). Hotels are

TABLE 6.8 Lodging/Resort REITs

Company Name	Ticker Symbol	Total Assets*	NAREIT Sub-Property Type
Host Hotels & Resorts	HST	$13,132	Full-Service Hotel
Park Hotels & Resorts Inc.	PK	11,620	Hotel
Service Properties Trust[a]	SVC	9,516	Limited-Service Hotel
Pebblebrook Hotel Trust	PEB	6,545	Hotel
RLJ Lodging Trust	RLJ	5,876	Full-Service Hotel
Apple Hospitality REIT Inc.	APLE	4,990	Hotel
Ashford Hospitality Trust	AHT	4,769	Full-Service Hotel
Sunstone Hotel Investors Inc.	SHO	3,899	Full-Service Hotel
Ryman Hospitality Properties	RHP	3,831	Full-Service Hotel
DiamondRock Hospitality Co.	DRH	3,315	Hotel
Xenia Hotels & Resorts Inc.	XHR	3,159	Hotel
CorePoint Lodging Inc.	CPLG	2,323	Limited-Service Hotel
Summit Hotel Properties Inc.	INN	2,149	Limited-Service Hotel
Hersha Hospitality Trust	HT	2,139	Limited-Service Hotel
Braemar Hotels & Resorts	BHR	1,767	Hotel
Chatham Lodging Trust	CLDT	1,454	Hotel
Sotherly Hotels Inc.	SOHO	499	Full-Service Hotel
Condor Hospitality Trust Inc.	CDOR	244	Limited-Service Hotel
InnSuites Hospitality Trust	IHT	18	Full-Service Hotel
Total for 19 REITs:		$81,244	

*Total Assets are as of September 30, 2019, in millions of dollars.

[a]During 2019, Service Properties Trust (NASDAQ: SVC) changed its name and ticker symbol from Hospitalities Properties Trust (NASDAQ: HPT).

Sources: Nareit, S&P Global Market Intelligence.

frequently classified by the quality-level of guest services offered, such as luxury, upper-upscale, upscale, midscale, or economy, or by their location such as urban, suburban, resort, and airport. The segmentation continues to expand as hotel operators introduce new "non-branded," boutique, and lifestyle-focused hotels to meet shifting consumer demand.

Hotel Revenue

Location and quality levels are key drivers of a hotel's maximum revenue per available room (RevPAR), which is the product of a hotel's average daily room rate (ADR) and its occupancy rate. Close proximity to a desirable attraction, such as a beach, a central business district, a large university, or a convention center can be a competitive advantage, enabling an operator to charge higher room rates and maintain higher occupancies than hotels that operate in secondary locations. The latter tend to be roadside, limited-, or economy-service hotels that compete primarily on price.

Hotel Expenses

Labor represents the most significant expense in hotel operations. As a result, hotels will have large fixed costs to operate the hotel since a minimum number of employees are required to open, run, and clean a hotel each day, regardless of occupancy levels. For this reason, hotels often reduce room rates to increase occupancy during off-seasons or in slow to declining economic times.

Technical Aspects Specific to Hotel REITs

Hotel REITs differ structurally from other equity REITs in that, according to REIT rules (see Chapter 8), hotel owners are not permitted to directly operate the properties they own. This is because earning profit from operating hotels is active (or "bad" taxable REIT income) and differs from the more passive business of collecting rent ("good" REIT income) on hotels leased to third-party operators. As a result, Hotel REITs must retain a third-party hotel manager to operate their hotels. The third-party hotel manager is in charge of all operating facets of the hotel, including hiring and managing the employees, revenue management, and maintenance. In exchange, the third-party manager receives a base management fee (typically 2–4% of hotel revenues) plus potentially an incentive fee if certain profitability thresholds are achieved. Hotel REITs generally retain asset managers to oversee the third-party hotel manager.

Risks and Rewards of Hotel REITs

Hotels are more like an operating company than a REIT because they have no leases to guarantee future revenues for some duration of time. Instead, Hotel

REITs have to "lease" their properties from scratch every day. During times of strong economic growth, hotels can increase prices immediately; as a result, during certain points in the economic cycle, Hotel REITs can achieve some of the highest annual total returns of any property type (see Chapter 10 for more detail). In addition, since the lease rate for hotel rooms can be reset daily, in a rising inflationary economy, Hotel REITs have an advantage as they can reprice their "leases" daily. As a result, Hotel REITs tend to be the least interest rate sensitive class of investment real estate. When it looks like the economy is coming out of a recession, Hotel REITs tend to outperform other REIT property types, as investors anticipate strong revenue growth and profitability.

In a declining economy, however, hotel operators often have to cut their daily rates, and a portion of their employees, to maintain profitability. Unsurprisingly, Hotel REITs tend to substantially underperform other REIT sectors when the economy is slowing or at risk of slipping into recession. They have cut their dividends during tough economic times more often than any other property type. More recently, during the COVID-19 pandemic, Hotel REITs drastically reduced or suspended their common dividends in order to preserve liquidity and weather the near-complete absence of demand associated with the business and travel shutdowns initially enacted to combat the virus.

During normal, non-crisis times, investors must still account for large swings in seasonal demand that can impact Hotel REIT performance; the highest RevPAR is typically achieved during summer months, but can differ depending on location and service level. Lastly, Hotel REITs face risks from alternative lodging providers (i.e., Airbnb, VRBO, and Homesharing). While these services tend to be more popular with younger travelers and families, hotels have begun to diversify their offerings to reduce the potential disruption risk.

MORTGAGE REITS

The FTSE Nareit All REITs index listed 40 mortgage REITs (mREITs) with total assets of $635 billion at September 30, 2019. Similar to banks and other financial institutions, mREITs lend money to real estate owners directly by issuing mortgages, or indirectly by acquiring existing loans or mortgage-backed securities. In contrast with equity REITs that derive the majority of their revenues from leases, mREIT revenue equals the principal and interest payments received from real estate-based loans. mREITs typically focus on either the residential or commercial mortgage markets. Chapter 7 focuses on mREITs and contains lists of residential and commercial mREITs that were publicly traded at the end of 2019.

Note: mREITs are not included in S&P Dow Jones Industrial's *Real Estate* GICS sector; they remained in *Financials.*

OFFICE REITS

In 2019, Nareit listed 20 companies as Office REITs, with total assets of $130 billion (Table 6.9). Office REITs own everything from high-rise buildings in major metropolitan areas such as New York City, to low- and mid-rise suburban office space in secondary office markets such as Charlotte, North Carolina. Within each market, location plays a major role in determining current rental rates, future rent increases, and property occupancy. Depending on the market, properties located in a city's central business district (CBD) may garner higher rents than suburban locations due to proximity to public transportation lines, industry resources, and/or the labor force targeted by corporations doing business there. In contrast, suburban office buildings may be attractive to tenants because of lower rent rates and their location relative to employee housing, ample parking, and worker preference to drive to work.

Office buildings are also classified based on building quality (construction and materials), conditions of their mechanical and other internal systems, in-building amenities (such as a gym or restaurant), and location. Newer buildings typically are deemed to be Class-A properties. Older buildings that have less efficient mechanical and electrical systems, or that are simply less aesthetically pleasing, tend to be classified as Class-B or Class-C. Although these ratings are subjective and vary from market to market, they are useful for benchmarking rents and property values on a local, regional, or national level. It is possible, for example, to have a Class-A building in a B or C market, and, therefore, only achieve rents that are competitive with other Class-B or -C buildings.

Lease Terms

Large office properties normally have multiple tenants – thus diversifying tenant risk. Office leases typically are full-service leases with an initial term of five to seven years plus one or more multiple-year renewal options. In a

TABLE 6.9 Office REITs

Company Name	Ticker Symbol	Total Assets*
Boston Properties Inc.	BXP	$21,289
Alexandria Real Estate	ARE	17,058
SL Green Realty Corp.	SLG	13,295
Kilroy Realty Corp.	KRC	8,624
Paramount Group Inc.	PGRE	8,580
Douglas Emmett Inc.	DEI	8,521
Hudson Pacific Properties Inc.	HPP	7,428
Cousins Properties Inc.	CUZ	6,704
Highwoods Properties Inc.	HIW	4,891
Office Properties Incm Tr	OPI	4,360
Brandywine Realty Trust	BDN	4,020
Columbia Property Trust	CXP	3,926
Empire State Realty Trust Inc.	ESRT	3,925
Corporate Office Properties Tr	OFC	3,855
Piedmont Office Realty Trust	PDM	3,752
Equity Commonwealth	EQC	3,731
Easterly Government Ppts Inc.	DEA	2,224
Franklin Street Properties	FSP	1,843
City Office REIT Inc.	CIO	1,190
CIM Commercial Trust Corp.	CMCT	660
Total for 20 REITs:		$129,876

*Total Assets are as of September 30, 2019, in millions of dollars.
Sources: Nareit, S&P Global Market Intelligence.

full-service lease (see Chapter 5, Leases), the landlord is responsible for all the operating expenses of the property, including landscaping, real estate taxes, and insurance, but generally the landlord is able to pass most expenses back to the tenant in the form of expense stops associated with the full-service lease and common-area maintenance, or CAM, charges. Office leases commonly include annual rent escalations (also called *bumps* or *step-ups*) that help insulate the landlord's profit margin from costs that rise with inflation.

A new concept of short-term daily leasing of space has developed over the last ten years and grown in popularity with WeWork (not public). In 2019, about 10% of all new office space in the US was leased to firms like WeWork that lease spaces for a long term, put in the tenant improvements, and then lease to start-up companies and others for a much higher price and for short durations. Also, the new accounting rules that went into effect in 2019 (see Chapter 5) require lessors (tenants) to record the liability associated with each long-term lease as debt. To minimize the liabilities related to leasing on their balance sheets, many firms now prefer to lease space for shorter terms.

Risks and Rewards of Office REITs

Office REIT returns are more cyclical than the average equity REITs due to periodic overbuilding. (Also see Chapter 10, REIT Performance in Various Market Conditions.) If demand for new space is not higher than the increase in supply, office vacancy in that market should rise and rental rates should decline. The office sector's longer building cycle is a primary contributing factor to historical overbuilding. During the two or more years it generally takes to complete an office tower, local demand for office space, which is a function of job growth and the local economy, can change materially and cause a building to sit vacant or mostly vacant until demand for office space recovers, or it may steal tenants from older buildings.

The way tenants use their space can also dramatically alter demand for office space, even in a growing economy. The advancement in communications over the past two decades has made working from home (WFH) a viable alternative for some workers. Although not all office cultures or industries lend themselves to allowing workers to perform their duties offsite, the ability to work remotely has dampened the overall need for office space in most locations. Densification, which is space planning for a greater number of employees in the same square feet of office space, and hoteling or "hot desking," which eliminates assigned seating for a portion of employees, are two additional trends that have dramatically reduced the need for office space since 2000. In 2000, employers generally budgeted 250 square feet of space per employee. Twenty years later, the range is between 125 and 200 square feet per employee (source: Cushman & Wakefield), representing at the mid-point a 22% average decrease in square feet per employee.

Densification and hoteling had largely run their course when the COVID-19 pandemic erupted in early 2020. The need for social distancing initially pushed hundreds of thousands of office workers into WFH situations. In mid-May of that year, when the CEO of Twitter Inc. (NYSE: TWTR) announced its employees could WFH "forever," REIT investors feared that demand for office space would be permanently impaired. Shortly thereafter, the *Wall Street Journal* quoted Twitter's CEO as confirming that many employees could continue to WFH – but also making it clear that the social media company did not plan "to close or shrink any of its offices" (*Wall Street Journal*, "When It's time to Go Back to the Office, Will It Still Be There?", May 16, 2020, Dana Mattioli and Konrad Putzier). The need for employees to be able to social distance in their workplaces and, therefore, maintain operations during future pandemics, is making employers rapidly rethink their highly dense usage of space. It will take years before investors know which trend – WFH or de-densification – has the greater influence on office demand. In the meantime, the way people use (or don't use) formal office space to do their jobs is likely to remain an ongoing challenge the office property sector faces.

RESIDENTIAL REITS

The Residential REIT sector encompassed 21 REITs with total assets of $150 billion. There are three subcategories of Residential REITs: Apartments (also called *multifamily,* and excludes condominiums), Manufactured Homes, and Single-Family Homes.

Apartment REITs

Nareit lists 15 Apartment REITs with total assets of $108 billion (Table 6.10). Historically, apartment REITs included only companies that owned traditional apartment buildings. More recently, however, the group expanded to include REITs that own student housing apartment complexes and single-family homes that are rented.

Traditional apartment buildings are classified as either garden-style (usually suburban locations) or high-rise buildings (usually downtown locations). Garden-style apartments contain multiple buildings that usually are one to four stories in height and are configured around the community amenities, typically a pool or other common area(s). High-rise apartment buildings are just that: high-rise buildings that contain apartments built in high-density cities or town centers where the cost of land and the monthly rental rates the landlord can charge support the additional cost per square foot associated with high-rise construction.

TABLE 6.10 Apartment REITs

Company Name	Ticker Symbol	Total Assets*	NAREIT Sub-Property Type
Equity Residential	EQR	$21,054	Multifamily
AvalonBay Communities Inc.	AVB	19,060	Multifamily
Essex Property Trust Inc.	ESS	12,998	Multifamily
MAA	MAA	11,248	Multifamily
UDR Inc.	UDR	8,698	Multifamily
American Campus Communities	ACC	7,669	Student Housing
Camden Property Trust	CPT	6,649	Multifamily
Aimco	AIV	6,539	Multifamily
Preferred Apartment Comm.	APTS	5,268	Diversified
Bluerock Residential Growth	BRG	2,090	Multifamily
Independence Realty Trust Inc.	IRT	1,653	Multifamily
NexPoint Residential Trust Inc.	NXRT	1,624	Multifamily
Investors Real Estate Trust	IRET	1,404	Multifamily
BRT Apartments Corp.	BRT	1,193	Multifamily
Clipper Realty Inc.	CLPR	1,138	Diversified
Total for 15 REITs:		$108,285	

*Total Assets are as of September 30, 2019, in millions of dollars.
Sources: Nareit, S&P Global Market Intelligence.

In both formats, apartment properties generally contain a mix of studio, one-, and two-bedroom apartment units. Properties also are classified as Class-A, -B, or -C. Class-A buildings include newer buildings in prime locations. Buildings in Class-B and -C categories tend to be older, offer residents fewer amenities, and, perhaps, are located in less desirable locations. Rental agreements for apartment units typically are for 12 months at a time. A tenant generally may cancel a lease, however, by providing one or more months' notice, typically in writing. The landlord is responsible for the cost of maintaining the property; however, similar to a full-service lease, the tenant's rent essentially covers costs paid by the landlord. Except in properties where it is possible to meter individual utilities, a landlord also factors into the rental rate reasonable costs for water and heating, ventilation, and air conditioning (HVAC) services.

Steady Demand for Apartment Units

Similar to office space, demand for apartments is highly correlated with employment trends. As employment in an area increases, demand for apartments to house new workers who in-migrate to that area also increases. In contrast to the office sector, demand for apartments also increases during recessions, when employment decreases, as some former homeowners sell their houses and go back to renting. When unemployment rises, apartment landlords tend to decrease monthly rents and/or offer concessions in the form of months of free rent and, depending on local competition, free garage parking and fitness center memberships in order to maintain occupancy levels. When the economy recovers and is expanding, apartment landlords take advantage of their shorter lease lengths to increase rents more aggressively each year and quickly stop offering concessions to attract or retain tenants.

Multifamily REITs that build apartments for student housing at universities benefit from higher undergraduate and graduate enrollment levels at the educational institutions they serve. During difficult economic times, such as during the Great Recession of 2008–09, enrollment levels tend to rise; conversely, during times of economic growth, they decline. Because demand can change quickly in response to the broader economy, it is important that student housing REITs are careful not to oversupply their markets.

Risks and Rewards of Apartment REITs

Because demand for apartments tends to be fairly steady, the main risk associated with this sector is the risk of oversupply. As rental rates for apartments increase, private developers and public REITs tend to develop more apartment buildings to take advantage of strong demand. As with any property type, too much supply results in lower rental rates and/or occupancy levels in a market. This in turn usually leads to a decline in the stock prices of Apartment REITs with meaningful exposure to the market(s) viewed as becoming overbuilt. Apartments are also able to access mortgages that are subsidized by the government-sponsored mortgage providers Fannie Mae, Freddie Mac, and Ginnie Mae. Lower mortgage interest rates have led to lower apartment cap rates.

Manufactured Housing REITs

There are only three Manufactured Housing REITs, with combined assets of $13 billion (Table 6.11). Commonly known as mobile homes, manufactured

TABLE 6.11 Manufactured Housing REITs

Company Name	Ticker Symbol	Total Assets*
Sun Communities Inc.	SUI	$7,398
Equity LifeStyle Properties	ELS	4,137
UMH Properties Inc.	UMH	1,010
Total for 3 REITs:		$12,545

*Total Assets are as of September 30, 2019, in millions of dollars.
Sources: Nareit, S&P Global Market Intelligence. These REITs generally use long-term triple-net leases and/or ground leases.

housing communities are a lower-cost alternative to home ownership, which makes them popular among retirees and lower-income workers. REITs in this property niche own land that is rented to individuals pursuant to a ground lease. Tenants purchase prefabricated houses that are placed in an approved location within the community. In addition to providing sites and utilities for the mobile houses, newer manufactured home communities may also include community-focused amenities, such as lighted streets, swimming pools, and a community recreation facility or clubhouse. The landlord (REIT) receives a monthly fee from each tenant for the right to locate his home on the property. Although individuals technically could move out in any given month, the relatively high cost associated with moving the building to a competing community tends to translate into a very high renewal rate and, in turn, a fairly stable income stream to the landlord.

Single-Family Home REITs

At the end of 2019, there were three REITs that owned single-family houses for rent, which Nareit recently carved out of specialty REITs and placed into their own sub-property type called Single-Family Home REITs (Table 6.12). This subcategory of Residential REITs grew out of the business opportunity the Great Recession of 2008–09 presented to buy houses at deeply discounted prices and lease them back to the former owners or new occupants. Many Millennials now rent these properties when they have children and want yards and good schools, but are not in a financial position to purchase a home. One of the risks to owning Single-Family Home REITs is the difficulty management teams have had in providing guidance; another is the heavy capital expenditure burden often associated with home ownership. While the

TABLE 6.12 Single-Family Home REITs

Company Name	Ticker Symbol	Total Assets*
Invitation Homes Inc.	INVH	$17,660
American Homes 4 Rent	AMH	9,140
Front Yard Residential Corp.	RESI	2,077
Total for 3 REITs:		$28,877

*Total Assets are as of September 30, 2019, in millions of dollars.
Sources: Nareit, S&P Global Market Intelligence. These REITs generally use triple-net leases.

tenants pay for daily upkeep (lawn maintenance, snow removal), the landlord (REIT) must pay for structural repairs (roof, windows, siding, driveway repaving) and systems upkeep. As such, adjusted funds from operations (cash flows) from these REITs may decline unexpectedly in some reporting periods.

RETAIL REITS

In 2019, the Retail REIT sector included 37 REITs with combined assets of $201 billion. Nareit tracks three subcategories of retail REITs: 19 Shopping Center REITs with $75 billion of assets, seven Regional Mall REITs with $78 billion of assets, and 11 Freestanding Retail REITs with total assets of $48 billion.

Initial lease terms to anchor tenants – the larger box tenants used to draw traffic to the retail center – generally are negotiated for 15 to 20 years. In-line tenants are the smaller shops in a center and generally lease their space for five to ten years. Retail landlords typically employ net or modified gross leases (please refer to Chapter 5). Retail landlords also may receive percentage rents in addition to their face rents and CAM fees. Percentage rents are calculated as a portion (typically 1% to 2%) of gross revenue a tenant achieves in any given year above the base (or initial) year revenue. For example, assume Tenant A generates revenue of $100 per square foot (PSF) during the first year of its lease. If Tenant A generates $110 in revenue PSF in the following year and the landlord has negotiated to receive 1% of rents above the base-year revenue, then the landlord will receive an additional $0.10 PSF in percentage rents. During times of economic expansion, landlords can enhance the overall yield on their properties from percentage rents. When economic growth slows or contracts, however, the landlord may receive no percentage rents, which would represent downside risk to the Retail REIT's earnings.

Shopping Center REITs

The term *shopping center* encompasses a range of formats, from grocery store-anchored neighborhood and community centers to power centers. According to the International Council of Shopping Centers (ICSC), neighborhood shopping centers range in size from 30,000 to 125,000 square feet and serve the area within a three-mile radius of their locations. Table 6.13 shows the 19 Shopping Center REITs tracked by Nareit.

TABLE 6.13 Shopping Center REITs

Company Name	Ticker Symbol	Total Assets*
Regency Centers Corp.	REG	$11,173
Kimco Realty Corp.	KIM	11,085
Brixmor Property Group Inc.	BRX	8,160
Federal Realty Investment	FRT	6,608
Acadia Realty Trust	AKR	4,330
SITE Centers Corp.	SITC	4,100
Weingarten Realty Investors	WRI	3,913
Retail Properties of America	RPAI	3,601
American Finance Trust	AFIN	3,457
Retail Opportunity Investments	ROIC	2,933
Urban Edge Properties	UE	2,874
Kite Realty Group Trust	KRG	2,714
Tanger Factory Outlet Centers	SKT	2,324
RPT Realty	RPT	1,866
Retail Value Inc.	RVI	1,686
Saul Centers Inc.	BFS	1,647
Cedar Realty Trust Inc.	CDR	1,223
Urstadt Biddle Properties Inc.[a]	UBA	994
Wheeler REIT Inc.	WHLR	489
Total for 19 REITs:		$75,176

*Total Assets are as of September 30, 2019, in millions of dollars.
[a]Nareit also lists Urstadt Biddle Properties, Inc. - Class A shares.
Sources: Nareit, S&P Global Market Intelligence.

Neighborhood and community centers are among the most defensive property types because, if well-located, they tend to remain well-leased regardless of broader economic trends. Anchor tenants at shopping centers generally are grocery and/or drugstores, designed to draw traffic to the center. Shopping center in-line tenants tend to sell necessary consumer items and services, such as barber shops, beauty shops, liquor stores, dry cleaning, and shoe repair. As a result, demand for neighborhood and community shopping center space tends to be fairly stable (or *inelastic*), as evidenced by their high historical occupancy rates that typically range between 89% and 94%. Similar to industrial properties, new supply of shopping centers tends to track demand due to the short development time. When 3,000 more households are built in an area, a new center is needed.

Power centers consist only of big-box, national retailers such as Bed Bath & Beyond, Petco, Dick's Sporting Goods, Best Buy, and Home Depot. According to ICSC, the average power center is between 250,000 and 600,000 square feet and has a primary trade area of five to ten miles. Although the goods sold at these stores are everyday in nature, they tend not to be true necessity items. Consumers, therefore, may substitute less-expensive brands during an economic downturn. Part of the major draw to power centers, however, is the convenience of shopping at a center that offers a series of anchor tenants clustered in one location. Successful tenants must now compete in the new Internet retail world.

Mall REITs

Malls are classified as regional or superregional, depending on how large they are and what population base they serve. According to ICSC, regional malls are generally between 400,000 and 800,000 square feet in size and have at least two anchor tenants. Super-regional malls are at least 800,000 square feet in size, have at least three anchor tenants, at least one of which offers luxury and/or fashion goods, such as Saks Fifth Avenue; and super-regional malls are the dominant shopping venue within a 25-mile radius. Malls also are classified as being Class-A or Class-B in quality, depending on location, the anchor tenants, and average household income in the surrounding trade area, all of which influence a mall's sales per square foot – an essential metric for comparing productivity among different malls. Table 6.14 shows the eight regional Mall REITs tracked by Nareit.

Anchor tenants may lease their space, though many prefer to own their stores. Since a landlord selects an anchor tenant primarily for that tenant's

TABLE 6.14 Mall REITs

Company Name	Ticker Symbol	Total Assets*
Simon Property Group	SPG	$33,844
Brookfield Property REIT Inc.	BPYU	19,171
Macerich Co.	MAC	8,776
CBL & Associates Properties	CBL	4,770
Taubman Centers Inc.	TCO	4,537
Washington Prime Group Inc.	WPG	4,228
Pennsylvania REIT	PEI	2,334
Total for 7 REITs:		$77,660

*Total Assets are as of September 30, 2019, in millions of dollars.
Sources: Nareit, S&P Global Market Intelligence.

ability to draw consumers to the mall itself, the choice of anchor tenants is crucial to the overall success of a project. In between anchor tenants are smaller retailers referred to as in-line shops. These tenants include national retailers such as Williams-Sonoma (NYSE: WSM), as well as regional and local retailers. Malls typically are located in close proximity to or within major metropolitan areas and/or areas that have above-average household income levels in order to maximize sales per square foot and profitability. With many department store anchor tenants doing poorly, landlords are replacing them with experience-based retail, such as restaurants, movie theaters, escape rooms, and indoor sports activities, including rock climbing gyms (e.g., Earth Treks) and even indoor soccer leagues (e.g., SoFive Soccer Centers).

Freestanding Retail REITs

Freestanding retail properties house a wide array of businesses, including fast-food and sit-down restaurants (such as Burger King and Olive Garden, respectively), drugstores, movie theaters, daycare services, automotive care, big-box (e.g., Walmart, Home Depot), and gas stations. REITs that own free-standing retail properties typically use triple-net leases with their tenants (see Chapter 5). By using triple-net leases, the tenants have full control over

TABLE 6.15 Freestanding Retail REITs

Company Name	Ticker Symbol	Total Assets*	NAREIT Sub-Property Type
Realty Income Corp.	O	$17,180	Single-Tenant
STORE Capital Corp.	STOR	7,813	Diversified
National Retail Properties	NNN	7,628	Single-Tenant
Spirit Realty Capital Inc.	SRC	5,664	Diversified
Seritage Growth Properties	SRG	2,793	Other Retail
Agree Realty Corp.	ADC	2,523	Single-Tenant
Essential Properties Realty Tr	EPRT	1,805	Single-Tenant
Four Corners Property Trust	FCPT	1,348	Single-Tenant
Getty Realty Corp.	GTY	1,194	Single-Tenant
Alpine Income Property Trust	PINE	150	Single-Tenant
Postal Realty Trust	PSTL	88	Single-Tenant
Total for 11 REITs:		$48,187	

*Total Assets are as of September 30, 2019, in millions of dollars.
Sources: Nareit, S&P Global Market Intelligence. These REITs generally use long-term triple-net leases and/or ground leases.

their property operations, including staying open late or all night for business. Alternatively, if these tenants rented space in a shopping center or mall, they would be subject to that center's operating hours and other criteria. Nareit tracks seven Freestanding Retail REITs, as shown in Table 6.15.

A handful of new Freestanding Retail REITs, including Seritage, Spirit, and STORE, have listed their shares since 2010. Growth in this once-sleepy subcategory of Retail REITs is being fueled by the increased comfort tenants have gained to lease rather than own their real estate. In a sale/lease-back transaction, an owner of a property sells it to a new owner/landlord, then leases back that same space, typically using a long-term triple-net lease. An increasing number of businesses are willing to monetize their real estate holdings through sale/lease-back transactions with REITs. By doing so, the businesses free up precious capital to deploy back into their operations while still maintaining fundamental control over their locations with long-term leases and lease renewal options.

Risks and Rewards of Retail REITs

As the 2019 holiday shopping season evidenced, and the response to the COVID-19 pandemic solidified, consumers increasingly are shopping for gifts and necessary items online rather than in retail stores (please refer to the discussion in Industrial REITs earlier in this chapter). Internet sales (*e-commerce*) are encroaching on the profitability of traditional brick-and-mortar stores. As e-commerce proliferates, traditional retailers – and the REITs who act as their landlords – will need to innovate to stay occupied and be profitable.

One effective strategy Retail REITs use to mitigate the risk of losing tenants and market share to e-commerce retailers, such as Amazon.com, Inc. (NASDAQ: AMZN), is to own the most attractive locations, often measured by the average household and discretionary income levels within a one-, three-, or five-mile radius of retail centers. Such attractive locations tend to support higher sales per square foot leased for their tenants, meaning the space they rent is more productive and profitable than secondary locations. When retailers close stores, they close their least productive ones (measured in sales revenues per square foot).

A second strategy landlords use to maintain the revenue per square foot at their centers is to lease space to tenants that offer necessary items (such as groceries and dry cleaning) or, at the other end of the consumption spectrum, luxury goods. A third strategy landlords can pursue to maintain a competitive edge is to redevelop existing properties that can capture the new retail concepts; experiential retail is the new winner that cannot be replaced with e-commerce. Simon Property Group (NYSE: SPG) in the Mall REIT category is known for reinvesting in its malls to stay ahead of retail trends; recent conversions include converting former retail square footage to office, residential, and recreational uses, such as outdoor parks. Online retail is also expanding back into brick-and-mortar locations for cost and convenience reasons. For example, Amazon is projected to open 250 Amazon grab-and-go locations in 2020.

COVID-19-related shutdowns had an immediate and bifurcated impact on retailers, who within most states were divided into "essential" and "non-essential" businesses. Grocery chains and big-box retail stores that often include a grocery component – for example, Target Corporation (NYSE: TGT) and Walmart (NYSE: WMT) – and home repair retailers such as The Home Depot (NYSE: HD), were deemed essential and were not negatively impacted by business shutdowns. In fact, these retailers generally saw increased demand and sales, as consumers had fewer alternatives for procuring essential goods. In contrast, non-essential retailers and enclosed malls, where social distancing could not be guaranteed, shuttered operations for several months. The long-term effects related to the shutdowns, including which retailers actually survive, are still to be determined, as are the ultimate impacts on the cash flows of REITs from whom these retailers lease space.

SELF-STORAGE PROPERTY MARKET

The FTSE Nareit All REITs Index classifies six companies as Self-Storage REITs with combined assets of $31 billion (Table 6.16). Similar to that which drives the apartment sector, demand for self-storage units is driven by population growth, people moving locations for jobs or other reasons, as well as the urge many people have to either archive things for future generations or the simple inability to throw anything away. Individuals who rent apartments or who live in condominiums tend to rent self-storage space. Businesses use self-storage to hold excess inventory. Customers select storage facilities based on the price, location, security, and suitability of space to their needs. Property owners rarely depend on one customer for large portions of revenue because individual consumers (rather than businesses) represent the majority of self-storage users. The storage units themselves are simple structures located near busy roads in order to ensure visibility. They require

TABLE 6.16 Self-Storage REITs

Company Name	Ticker Symbol	Total Assets*
Public Storage	PSA	$11,414
Extra Space Storage Inc.	EXR	8,318
Life Storage Inc.	LSI	4,189
CubeSmart	CUBE	3,950
National Storage Affiliates Trust	NSA	3,111
Global Self Storage	SELF	58
Total for 6 REITs:		$31,040

*Total Assets are as of September 30, 2019, in millions of dollars.
Sources: Nareit, S&P Global Market Intelligence.

little capital expenditures outside of roof or parking lot/pavement repairs and air conditioning. Management has become important in attracting and retaining clients over the past decade with national chains producing effective marketing.

Risks and Rewards of Self-Storage REITs

Self-storage units are rented on a month-to-month basis, which can create volatility in rental rates during times of weak or robust demand. Historically, oversupply has been the primary risk associated with this sector. Although the facilities take little time to construct, highly fragmented ownership historically led to less transparent demand-and-supply information than for other commercial property types. As the REITs in this space have grown primarily by acquiring existing local properties, the sector's supply issues have waned and the sector has tended to outperform other property types.

CONCLUSION

REIT performance varies by property sector, as each type of real estate is impacted differently by tenant preferences, technology changes, and larger economic trends. Chapter 10 provides a more in-depth analysis of how REITs have performed in different market conditions in the past, including a comparison by property sector. Any investment strategy that diversifies by property type should produce good results.

CHAPTER 7

Mortgage REITs

OVERVIEW OF MORTGAGE REITS

Mortgage real estate investment trusts (mREITs) are companies that finance residential and commercial real estate. In addition to providing long-term funding for the homeowner or commercial property owner, mREITs may originate and service loans, perform capital markets activities like securitizations, and restructure or recapitalize troubled credits. Most public mREITs are listed on stock exchanges like the NYSE or Nasdaq. By purchasing common stock of mREITs, investors can access the $15.6 trillion market of home and commercial mortgage investments through a liquid, transparent, exchange-traded company (see Figure 7.1).

As Figure 7.2 shows, mREITs pay a high dividend yield, typically representing a premium of 500 to 800 basis points to the dividend yield of equity REITs. While high leverage and credit risks caused several mREITs to encounter financial difficulty during the Global Financial Crisis (GFC) of 2007–08, other mREITs weathered the crisis and even accelerated their growth by making advantageous investments in the aftermath.

Size and Composition of the mREIT Sector. As of December 31, 2019, there were 40 mREIT constituents in the FTSE Nareit Mortgage REITs Index, including 24 that provide financing for residential real estate (see Table 7.1) and 16 that fund commercial real estate (see Table 7.2). The equity market capitalization of the residential mREITs was $55.2 billion, and the market cap of commercial mREITs was $27.8 billion, resulting in a total market cap of $82.9 billion for the overall mREIT sector.

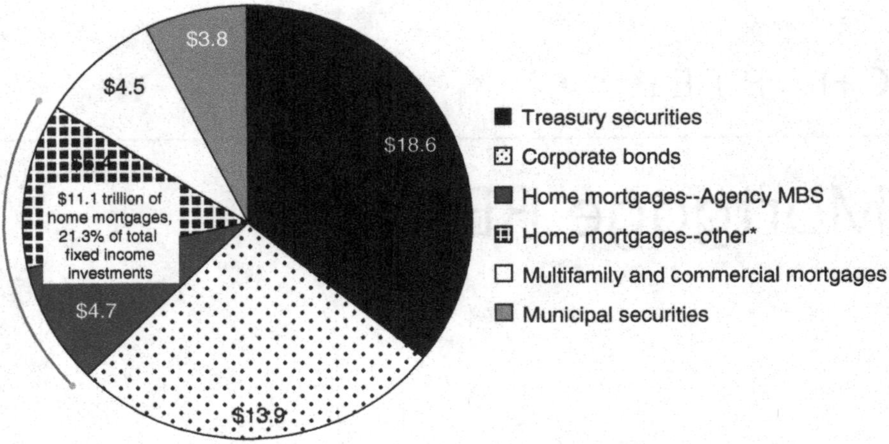

FIGURE 7.1 Fixed Income and Mortgage Investment Universe
* Includes private-label MBS and whole-loan mortgages.Trillions of dollars.
Source: Federal Reserve Board, *Financial Accounts of the United States*, 2019:Q3, Nareit.

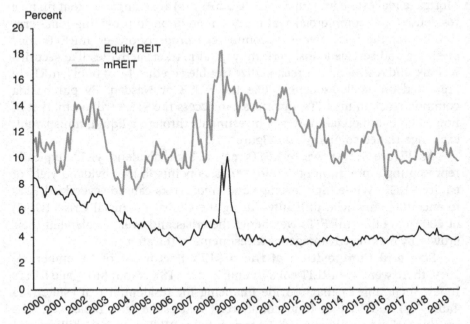

FIGURE 7.2 Dividend Yield of mREITs versus Equity REITs
Source: Nareit.

TABLE 7.1 Residential mREITs

Company Name	Ticker Symbol	Total Assets*
Annaly Capital Management	NLY	$128,956
AGNC Investment Corp.	AGNC	109,761
New Residential Investment Corp.	NRZ	41,348
Two Harbors Investment Corp.	TWO	32,164
Chimera Investment Corp.	CIM	28,632
Invesco Mortgage Capital	IVR	24,061
New York Mortgage Trust	NYMT	19,759
Redwood Trust	RWT	15,476
ARMOUR Residential REIT	ARR	13,223
MFA Financial, Inc.	MFA	13,105
Capstead Mortgage Corp.	CMO	11,535
PennyMac Mortgage Investment Tr	PMT	10,745
Dynex Capital, Inc.	DX	5,487
Western Asset Mortage Cap'l Corp.	WMC	5,254
AG Mortgage Investment Trust	MITT	4,749
Anworth Mortgage Asset Corporation	ANH	4,582
Ready Capital Corp.	RC	4,123
Arlington Asset Investment Corp.-Class A	AI	4,100
Orchid Island Capital	ORC	3,727
Ellington Financial, Inc.	EFC	3,627
Cherry Hill Mortgage Investment Corp.	CHMI	2,876
Ellington Residential Mortgage REIT	EARN	1,674
Great Ajax Corp.	AJX	1,554
Hunt Companies Finance Trust	HCFT	657
Subtotal for 24 Residential mREITs:		$491,177

*Total Assets are as of September 30, 2019, in millions of dollars.
Sources: Nareit, S&P Global Market Intelligence.

TABLE 7.2 Commercial mREITs

Company Name	Ticker Symbol	Total Assets*
Starwood Property Trust	STWD	$74,434
Blackstone Mortgage Trust, Inc - Class A	BXMT	15,082
Colony Credit Real Estate, Inc. - Class A	CLNC	7,444
Ladder Capital Corp. - Class A	LADR	6,620
Apollo Commercial Real Estate Finance	ARI	6,352
TPG RE Finance Trust	TRTX	5,863
iStar Inc.	STAR	5,580
Arbor Realty Trust, Inc.	ABR	5,396
KKR Real Estate Finance Trust	KREF	5,211
Granite Point Mortgage Trust	GPMT	4,308
Exantas Capital Corp	XAN	2,472
Hannon Armstrong Sustainable Infra. Cap'l	HASI	2,279
Ares Commercial Real Estate Corp	ACRE	1,675
Jernigan Capital, Inc.	JCAP	776
Tremont Mortgage Trust	TRMT	218
Sachem Capital Corp	SACH	109
Subtotal for 16 Commercial mREITs:		$143,820

*Total Assets are as of September 30, 2019, in millions of dollars.
Sources: Nareit, S&P Global Market Intelligence.

Investing in mREITs. An individual may buy shares in mREITs, which are listed on major stock exchanges, just like they do for any other public stock. Shares can also be purchased in a mutual fund or exchange-traded fund (ETF). (Mutual funds and ETFs are discussed further in Chapter 10.) Investors have historically found value in mREITs primarily because of their history of relatively high dividends. This high dividend yield makes mREITs particularly attractive for investors who desire current income from their portfolio, including retirees.

RESIDENTIAL mREITS

Agency mREITs. Most residential mREITs today focus their investments on mortgage-backed securities (MBS) issued by Fannie Mae, Freddie Mac, and Ginnie Mae. These mREITs are often called *Agency mREITs,* in reference to the status of Fannie Mae, Freddie Mac, and Ginnie Mae as US Government Sponsored Enterprises (GSEs). The MBS securities the GSEs issue are bonds composed of – that is, backed by – residential home mortgages that lenders issued to homeowners who have good credit (also referred to as *prime borrowers*). Most Agency MBS do not bear credit risk, as the GSEs guarantee the timely repayment of principal. Fannie and Freddie have recently begun issuing some credit-linked bonds to pass credit risk on to the investors. Total amounts outstanding of these credit risk-sharing securities, however, are small relative to the total size of the Agency MBS market. (Chapter 9 discusses MBS and other real estate debt securities in greater detail.)

mREITs and other investors in Agency MBS are subject to other risks, however. Homeowners generally have the right to prepay their mortgage without penalty, either to refinance at a lower interest rate or in case they have sold the home and moved. Investors in Agency MBS are thus subject to the risk of unpredictable cash flows, including the need to reinvest prepayment proceeds at a time when market yields may have declined. These risks associated with changes in interest rates and the tools that mREITs use to mitigate them are discussed below.

Non-Agency mREITs. Prior to the GFC, several mREITs focused on investments other than Agency MBS. These comprised non-Agency MBS including those backed by subprime mortgages issued by banks and other financial institutions other than Fannie Mae and Freddie Mac, also referred to as *Private-Label Securities* (PLS), as well as residential whole loans (which are less liquid than MBS, and are discussed later in this chapter), mortgage servicing rights and commercial real estate debt, in addition to holding Agency MBS. These firms were often referred to as *non-Agency mREITs.*

At the end of 2006, prior to the GFC, non-Agency mREITs constituted over 70% of the market capitalization of the residential mREIT subsector. Most experienced losses due to defaults by homeowners during the GFC, and 19 of the 25 residential mREITs in operation prior to the GFC went out of business during the GFC. The performance of these mREITs through the GFC impacts the long-run reported total return of the overall mREIT sector and of the residential mREIT subsector.

Other Residential mREIT Investments and Activities. Several mREITs invest in mortgage servicing rights (MSR), which entails collecting monthly mortgage payments from homeowners and forwarding the payments to the investors who hold MBS backed by these mortgages. Mortgage servicing is an essential service in the mortgage business and provides fee income to the entity that performs the servicing. There are financial risks to investing in MSR, however, as the need to service a mortgage (and the stream of fee income for doing so) vanishes if the mortgage is prepaid or refinanced. mREITs that invest in MSR often hedge these risks using similar techniques to those applied to prepayment and interest rate risks on the MBS themselves, which are discussed in the following section.

In addition to investing in residential mortgages and MBS and MSR, some residential mREITs also invest in commercial mortgages and MBS. Lastly, most residential mREITs do not originate mortgages (the primary mortgage market); they do, however, invest in MBS that include mortgages originated by other institutions (the secondary mortgage market).

COMMERCIAL mREITS

Commercial mREITs engage in a wide range of activities related to originating, funding, servicing, and restructuring loans secured by commercial real estate. Some commercial mREITs specialize in one or two of the following activities, while others enter into a large number of these activities:

- **Commercial mortgage-backed securities (CMBS).** CMBS are similar to the residential mortgage securities that are issued by Fannie Mae and Freddie Mac or private-label issuers, but contain loans secured by commercial and multifamily properties. CMBS are liquid, traded investments that can be bought or sold easily. The collateral backing the CMBS includes a large number of loans. This helps diversify exposure across many borrowers, geographic regions, and types of properties.
- **Whole-loan commercial mortgages.** Whole loans are the old-fashioned way of investing, where the entity that originated the loan also keeps it on its own balance sheet, funding and servicing the mortgage. Whole loans are less liquid than CMBS and retain higher concentrations to specific borrowers, properties, or regions.

- **Originating and underwriting commercial mortgages.** Commercial mREITs, in contrast to their residential counterparts, may originate and underwrite loans.
- **Servicing.** Many commercial mREITs service loans and CMBS. Several are involved in special servicing of CMBS that have gone into default.
- **Restructuring and workouts.** Some commercial mREITs work with borrowers to restructure loans that have fallen delinquent. They are often able to improve cash flows from the mortgage by avoiding some of the costs that may arise in the event of a default.
- **Securitizations.** Some commercial mREITs carry out the process of securitization, which entails assembling a large number of commercial mortgages into a pool structure, creating CMBS backed by this pool, and selling/distributing the CMBS to investors.
- **Real estate.** Some commercial mREITs hold an equity interest in commercial properties as investments.

FUNDING SOURCES FOR mREITS

mREITs, like most investors in mortgages and MBS, use both equity and debt to fund their portfolios. Higher amounts of debt, or greater leverage, increase the size of a portfolio that a given equity investment can acquire. Leverage can boost returns to equity investors but can also raise risks as the use of leverage can magnify losses during a downturn.

Sources of capital include: common equity; preferred shares; long-term debt; repurchase agreements (short-term debt financing discussed later in this chapter); and bank loans.

mREIT RISKS AND RISK MANAGEMENT

Like any financial business, mREITs face certain risks. Most employ techniques to mitigate these risks. No risk management strategy, however, can eliminate 100% of the risks, and indeed, during the GFC, several mREITs came under severe pressure and some failed. Since the crisis, however, most mREITs have chosen more conservative business models that are less vulnerable to the types of risk that caused difficulties during the GFC.

The main types of risks faced by mREITs include:

- **Interest rate risk.** Managing the effects of changes in short- and long-term interest rates is an essential element of mREITs' business operations. Changes in interest rates can affect the net interest margin, which is the difference between an mREIT's average investment yield and its average cost of capital (or *weighted average cost of capital* [WACC], discussed in Chapters 10 and 11) and is every mREIT's fundamental source of earnings. Changes in interest rates may also affect the value of an mREIT's mortgage assets, which affects corporate net worth. Similar to how US Treasuries are valued, when the underlying interest rate increases, the value or price of the Treasury bill, note, or bond decreases.

  mREITs typically manage and mitigate risk associated with their short-term borrowings through conventional, widely used hedging strategies, including interest rate swaps, swaptions, interest rate collars, caps or floors, and other financial futures contracts. mREITs also manage risk in other ways, such as selecting specific MBS investments based on the likely prepayments of mortgages in the pool under alternative interest rate environments, adjusting the average maturities on their assets as well as their borrowings, and selling assets during periods of interest rate volatility to raise cash or reduce borrowings.
- **Credit risk.** The bulk of mortgage securities purchased by residential mREITs are Agency securities backed by the federal government, which present limited credit risk. Commercial mREITs may be exposed to credit risk through their private-label residential MBS and CMBS. The degree of credit risk for a particular security depends on the credit performance of the underlying loans, the structure of the security (that is, which classes of security are paid first, and which are paid later), and by the degree of over-collateralization (in which the face amount of the mortgage loans held as collateral exceeds the face amount of the residential MBS or CMBS issued).
- **Prepayment risk.** Changes in interest rates or borrower home sales affect the probability that some borrowers will refinance or repay their mortgages. When such a refinancing or repayment occurs, the investor holding the mortgage or MBS must reinvest the proceeds into the prevailing interest rate environment, which may be lower or higher. Investors also lose the investment premiums of MBS that prepay at par. mREITs seek to hedge prepayment risk using similar

tools and techniques as those they use to hedge against interest rate risks.

- **Funding or liquidity risk.** mREIT assets are mainly longer-term MBS and mortgages, while their liabilities may include a significant amount of short-term debt, especially among residential mREITs. This term mismatch requires that they roll over their short-term debt before the maturity of their assets. Their ability to do so depends on the liquidity and smooth functioning of the short-term debt markets, including the repo market. The repo market is extremely liquid, with an estimated $2 trillion in outstanding instruments and several hundred billion dollars in daily trading volume. Banks and dealers also use the repo market as an important source of market liquidity. In the financing markets, the liquidity of the Agency MBS and TBA (or *To Be Announced*) markets is comparable to the market for Treasuries. (The TBA market trades forward contracts of Agency MBS to be delivered at a future date and at a predetermined price, but without specifying which exact mortgage securities will be delivered.) Commercial mREITs tend to match the duration of their assets and liabilities and face little roll over risk.

mREITS AND THE GREAT FINANCIAL CRISIS OF 2007–08

mREITs grew rapidly during the housing boom that preceded the GFC. Total mortgage and MBS holdings of mREITs increased from less than $20 billion in 2000, to greater than $100 billion in mid-2007. Much of this growth resulted from increased holdings of non-Agency MBS. These securities included not only MBS backed by "jumbo" mortgages that exceed the upper size limit on mortgages that the GSEs are authorized to securitize ("conforming mortgages" and "conforming loan limit"), but also MBS backed by subprime and Alt-A mortgages.

Total mREIT holdings of non-Agency MBS were $7 billion, less than 20% of the total MBS position of mREITs in 2002; by 2006, however, the non-Agency share had risen to $45 billion, and were roughly half of total MBS holdings (Figure 7.3).

A number of developments brought the credit exposure of the non-Agency MBS into crisis in 2008–09. The credit underwriting of the predominantly subprime and Alt-A mortgages backing these non-Agency MBS had often been lax, and many of the homeowners who borrowed in the subprime mortgage market were unwilling or unable to continue

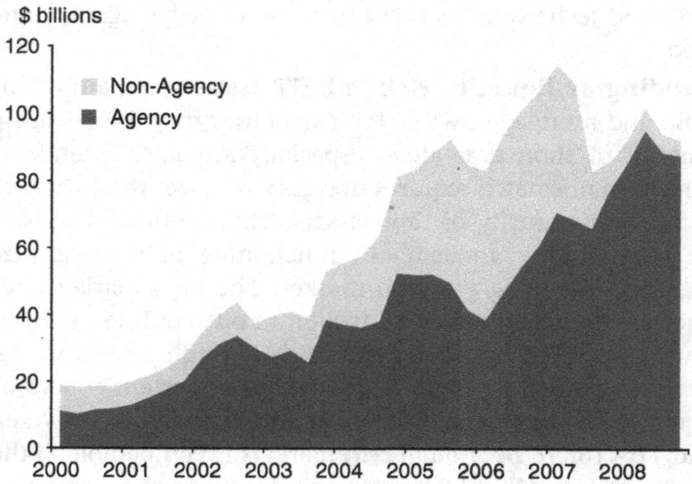

FIGURE 7.3 Mortgage Assets of Home Financing mREITs
Source: S&P Global Market Intelligence, Nareit.

making payments. There was a notably sharp increase in failure to make payments when "teaser" interest rates reset to a market-based interest rate. Furthermore, home prices began falling as the GFC proceeded, eroding the value of the collateral and contributing to large losses for many lenders, including mREITs holding non-Agency MBS.

The decision whether or not to take on credit risk was a major determinant of whether the mREIT survived the GFC. Indeed, most mREITs that focused on non-Agency MBS failed during the crisis, and the MBS in their portfolios represented 87% of the total non-Agency MBS held by mREITs (Figure 7.4, hashed lightest gray area). In contrast, all the major Agency mREITs survived the GFC, and over 94% of Agency MBS held by mREITs were on the balance sheets of those that survived the GFC.

mREITS SINCE THE GREAT FINANCIAL CRISIS

Recapitalizing the Agency MBS Market. The mREIT sector grew even more rapidly following the onset of the GFC. Most traditional investors in MBS, including commercial banks, investment banks, and the GSEs, Fannie Mae and Freddie Mac, came under severe funding pressure, in particular related to their portfolios of MBS. Many investors were forced to trim their holdings or liquidate their portfolios, putting downward pressure on asset

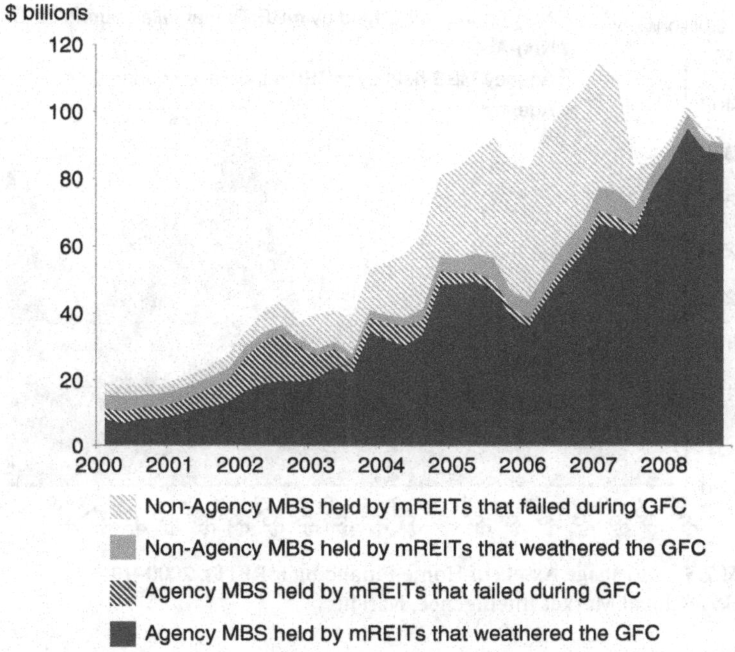

FIGURE 7.4 Mortgage Assets of Home Financing mREITs and Failures During GFC
Source: S&P Global Market Intelligence, Nareit 2018.

prices and raising concerns about fire sales. During this period, several mREITs stepped in to purchase Agency MBS, helping to stabilize asset prices. The Federal Reserve also began purchasing Agency MBS, as well as Treasury securities, to improve market liquidity. mREIT holdings of Agency MBS rose from less than $90 billion at the end of 2008, to $380 billion in 2012 (Figure 7.5). To a certain extent, the investments by mREITs in Agency MBS helped reinforce the federal government's efforts to calm the crisis.

mREITs issued common stock to help fund these investments. Equity issuance during the early period of most portfolio growth, 2010 through 2013, totaled $51 billion, and the total amount raised from 2009 through 2019 was $93 billion (Figure 7.6). One of the contributing factors to the financial crisis was excessive use of debt and high leverage; that is, a lack of permanent equity capital to support mortgage investments, including those by the commercial banking and investment banking sectors. By raising significant amounts of equity capital, the mREIT sector helped recapitalize the mortgage and MBS sector.

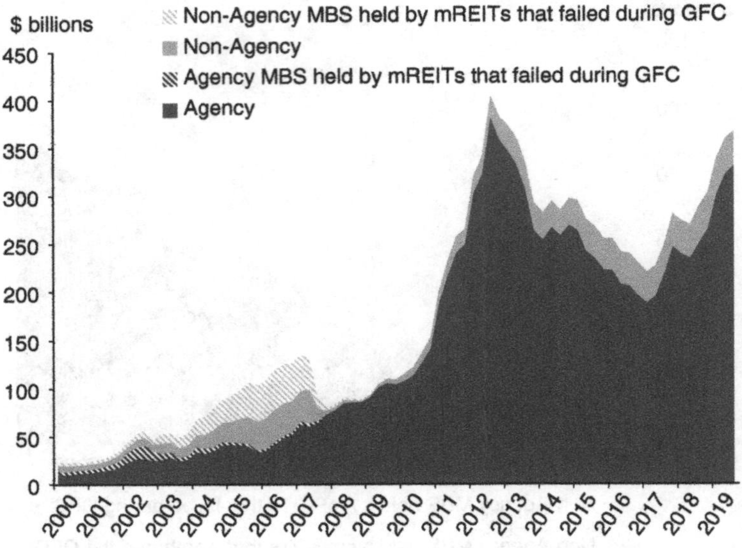

FIGURE 7.5 Mortgage Assets of Home Financing mREITs, 2000–19
Source: S&P Global Market Intelligence, Nareit.

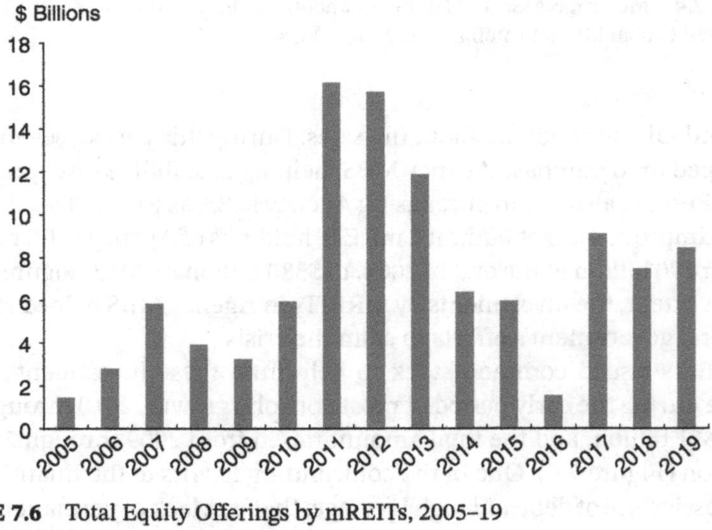

FIGURE 7.6 Total Equity Offerings by mREITs, 2005–19
Source: Nareit.

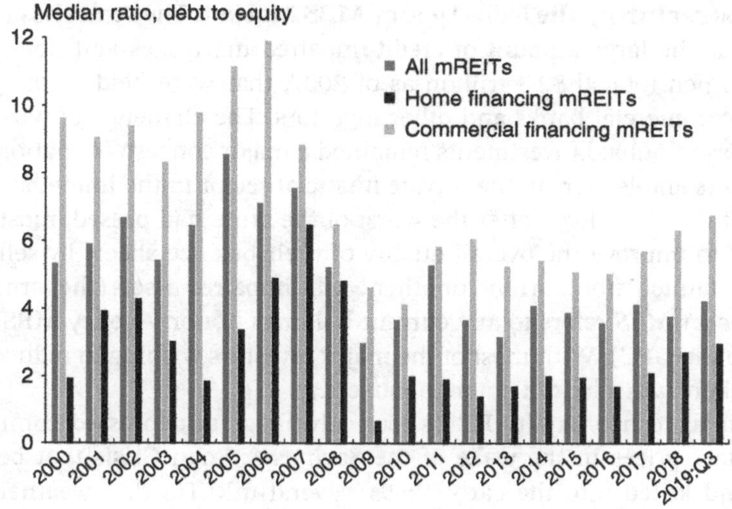

FIGURE 7.7 mREIT Median Debt-to-Book Equity Leverage Ratios
Source: S&P Global Market Intelligence, Nareit.

The $93 billion of equity capital that mREITs raised not only facilitated balance sheet growth, but also allowed them to strengthen their own balance sheet positions. Prior to the GFC, the median leverage ratio of mREITS was 8.5× debt-to-book equity (see dark gray bars in Figure 7.7). Debt-to-book equity is the book value of debt divided by book value of equity, where the debt and equity values are those presented on a REIT's consolidated balance sheet in its 10-Q and 10-K SEC filings. Book equity can also be calculated by subtracting book debt from the total book assets listed on the balance sheet:

$$\frac{\text{Debt}}{\text{Book Equity}} = \frac{\text{Book Debt}}{(\text{Total Book Assets} - \text{Book Debt})}$$

Among home financing mREITs, which tend to use higher leverage than the commercial mREIT sector, the median leverage ratio was 11.9× in 2006 (black bars in Figure 7.7); the median leverage ratio of commercial mREITs reached a peak of 6.5× in 2007 (light gray bars in Figure 7.7). Since the GFC, however, leverage ratios have declined sharply. The median leverage ratio among all mREITs dropped to as low as 3×, and has subsequently risen slightly, to 4.2× as of the third quarter of 2019. This reflects a median leverage ratio of 6.8× and 3.0×, respectively, for the home financing and commercial mREIT subsectors.

Restructuring the Non-Agency MBS Market. The central issue of the GFC was the large amount of credit-impaired mortgages and non-Agency MBS, which totaled $2.3 trillion as of 2007, that were held in the portfolios of commercial banks and other investors. The challenge of what to do with these troubled investments remained a major concern for national policymakers and leaders in the private financial sector in the immediate aftermath of the GFC. Even after the worst of the crisis had passed, most banks wanted to improve the overall quality of their balance sheets by selling off those defaulted, non-current, or other credit-impaired assets (the term *legacy non-Agency MBS* refers to any current holdings of non-Agency MBS issued prior to the GFC). With most of the major investors wishing to reduce exposures, there was a lack of potential buyers.

Similar to how equity REITs took advantage of depressed commercial real estate prices in the wake of the Savings & Loan Crisis that began in 1986 and lasted into the early 1990s, several mREITs that weathered the GFC bought legacy non-Agency MBS from banks and other investors at highly opportunistic prices. Total non-Agency MBS held by mREITs began increasing from a low of $4.3 billion in early 2009, to $25 billion in 2012. Holdings of non-Agency MBS rose a bit more but have been stable at $30 billion to $38 billion since 2015. Many of these assets were purchased at a deep discount to their face value, often less than 50 cents on a dollar, reflecting the troubled credit of the mortgages underlying the MBS. The estimated face value of these legacy non-Agency MBS represents as much as 15% of total legacy non-Agency MBS outstanding as of 2019 (total outstanding non-Agency MBS had a face value of $452 billion as of September 30, 2019).

Some of the mortgages underlying legacy non-Agency MBS are re-performing; that is, homeowners who may have struggled financially during the crisis and fallen delinquent, subsequently resumed making payments on the mortgages. Others have been restructured to help the owner remain in the home and avoid the costs of going through foreclosure and home sale (in essence, the borrower and lender agree to share the costs of past delinquent payments, in an effort to enable the homeowner to make payments in the future). Still others of these are mortgages that have been re-securitized, that is, packaged into a new pool of mortgages to back a newly issued MBS.

By purchasing these legacy non-Agency MBS and mortgages at a discount and taking measures to improve the chances that the homeowner will make payments in the future, mREITs have been able to earn an attractive rate of return on these legacy assets.

TOTAL RETURN OF AGENCY mREITs

The FTSE Nareit Mortgage REITs Index is a float-adjusted market capitalization-weighted index of returns of the mREIT constituents of the index. For the period beginning prior to the GFC, this includes a heavy weighting of the return of non-Agency mREITs, which, as mentioned previously, constituted 70% of the market cap of the home financing subindex. Most of these constituents experienced significant losses and negative returns during the GFC, pulling down the reported returns of the mREIT sector.

While this index is appropriate to measure the performance of the sector as it existed prior to the GFC, the current composition of the industry is very different. As noted above, no mREITs invest in original-issue subprime MBS – indeed, there are virtually no subprime mortgages being originated in the United States. Rather, the mREIT sector today is composed of firms that invest primarily in Agency MBS, other mREITs that invest in Agency MBS and also legacy non-Agency MBS (purchased at deep discounts), plus the commercial mREITs.

Nareit constructed an index of total returns of the Agency mREITs that were in operation through the GFC as well as those that formed subsequent to the GFC. The total return of these Agency mREITs over the past 15 years has been comparable to investment returns in other sectors, including equity REITs and the Russell 3000 Stock Index:

- The 15-year annualized total return of the FTSE Nareit Mortgage REITs Index was 1.2% (through December 31, 2019), compared to a 7.8% return for the FTSE Nareit All Equity REITs Index and a 9.0% return for stocks in the Russell 3000 Index.
- The Agency mREITs posted an annual return of 6.8% over this period, significantly outperforming the FTSE Nareit mREIT Index.

The difference in total return performance between the index that included the non-Agency mREITs prior to the GFC of 1.2% and the Agency mREIT returns of 6.8% reflects the different business models of a large portion of the sector prior to the GFC that took on significant credit risks, and those mREITs that did not bear credit risks but rather focused on investments in Agency MBS. The sector today holds little or no credit risk, suggesting that this Agency mREIT index is appropriate for investors in today's mREITs.

CURRENT REGULATORY ISSUES REGARDING mREITS

As of early 2020, there were two regulatory matters regarding mREITs. First, several mREITs had borrowed from the Federal Home Loan Bank (FHLB) system through captive mortgage company subsidiaries. The FHLB was established to help provide funding and liquidity to the home mortgage market, and most members in the system were banks and other depositories, and insurance companies. The FHFA in 2016 restricted access to the FHLB by limiting membership by captive insurance companies, including those owned by mREITs. Those mREITs that had borrowed from the FHLB through a captive subsidiary were given a time window, ranging from two to five years, to repay those borrowings. There have been discussions, however, over whether to allow mREITs to borrow from the FHLB to help further their role in financing the home mortgage market.

The second regulatory matter has been the eligibility of REITs to invest in certain MBS that transfer some of the credit risk of the mortgages from the GSEs to investors. The GSEs introduced such securities following the GFC to help reduce concentrations of risk that could threaten financial stability in a future crisis. The structure of these credit risk transfer (CRT) securities, however, may preclude REIT investment depending whether these securities are classified as a "whole pool certificate" or a "partial pool certificate." As of publication, this matter has not been resolved and the eligibility of CRT securities for REIT investment is uncertain.

CONCLUSION

The mREITs sector has grown rapidly over the past decade, and the composition of the sector has changed as well, especially among mREITs that finance residential real estate. mREITs that had taken on exposures to credit risk prior to the GFC have exited the sector, while those that invest in mortgage securities guaranteed by the government agencies constitute nearly all of the home financing mREIT subsector. In the wake of the GFC and in the years since, mREITs proved to be vital participants in the US financial industry, having helped banks recapitalize their balance sheets and return to financial health, and also providing greater liquidity to support home ownership and commercial real estate investments needed to support a growing US economy.

PART II

INVESTING IN REITs

Part II of this book builds on the basic information conveyed in Part I. Chapters 8 through 11 are geared toward investors who want to take their academic understanding of REITs accumulated in Chapters 1 through 7 and apply it to actual companies for investment purposes. This includes individuals and money managers who are new to REITs, and financial advisors who want to better serve their clients by mastering the basics of REIT analysis. Chapter 8 discusses important technical aspects specific to REITs, including their ability to issue OP units (a non-tradeable equity) when acquiring privately held real properties and also the compliance aspects of qualifying for and maintaining REIT status. Chapter 8 concludes by comparing publicly traded REITs and their public non-listed REIT (PNLR) cousins, which differ primarily in the aspect of liquidity. Chapter 9 provides an overview of the types of public and private alternatives REITs have for raising debt capital. Chapter 10 summarizes how REITs, as an industry, have performed in different stock market and interest rate environments. Lastly, Chapter 11 provides calculations for analyzing REITs. Metrics includes how to assess REIT profitability and cash flow, balance sheet strength, portfolio risk/strength, weighted average cost of capital, and net asset value.

CHAPTER 8

Getting Technical

Before discussing the various metrics used to analyze REITs in Chapter 11, there are a few technical items specific to REITs that are important to understand.

REIT STRUCTURES

As discussed at the outset of this book, REITs are companies that own or finance income-producing commercial real estate (a similar structure to a mutual fund). The majority of REITs are equity REITs, which generally derive the bulk of their income from rental revenue paid by tenants. Prior to 1992, equity REITs owned their commercial properties directly or through joint ventures. As Figure 8.1 illustrates, a REIT raises capital by issuing equity (common and/or preferred) and debt (such as bonds or mortgages). The investing public buys the REIT's securities, and the REIT invests the monies into rentable properties. The REIT then pays interest payments to its debt investors and pays a dividend to its shareholders. Besides their current returns and the possibility that their equity investments will appreciate in price, investors in the REIT receive professional management and investment access to large properties they could not buy on their own.

With a traditional REIT structure (Figure 8.1), common shareholders essentially own a portion of the REIT's business enterprise, prorated according to how many shares they owned relative to the REIT's total shares outstanding. If an investor owns 5% of a REIT's outstanding common shares, they essentially own 5% of that REIT's assets and operations.

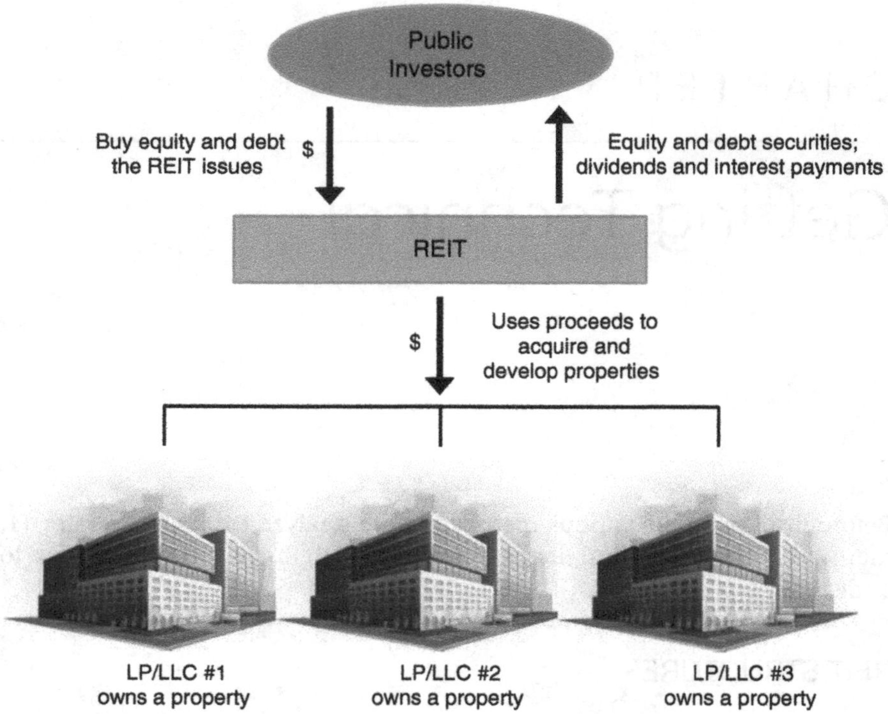

FIGURE 8.1 REIT Structure

UPREITs

Beginning in 1992, REITs' corporate ownership structure underwent a revolutionary change with the introduction of the Umbrella Partnership REIT (UPREIT) structure and the Operating Partnership Unit (OP unit). Taubman Centers, Inc. (NYSE: TCO) is credited for innovating the UPREIT structure with its 1992 initial public offering (IPO). An UPREIT uses Section 721 of the Tax Code to allow the owner(s) of investment property(s) to transfer their ownership to an UPREIT in exchange for partnership units, thereby deferring the recognition of capital gains tax associated with the property(s) exchanged (721 Exchange). Figure 8.2 illustrates a typical 721 Exchange.

The UPREIT structure differs from that of a traditional REIT in two ways. First, and as shown in Figure 8.3, the REIT does not own its properties directly. Instead, the REIT owns (usually a great majority of) units

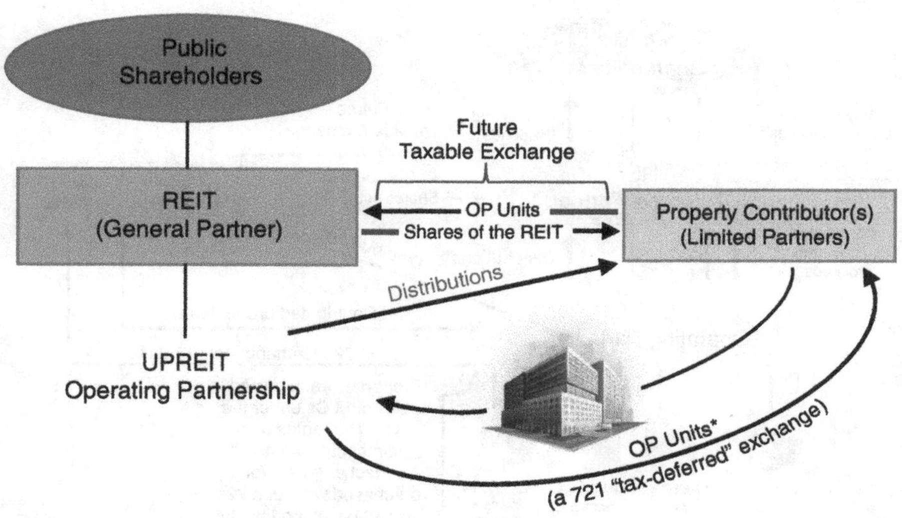

FIGURE 8.2 721 Exchange
* The UPREIT OP will pay the purchase price of the property with OP units or a combination of OP units, cash, and often the assumption of debt on the properties being sold.

in a limited partnership called an umbrella operating partnership (the OP), which in turn owns and operates the properties. Note that, like a traditional REIT, the OP still uses individual LPs or LLCs to own each property. As Figure 8.3 also illustrates, the UPREIT owns an interest in and is the sole general partner of its OP. When a REIT that uses an UPREIT structure issues new common or preferred equity shares to public investors, it contributes the proceeds to its OP in exchange for additional OP units. The OP technically is the legal entity that buys and/or develops properties and operates them. From the money it earns from operating the properties, the OP "distributes" money back to the REIT, which pays dividends to its shareholders (and interest payments to its lenders). The OP, therefore, is a pass-through mechanism that is transparent to public shareholders.

The second difference between traditional REITs and UPREITs is that the latter have an additional currency besides cash and common stock with which the management teams can acquire properties – the OP unit.

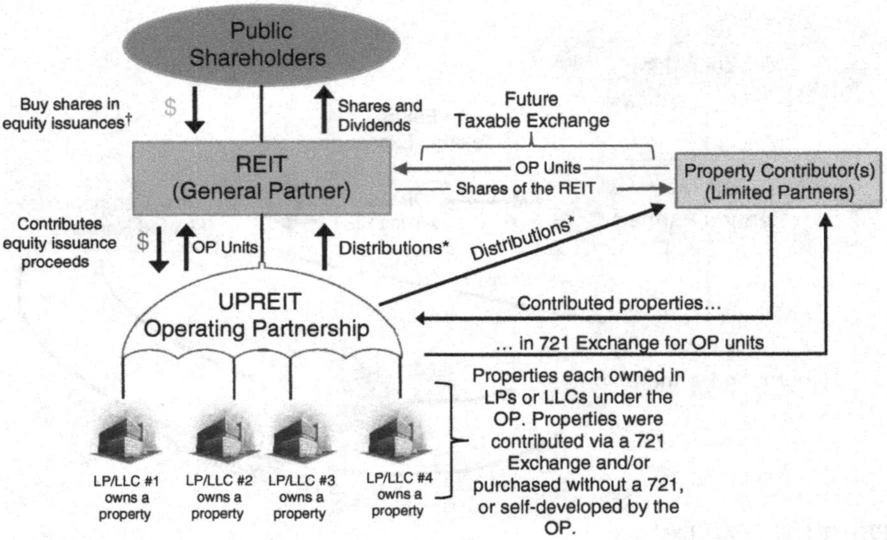

FIGURE 8.3 UPREIT Corporate Structure

†The REIT issues common and/or preferred shares to investors and contributes the proceeds to the UPREIT OP. When an UPREIT issues debt capital (secured or unsecured), it does so at the OP level.

* Public shareholders receive dividends from the REIT. The REIT (as the OP's general partner) and the OP unitholders (limited partners) receive distributions from the OP.

Note: If one individual contributes a property via a 721 Exchange, the OP owns it through an LP. If a group of individuals contributes the property(s), then the OP owns them in an LLC (Limited Liability Corporation).

OP UNITS

As is the case for all US partnerships, the operating partnership of an UPREIT can issue OP units to the seller of property as a form of consideration, similar to issuing common shares. OP units today are economically the same as shares of common stock in that the distribution the OP unit holders receive for each OP units equals the dividend paid to each common shareholder. Unlike common stock, OP units are not publicly traded, and the OP unitholder generally cannot vote regarding UPREIT corporate governance matters. (Historically, some of the initial UPREITs like Taubman Centers, Inc. issued "tracking shares" to its founders, which associated their OP units not only with voting rights, but often with super-voting rights, wherein each OP unit represented more than one vote. Tracking shares created conflicts of interest with the public shareholders and were phased out.) In nearly every instance, OP unitholders can – at their sole option and at a time of their choosing – convert each OP unit into one share of publicly tradeable common stock of the REIT or, depending on the terms of the conversion rights, for cash. (Technically, each OP unitholder has a "put" right with the REIT.) When unitholders convert their OP units in the UPREIT into common shares, they become shareholders of the REIT. As Figure 8.3 illustrates, converting OP units into common shares also normally triggers a taxable event to the selling unitholder, who owns the units with a tax basis that tracks their original basis in the contributed property, thus triggering a capital gains tax. This is why it is rare for unitholders to convert units into shares while they are alive – the mechanism is generally seen as a wealth transfer estate planning tool.

OP units were created to defer taxes for property sellers. Generally, the IRS views the contribution of limited partnership units of real property in exchange for partnership interests, including OP units, as a 721 tax-deferred event. As a result, the party that contributed real estate in exchange for OP units may be able to defer the recognition of capital gains (and the associated taxes) until such time as they convert their OP units into shares of the REIT or cash, and upon death the heirs get a stepped-up basis, removing the capital gains tax all together. Note that this does not avoid inheritance tax.

The partnership structure of the OP enables the IRS to view OP units in the UPREIT as Section 721-exchangeable for the owner's former partnership interest in the contributed property(s). The nature of the investment stays the same: one partnership interest is exchanged for another; whereas if actual common shares were used in payment, it would be a partnership interest being given up in exchange for stock – which is not a like-kind exchange and would trigger the tax event to the property contributor. Said more simply, by accepting an UPREIT's OP units rather than cash or common stock as payment for a property, the seller of the property may defer the capital gain tax liability that otherwise would have been triggered at the time of the asset sale.

A 721 Exchange is similar to a 1031 Exchange, but with more benefits. Like a 1031 Exchange, the 721 Exchange allows for tax-deferred exchanges of property. Unlike a 1031, however, 721 Exchanges also allow the property contributors to diversify their investment – because as OP unitholders the distributions they receive are based on the results of the OP's entire portfolio. A 721 Exchange also creates a future liquidity event for the property contributor; as previously discussed, however, converting OP units into shares of the REIT normally triggers capital gains and possibly other taxes.

Because OP units enable REITs to acquire properties on the same basis as regular contributions of properties to partnerships, since 1992 most REITs have adopted the UPREIT structure for their IPOs, and many REITs that were publicly traded before 1992 have adopted the UPREIT structure over time. Those that have not converted have, when necessary, used a downREIT structure (discussed later in the chapter) to structure 721 Exchanges to acquire privately owned properties.

OP Units and Estate Planning

Private real estate operators typically own their assets in LPs with each limited partner (investor) having rights to his or her *pro rata* share of the partnership's profits and losses. The US Tax Code allows landlords to depreciate the value of a property (excluding land value) over the "useful life" of the building. In the cases where private landlords have owned their properties for a number of years and have completed one or more cash-out mortgage refinancings (which are non-taxable events), for income tax purposes they likely have a very low or even negative basis in each asset. Consequently, the sale of their assets at current market values would trigger a large capital gain on sale, resulting in a significant tax liability.

With the use of cash-out refinancing, a property investor may have gotten back all of his or her contributed equity capital, perhaps several times over, therefore having a negative tax basis in the investment. Sometimes this basis is so low, and the levered equity remaining in the partnership is so little after refinancing, that the tax liability on sale of the asset can exceed the cash proceeds to the owner. This is considered a "locked-up" or "tax-impaired" property – an asset that would make no sense for an investor to sell for almost any reason. The use of UPREIT units essentially solves this problem by allowing a "sale" to a REIT without triggering the tax event, but allowing the former "owner/partner" to move on and own a smaller piece of the REIT's bigger overall portfolio that now includes the asset(s) he or she contributed – thus diversifying their investment from one property to a large diversified pool of properties with professional management.

Because the IRS views OP units comparably to other partnership contributions, sellers may defer their current tax liabilities* by accepting an UPREIT's OP units as part of the sales price, instead of cash or common stock. Equally important is the fact that, when unitholders die, their heirs may step-up the basis in those OP units to the then-current market value of the REIT's common stock (no appraisal necessary) and immediately convert the OP units into common shares, thereby avoiding triggering capital gains and related taxes. However, this does not avoid inheritance taxes.

OP UNITS POSSIBLE CONFLICTS WITH PORTFOLIO MANAGEMENT

The creation of the UPREIT structure was a watershed event that directly contributed to the REIT industry's rapid growth, particularly in the 1990s. As Table 1.1 in Chapter 1 shows, the market capitalization of equity REITs increased dramatically from $9 billion at the end of 1991 (before UPREITs) to $147 billion at the end of 2001, representing compound annual growth of 32.6%. As beneficial as the UPREIT structure has been to the REIT industry's growth, investors should be aware of the little-understood but key element the UPREIT tax-deferral structure includes that can generate potential conflicts of interest between the UPREIT partnership unitholders and the REIT's common shareholders. Specifically, the UPREIT takes the property(s) contributed in exchange for partnership units at the new acquisition price basis for tax purposes, and the old, lower tax basis and the related tax deferral remains with the property contributor (seller). Consequently, if the REIT resells the asset, the tax indemnification clause in the 721 Exchange means not only that the resale of the property will trigger the full deferred tax liability, but also that the REIT (not the original seller) will have to pay it.

For this reason every UPREIT transaction between a REIT and contributing partners includes a tax indemnification clause stating that if the REIT sells the acquired asset during a specified period of time, typically five, seven, or ten years (with the predominate number of lock-up years being seven), the REIT must either (1) perform a 1031 Exchange with proceeds from the sale of the original asset into a replacement property in order to continue deferring the seller/contributors' tax liability; or (2) pay the taxes incurred by the original contributor that arise out of the property sale. This UPREIT

*Note: Before entering into a transaction, sellers of property should consult with their tax accountant to determine their ability to defer taxes according to then-current US Tax Code.

sale clause is overt – that is, everyone knows that a contributed asset will not likely be sold during the lockup period. This understanding is a possible negative in terms of portfolio management flexibility in that the REIT's leadership is incentivized to manage its portfolio with consideration of external tax impacts. The more insidious conflict element in UPREIT transactions is that if management and/or the board is the property contributor, which is often the case, they remain personally on the hook for the deferred tax liability even after the asset lockup period burns off; the conflict is that they may be motivated to hold on to properties that in an unconflicted scenario the REIT might otherwise decide to sell, in some cases holding on to properties that are well past their "sell-by" date just to avoid paying taxes.

As time passes, the tax encumbrances associated with many 721 Exchanges burn-off. Additionally, there are some instances where an UPREIT's management team has negotiated only a "best effort" not to resell an asset until after a certain number of years, leaving them fundamentally free to resell the asset if that is the correct asset management tactic. Accordingly, not every UPREIT has tax-impaired properties embedded in its OP – but investors should definitely be curious if a management team continues to own an asset that is under-performing (as measured by occupancy, for example) and/or is a strategic misfit when compared to the rest of the company's portfolio.[1]

DOWNREITs

In some instances, REITs whose shares were publicly listed before 1992 found it too costly to convert to an UPREIT structure. For example, the legal process of contributing properties from the REIT to a new Umbrella Partnership could trigger potentially massive state-level transfer taxes. To compete with UPREITs in bidding for privately held assets, some REITs began acquiring assets using downREIT structures which could issue downREIT units and offer similar tax deferrals. The downREIT structure is a joint venture between the REIT and the property contributors, where the downREIT (structured as an LP or LLC) issues downREIT units in exchange for the property contributor's investment property(s). Unlike UPREIT OP

[1]Note that David M. Fick, CPA, who served as Chief Financial Officer of a retail REIT, then as an influential equity research analyst covering REITs, and currently teaches real estate capital markets at Johns Hopkins Carey Business School, contributed the bulk of the content in the two preceding paragraphs, as well as edits to the discussion of OP units.

units, the value of the downREIT units are not tied to the REIT's common share price on the day the downREIT transaction is executed. Instead, the downREIT unit is tied to the value of the fair market value of the property(s) contributed. As Figure 8.4 shows, the REIT owns assets directly, as well as through a downREIT structure (which is also referred to as a *baby REIT*).

The downREIT structure does have drawbacks, beginning with being more restrictive than 721 Exchange agreements on allowing the REIT to sell the downREIT's properties in the future. Second, downREIT unitholders historically had different voting rights than public shareholders of the REIT, which proved to be an unsustainable conflict and has since been corrected. A third conflict is that the conversion ratio for downREIT units is based on the value of the joint venture's asset. Their value is not tied to the performance of the REIT and could have appreciated much more than the REIT's directly owned assets (or, conversely, the venture's assets could have under-performed). From the downREIT unitholder's perspective, the distribution that downREIT OP unitholders receive is based on the economics of the properties in that downREIT – not on the performance of

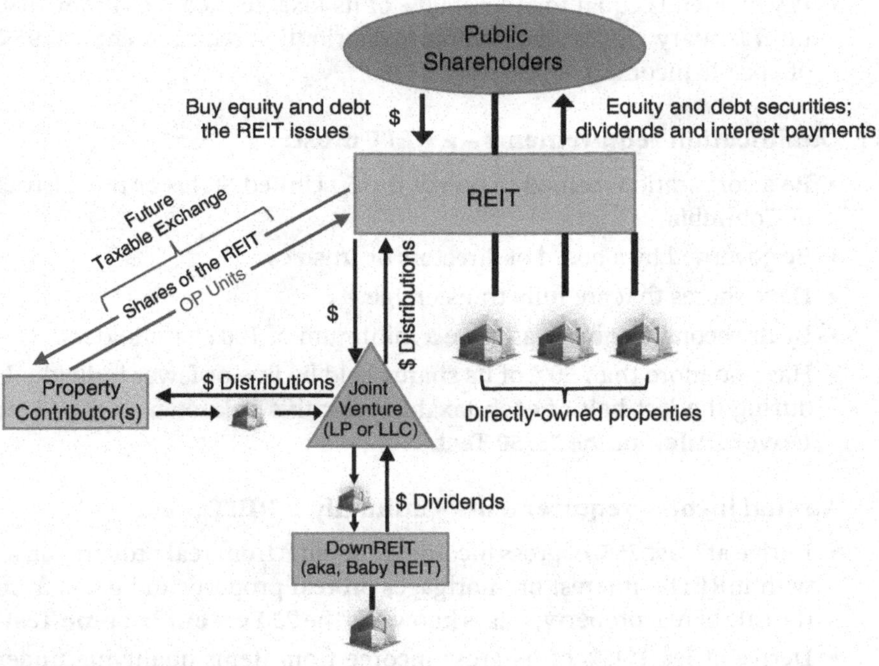

FIGURE 8.4 DownREIT Corporate Structure

the REIT's entire portfolio. Accordingly, the downREIT unitholders, current returns can differ greatly from those of the REIT shareholders.

Advances in REIT governance practices and disclosure have eliminated or mitigated many downREIT conflicts. Despite its limitations, the down-REIT structure has been a useful tool that traditional REITs like Kimco Realty (NYSE: KIM) employ, when necessary, to acquire assets in a manner that defers capital gains taxes for the seller.

QUALIFYING AS A REIT

Just as The Walt Disney Company (NYSE: DIS) and Apple, Inc. (NASDAQ: AAPL) must comply with aspects of the Internal Revenue Code (the Tax Code) that govern C-corporations, a REIT must adhere to certain provisions in order to qualify for and maintain its tax status. A summary of the principal provisions of the Tax Code for REITs follows:

Distribution requirements – a REIT must:

- Pay dividends equal to at least 90% of its taxable income. (From 1980 until January 1, 2001, the minimum distribution requirement was 95% of taxable income.)

Qualification requirements – a REIT must:

- Be a corporation formed in one of the 50 United States or the District of Columbia.
- Be governed by a board of directors or trustees.
- Have shares that are fully transferable.
- By its second taxable year, have a minimum of 100 shareholders.
- Have no more than 50% of its shares held by five or fewer individuals during the last half of each taxable year; this is known as the **"5 or Fewer Rule,"** or the **"5/50 Test."**

Annual income requirements – annually, a REIT must:

- Derive at least 75% of gross income from rents from real property or, as with mREITs, interest on mortgages on real property and gains from the sale of real property; this is known as the **75 Percent Income Test.**
- Derive at least 95% of its gross income from items qualifying under the previously defined 75 Percent Income Test, plus dividends and

interest income, and gains from the sale of stock or other non-real estate investments (the **95 Percent Income Test**).

- Derive 5% or less of its income from non-qualifying sources, such as third-party management or leasing fees provided to properties the REIT does not own. As a result, REITs often use a structure known as a taxable REIT subsidiary (TRS) to pursue real estate-related business opportunities that enhance management's ability to deliver higher levels of tenant services. Because the TRS is taxed like a regular operating company, the REIT is allowed to own up to 100% of each TRS's stock. Many REITs use TRS to develop properties (which have no revenue during construction) and use construction financing, then sell the property to the REIT at cost – so the REIT has a good cash flow return upon purchase.

Quarterly investment requirements – at the end of each quarter, a REIT must:

- Invest at least 75% of its total assets in real estate assets, mortgage loans, cash, and government securities.
- Not own more than 10% of another company, other than another REIT, a qualified REIT subsidiary (QRS), or a TRS. In the case of TRS, no more than 20% (down from 25% before 2017) of a REIT's total asset value may reside in one or more TRS.
- A REIT cannot own stock in any corporation other than a TRS whose value exceeds 5% of the REIT's total asset value.

Note that a REIT's board of directors/trustees votes on which methodology it will use to measure *total asset value*. Methodologies include using gross asset value (also known as *undepreciated book value*), or methods prescribed by the REIT's lenders.

EXTERNALLY ADVISED AND MANAGED REITs

Among the 219 REITs that composed the FTSE Nareit All REITs Index at the end of 2019, there is a small population of publicly traded REITs that are externally advised and managed, which is similar to how REITs were structured before the 1986 Tax Act (see the section in Chapter 10, Improvements to the REIT Structure).

The externally advised structure may have conflicts of interest between the REIT advisor and REIT shareholders that can lead to suboptimal capital allocation decisions and, by extension, lower returns for shareholders. First, externally advised REITs do not have any employees; instead, they pay a fee to an external, third-party advisor, whose employees oversee the REIT's daily operations. Second, the advisor also earns a fee on any assets the REIT acquires. An incentive for the advisor may be to maximize the amount of properties the REIT owns, not to maximize the performance or profitability of those assets. The conflict between the advisor and shareholders may not be apparent immediately, but over time, research has shown that the average annual total returns of externally managed REITs often lag that of the industry.

To learn if a REIT is an externally advised or managed REIT, be sure to read the "Company Description" located in the first few pages of any recent form 10-Q or 10-K that the REIT has filed with the SEC. If the company states that it is "a self-advised, self-managed real estate investment trust," then it does not have the fee-oriented conflicts of interest just described.

PUBLICLY TRADED, PUBLIC NON-LISTED, AND PRIVATE REITS

The focus of the chapters leading up to this point has been to provide information on publicly traded REITs. Since the mid-1990s, however, private REITs and REITs that are public but not listed (PNLR) on any exchange have proliferated. During 2015, the Financial Industry Regulatory Authority (FINRA) modified NASD Rule 2340 regarding Customer Account Statements to improve disclosure issues previously associated with PNLRs (FINRA's 2015 Regulatory Change). Since this change went into effect in April 2016, PNLRs' disclosure closely parallels that of publicly traded REITs, leaving liquidity as the primary difference between the two organizational structures. Table 8.1 summarizes the similarities and differences between publicly traded REITs, PNLRs, and private REITs, and the paragraphs that follow provide additional detail.

Volatility versus Liquidity

Investors who invest in PNLRs and private REITs rather than publicly traded REITs often cite the lack of daily price changes (or *volatility*) as a key criterion underlying their choice. The trade-off for this semblance of stability is liquidity. Shareholders of publicly traded REITs own liquid investments that can

TABLE 8.1 Comparison of Public versus Non-traded and Private REIT Structures

	Publicly Traded REITs	Public Non-listed REITs	Private REITs
Overview	REITs that register with the SEC and choose to list their shares for trading on a national stock exchange.	REITs that are registered with the SEC and choose not to list their shares for trading on a national securities exchange. Offerings are subject to review by state securities regulators, commonly referred to as "Blue Sky" review.	Private REITs, sometimes called private placement REITs, are offerings that are exempt from SEC registration under Regulation D of the Securities Act of 1933 and whose shares intentionally do not trade on a national securities exchange. Private REITs generally can be sold only to institutional investors, such as large pension funds, and/or to "accredited investors" generally defined as individuals with a net worth of at least $1 million (excluding primary residence) or with income exceeding $200,000 over two prior two years ($300,000 with a spouse).
Liquidity	Shares are listed and traded on major stock exchanges and can be bought and sold instantly during market hours through financial advisors and online brokerage houses. Most publicly traded REITs are listed on the NYSE.	Shares are intentionally not listed on national securities exchange. Liquidity options vary and may take the form of share repurchase programs or secondary marketplace transactions, but are generally limited. "Net Asset Value (NAV) REITs" provide enhanced liquidity by offering periodic, e.g., daily or monthly, repurchase offers at net asset value for up to 20% of outstanding shares annually. Traditionally, public non-listed REITs have aimed at providing liquidity through an event such as listing on a national securities exchange, selling all or substantially all its assets, or entering into a merger or business combination.	Shares are not traded on a public securities exchange and are not generally liquid. Redemption programs for shares vary by company and may be limited, non-existent, and/or subject to change.

TABLE 8.1 *(continued)*

	Publicly Traded REITs	Public Non-listed REITs	Private REITs
Transaction Costs	Brokerage costs the same as for buying or selling any other publicly traded stock.	Brokerage costs vary by REIT and by share class and may include upfront commissions and/or trail fees.	Brokerage costs vary by company and may include formation fees.
Management	Typically self-advised and self-managed. (The costs of external advisory and management services are replaced by employee overhead.)	Typically externally advised and managed, although many have internal management before a liquidity event. Externally advised REITs generally pay fixed annual asset management fees and may also pay performance-based incentive fees for these services.	Typically externally advised and managed. Private REITs generally pay fixed annual asset management fees and pay a share of profits at liquidation to advisors.
Minimum Investment	One share.	Typically \$2,500–\$5,000 initial investment.	Typically \$1,000–\$25,000; private REITs that are designed for institutional or accredited investors generally require a much higher minimum investment.
Independent Directors	Stock exchange rules require a majority of directors to be independent of management. NYSE and NASDAQ rules call for fully independent audit, nominating, and compensation committees.	Subject to state "Blue Sky" securities regulations that generally follow the North American Securities Administrators Association (NASAA) *Statement of Policy Regarding REITs*, which recommends that boards consist of a majority of independent directors and that a majority of each board committee consist of independent directors.	Generally exempt from regulatory requirements and oversight, unless managed by a registered investment advisor under the Investment Advisers Act of 1940.
Investor Control	Investors re-elect directors.	Investors re-elect directors.	Investors generally re-elect directors.

Corporate Governance	Specific stock exchange rules on corporate governance.	Subject to the same state law corporate law provisions as Stock Exchange-listed REITs as well as state securities laws and regulations which generally follow the North American Securities Administrators Association (NASAA) *Statement of Policy Regarding REITs*.	Not required other than the Internal Revenue Code's requirement that a REIT needs to have a board of directors or board of trustees.
Disclosure Obligation	Required to make regular financial disclosures to the investment community, including quarterly and yearly audited financial results with accompanying filings to the SEC.	Required to make regular financial disclosures, including quarterly unaudited and annual audited financial results under the Securities Exchange Act of 1934, including 10-Qs, 10-Ks, 8-Ks, and proxy statements. Pursuant to FINRA Notice 15-02, Financial Industry Regulatory Authority (FINRA) rules require additional broker-dealer disclosure of net asset valuation and valuation methodology.	Exempt from SEC registration and related disclosure requirements under Regulation D.
Performance Measurement	Numerous independent performance benchmarks available for tracking public REIT industry. Wide range of analyst reports available to the public.	FINRA rules require that investors be furnished with per-share net asset value estimates within 2 years and 150 days from escrow break and annually thereafter. Independent publications track activities and results of public non-listed REITs.	No public or independent source of performance data available for tracking private REITs.

Sources: National Association of Real Estate Investment Trusts® (Nareit) and Robert A. Stanger & Company, Inc.

be sold instantly in the stock market. It can take weeks or months to redeem an investment in a private REIT or PNLR; in some instances, redemptions may be forbidden for a specified period of time. If investors need immediate liquidity, they should avoid investing in private REITs and/or PNLRs.

Transparency and Corporate Governance

Publicly traded REITs and PNLRs must file quarterly and annual periodic statements with the SEC. Accordingly, shareholders in these REITs enjoy a high level of transparency regarding the costs and fees both types of REIT incur over the course of managing their portfolios. In contrast, private REITs do not have to disclose their financial statements.

Costs and Fees

Publicly traded REITs and PNLRs list their costs (both property level and corporate general and administrative expenses [G&A]) in their quarterly financial statements, which analysts and investors can scrutinize to determine how efficiently the management team is managing its properties and the company in general. In contrast, private REITs are not compelled to disclose any such information.

PNLRs historically were criticized for charging large upfront fees of 12% or more, in part to pay financial advisors' commissions for marketing their shares. (Note that publicly traded REITs pay investment banking fees and brokerage commissions during their IPO and subsequent capital raises, as well.) During the investment period, PNLRs may also charge fees for property acquisition and asset management. These fees are described in detail in the PLNR's prospectus.

The real problem with the upfront fees charged by PNLRs is that, historically, they were not transparent on investor statements. When an investor would buy a share in a PNLR, typically for $10, the value per share listed on the investor's statement would be the gross $10, not an amount that was net of fees and other costs, which typically consumed about $1.20 per share. Said another way, the PNLR investor did not realize their initial investment value was immediately reduced by these costs.

As mentioned earlier, FINRA addressed these and other disclosure issues associated with PNLRs by modifying NASD Rule 2340. Effective in April 2016, PNLRs now provide customer statements that show the shareholder's net investment (i.e., subtracting commissions) for the first couple of years, and then show the shareholder's share of net asset value (NAV) of the PNLR thereafter. Alternatively, the PNLR must provide NAV at least annually, though many give NAVs monthly or daily. (Note, most publicly traded REITs do not provide disclosure on their NAV.) Investors in PNLRs now have a better line of sight on how efficiently their investments are put to use. As a result, the major difference between publicly traded REITs and PNLRs is liquidity.

Strong Demand for PNLRs

Since FINRA's 2015 Regulatory Change improved PNLRs disclosure, many institutional real estate investment managers have entered the PNLR field. Because defined benefit pension plans are not growing in number, some of these managers are attempting to enter the individual investor market. Major firms like Blackstone, Jones Lang LaSalle, and Nuveen have started PNLR funds. The majority have done so using either the daily or monthly NAV REIT structure. These NAV REITs offer multiple share classes with low to no upfront fees, although additional trailing fees are charged for some share classes.

Robert A. Stanger & Co., Inc. (Stanger, https://rastanger.com) is a nationally recognized investment banking firm specializing in providing financial advisory, investment banking, fairness opinion, and asset and securities valuation services to partnerships, REITs, and real estate advisory and management companies. Stanger is also well known for *The Stanger Report,* a nationally recognized newsletter focused on direct participation program and non-traded REIT investing. Stanger tracks and publishes the performance of the more traditional lifecycle non-traded REITs and NAV REITs.

Lifecycle REITs are designed to be limited-life products that undergo a lifecycle of fundraising followed by a liquidity event of some form. They generally provide their first independent appraisal-based NAV at a maximum of two years and 150 days after fundraising escrow break, and at least annually thereafter. There were approximately 50 Lifecycle REITs at the end of 2019, each with either one or two classes of shares. Table 8.2 ranks the lifecycle REITs' top-performing share class according to their one-year total returns as of December 31, 2019.

NAV REITs are perpetual-life products that continue fundraising indefinitely while providing updated NAVs on a daily or monthly basis. The NAV REITs typically have between three and five classes of shares, with most having four. Table 8.3 ranks the NAV REITs' top-performing share class total

TABLE 8.2 Top 10 Performing Lifecycle REIT Shares in 2019

Lifecycle REIT Performance – Ranked	Annualized Total Return		
	1-Year	2-Year	3-Year
Industrial Property Trust Inc. - Class A*	16.80%	16.72%	18.02%
Steadfast Apartment REIT Inc.	10.48%	9.47%	9.35%
Cole Office & Industrial REIT (CCIT II) Inc. - Class A	10.41%	9.61%	9.65%
KBS Real Estate Investment Trust III Inc.	9.61%	9.10%	11.90%
Carey Watermark Investors 2 Incorporated - Class A	9.02%	9.56%	9.29%
Moody National REIT II Inc. - Class A	8.39%	3.99%	9.71%
RW Holdings NNN REIT Inc.	8.29%	9.66%	8.84%
Strategic Storage Trust IV Inc. - Class A	7.84%	7.31%	–
Pacific Oak Strategic Opportunity REIT Inc.	7.54%	9.72%	7.48%
Pacific Oak Strategic Opportunity REIT II Inc. - Class A	7.45%	9.16%	7.63%

Note: Returns are calculated without sales load and with reinvestment where available. Rankings are based on the share class with the highest total return.

Source: Reproduced by permission from Robert A. Stanger & Company, Inc. As of December 31, 2019.

returns for 2019. (Note that as of December 31, 2019, there were only 10 NAV REITs that had at least one full year of operations.)

As highlighted earlier, since FINRA's 2015 Regulatory Change the main difference between PNLRs and publicly listed REITs is liquidity. Figure 8.5 compares the cumulative returns since 2016 of Stanger's lifecycle and NAV REIT indices with that of two well-known publicly traded REIT indices, namely, Cohen & Steers Realty Majors Portfolio and the FTSE Nareit Equity REIT Total Return Index. The cumulative performance of the NAV REITs closely tracks that of publicly traded REITs.[2]

[2]Special thanks to Kevin Gannon and Nancy Schabel at Robert A. Stanger & Company, Inc., for their assistance in analyzing the differences between publicly traded, public non-listed, and private REITs.

TABLE 8.3 Top 10 Performing NAV REIT Shares in 2019

	Annualized Total Return		
NAV REIT Performance – Ranked	**1-Year**	**2-Year**	**3-Year**
Starwood Real Estate Income Trust Inc. - Class I	13.59%	–	–
Blackstone Real Estate Income Trust Inc. - Class I	12.23%	10.26%	–
Nuveen Global Cities REIT - Class I	9.19%	–	–
Hines Global Income Trust Inc. - Class AX	8.54%	9.69%	11.18%
RREEF Property Trust- Class I	8.23%	7.98%	8.12%
FS Credit Real Estate Income Trust Inc. - Class I	6.70%	–	–
Black Creek Diversified Property Fund Inc. - Class I	6.03%	5.80%	4.72%
Jones Lang LaSalle Income Property Trust Inc.- Class M-I	5.89%	7.07%	7.53%
CIM Income NAV Inc.- Class I	4.12%	3.96%	4.98%
Griffin Capital Essential Asset REIT Inc. - Class I	3.72%	5.54%	–

Note: Returns are calculated without sales load and with reinvestment where a DRIP (dividend reinvestment program or plan) is available. Rankings are based on the share class generating the highest total return. Griffin Capital Essential Asset REIT's Class I share returns and not Class E share returns were displayed in order to capture the history of the NAV fund as opposed to the legacy GCEAR I fund.

Source: Reproduced by permission from Robert A. Stanger & Company, Inc. As of December 31, 2019.

CONCLUSION

Many REITs have a unique currency – the OP unit – that is similar to common shares except it is not publicly traded. By issuing OP units as part of the overall consideration for purchasing privately held property, a REIT can structure a tax-efficient sale for the seller, thereby creating an advantage over other non-REIT bidders. The OP unit can, however, create a conflict of interest between the unitholders and common shareholders in that the REIT's management may have a disincentive to sell the assets in the future, because doing so may trigger a tax liability that the REIT must pay.

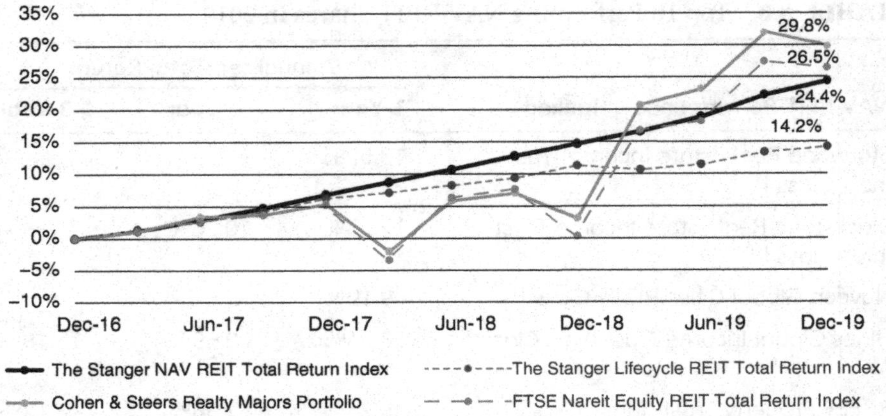

FIGURE 8.5 Cumulative Return Comparisons among Select PNLR and Traded REIT Indices

Source: Reproduced by permission from Robert A. Stanger & Company, Inc. As of December 31, 2019.

Investors have many choices for investing in REITs. There are publicly traded REITs, which are the subject of this book, and there also are public non-listed (PLNRs) and private REITs, each with their own benefits and risks. Investors can invest in different REIT structures to align with their individual investment objectives.

CHAPTER 9

Real Estate Debt and Fixed Income Securities

Like any other real estate investor, REITs can purchase properties with cash and/or with debt. REITs can issue debt in several forms, providing them much greater financial flexibility than individual real estate investors. There are private issuances of debt, meaning the debt securities are not listed on an exchange and are owned/invested in by the lending institution that underwrote them. Forms of private debt that REITs can issue include regular individual property mortgages, bank lines of credit, corporate bonds, and bank term loans. (Note that a corporation can issue any type of loan privately, including senior unsecured notes; private issuance may provide more flexible lending terms than a public issuance and, depending upon the spread over US Treasuries or LIBOR at that time, lower costs.) REITs can also issue public debt securities, consisting primarily of senior notes (bonds) and preferred stock. This chapter addresses the many forms of debt capital REITs can raise.

PRIVATE REAL ESTATE DEBT

Private real estate debt consists of loans for which REITs contract directly with their lenders – typically a syndicate (group) of several banks. The majority of *direct lending* used by REITs is in the form of property mortgages, lines of credit, and bank term loans.

Property Mortgages

REITs and individual investors can acquire a mortgage for individual properties through national, regional, or local banks, insurance companies and CMBS conduits, or mortgage companies. Mortgage amounts and rates are based upon the characteristics of the property, including location, rental income, tenant quality, and building quality. The lender also analyzes the owner/borrower regarding their ability to manage the property and pay the mortgage as well as their track record with other properties.

Mortgages on commercial properties come with restrictions not found in home mortgages. Whereas residential/personal property mortgages can be up to 30 years in duration with the ability to be repaid without penalty at any time, commercial mortgages are usually no more than ten years long (called a *ten-year balloon* even though the amortization period may be longer) and have restrictions on early repayments. (Public policy has long mandated that individual home borrowers have the flexibility to pay off mortgages and freely move residences.) Commercial mortgage restrictions are either: (1) a lock-out clause that prevents prepayment until a certain length of time has passed – typically at least five years; (2) a prepayment penalty for paying the loan early in the form of a decreasing interest rate for early prepayment in years one through six; or (3) a yield maintenance clause where a surcharge amount equal to the interest income lost by the lender must be paid. Yield maintenance can be calculated using online calculators or websites of firms that complete the calculations for viewers. Two simple examples are as follows:

I. Penalty for selling a commercial property before the end of the mortgage's term:

A commercial property borrower wants to sell the property securing a mortgage, is six years into a ten-year term, pays an annual percentage rate of interest of 6% on a $1,000 principal (*face*) amount – the lender would be paid a yield maintenance penalty, which is the prepayment fee that borrowers pay lenders to reimburse them for the loss of interest resulting from the loan prepayment. This provision allows the lender to obtain the same yield as if the borrower had made all the scheduled mortgage payments until the loan maturity. In the case of the 6% loan, the prepayment penalty would be $240, calculated as the present value of the remaining payments on the loan, multiplied by the amount of time left until the original maturity:

- Annual interest payment due of 6% × $1,000, or $60
- Ten years of payments = $600

- Less six years' interest already paid (6 years × \$60= \$360)
- Four annual payments of \$60 equals a future value of \$240 due to the lender
- Discount the future value of payments using the yield on four- or five-year benchmark rates, such as Treasuries, plus an appropriate spread as a discount rate (3%, for example): PV = \$240 ÷ [(1 + 3%)^4 years]
- Equals a yield maintenance penalty of approximately \$213

Because the penalty for paying off the mortgage early is high, sellers like the one in this example would be better served to negotiate with the buyer to assume the existing commercial mortgage as part of the purchase price. Note that yield prepayment differs from *defeasance,* which entails a substitution of collateral (such as Treasury bonds) and a possible assumption of the loan by the successor borrower.

II. Penalty for refinancing to a lower interest rate during the mortgage's term:

Interest rates decline in year six of a ten-year loan, and the borrower wants to refinance a 6% loan to the new 4% rate. The lending institution calculates a present value calculation of the difference between the payments they would have received over the full term at the higher interest rate (e.g., \$240) versus the new lower interest rate (e.g., \$160), equaling \$80.

- Original mortgage payments of \$60 (from example above) for another four years, equal to \$240
- New annual interest payment 4% × \$1,000 = \$40 for four years = \$160
- \$60 old payment − \$40 new payments for four years = \$20 × 4 = \$80
- (Alternatively, future payments of \$240 − \$160 = \$80 difference)
- Discount the future value of the difference using a discount rate (3%, for example): PV = \$80 ÷ [(1 + 3%)^4 years]
- Equals a yield maintenance penalty of approximately \$71

The goal of a yield maintenance prepayment penalty is to provide the lender with compensation for the interest income it would have received if the loan had been outstanding the full term at the original higher rate.

There are several reasons why commercial mortgages are less attractive financing vehicles for REITs. Monetary penalties for early prepayment or refinancing, as well as the time it takes to negotiate a mortgage loan (typically at least six weeks), the documentation process, which includes appraisals, estoppels, title insurance, etc., all slow down a REIT's ability to actively manage their portfolios, including deciding to sell a property or exit an entire market.

Lines of Credit

Just like other operating companies, most REITs establish a line of credit (also called a *revolver*) with a bank or group of banks that allows them to access cash on any given day to finance operating needs or property purchases. A line of credit is like a credit card where the borrower uses funds for a purpose and interest is charged on the outstanding balance, then the balance due can be paid off at any time. Credit lines also have a maintenance or *commitment* fee (approximately 25 basis points) levied against the entire capacity of the credit line, in addition to the REIT interest rate a REIT pays on any balances drawn. A REIT's interest rate on its line of credit is based on the sum of the company's credit spread over a short-term (typically 30 days to one year) benchmark rate, such as LIBOR or the newly introduced SOFR (secured overnight financing rate).

Most REITs have a line of credit capacity that is approximately 10% of their market capitalization, thus a $1 billion REIT might have a $100 million line of credit. If a REIT is purchasing a property for $40 million, they can write a purchase offer as a cash offer to close quickly. They call their bank and ask to have $40 million from the line of credit transferred into their account to close on the property. Afterward, they can decide how to finance the property over a longer term. This short-term debt comes smoothly and flexibly to the REIT for its operating activities. If they sell another property a week later, they can pay back the line of credit and it is then available all over again.

Note that REITs typically do not draw down the full capacity of their line of credit; doing so would concern lenders and stockholders. Accordingly, REITs refinance the amounts drawn on their lines of credit periodically with equity, a new mortgage, corporate bond, or other longer-term, often fixed rate debt, which is addressed in the chapter. Refinancing lines of credit balances with longer-term debt is also called *terming out the line.*

REITs grow their portfolios through acquisitions and development and finance those properties long term through new stock equity issuance and corporate debt. However, the long-term equity and debt is usually issued in large numbers with issuance timed to take place during favorable market conditions. Thus, a REIT might purchase three properties at $30 million each and then issue new stock worth $120 million and use the stock proceeds to pay the

$90 million line of credit down to zero and use the extra $30 million to purchase the next property. Alternatively, the REIT may term out its line balance with mortgages or by issuing corporate debt.

Bank Term Loans (Secured and Unsecured)

Bank term loans allow REITs to borrow large amounts of money for medium durations of time, often without collateral. Bank term loans typically are five to seven years in duration and carry a floating rate of interest tied to LIBOR or another benchmark. (REITs will often swap the term loan's interest to a fixed rate for the duration of the term.) The exact terms of a term loan are negotiable, including whether a REIT needs to commit any properties to collateralize the loan, and ultimately depend on the borrower's/REIT's credit profile and history with its lenders. REITs that borrow using bank term loans often are able to issue investment grade unsecured senior notes, but may choose a term loan because it offers a lower all-in interest rate; or, they are on the cusp of being able to issue investment-grade rated debt, and term loans enable them to keep their properties unencumbered.

PUBLIC REAL ESTATE DEBT

Corporate Debt (Unsecured and Secured)

Most publicly traded companies issue corporate debt to fund their activities. Operating companies pledge the first portion of their revenues and their assets (inventory and/or receivables) to pay interest on their debt and repay the principal by issuing new debt when the old debt matures. To issue secured debt, REITs have "hard assets" in their properties and can take a number of properties and pledge them as collateral for their corporate debt. REITs will designate a number of properties with a private market value – say $1 billion – to use as collateral for a $400 million secured corporate bond issuance. This is like a 40% loan-to-value ratio mortgage.

The main advantage of unsecured REIT corporate debt is that the individual properties are not tied up with mortgage restrictions, such as lock-out clauses or prepayment penalties. In addition, even if the corporate debt is secured, the REIT is allowed to sell a property from the collateral pool and substitute another property of equal or greater value into the pool. This gives REITs much greater financial flexibility than individual investors – though the substitution process is still time-consuming.

CMBS Issuance

Commercial Mortgage Backed Securities (CMBS) were first created in 1988. The idea of pooling a number of mortgages together and creating a security that allowed investors to invest in a diversified pool of mortgages was first created in the 1960s for single-family home mortgages. With government support this concept worked well as standard underwriting of a home mortgage was easy to establish. The bonds issued to raise the money for the mortgages contain the same interest rate paid and risks taken. However, commercial properties are all unique, so standard underwriting is much more difficult. The commercial concept pools mortgages from different properties that may also be different property types. Various classes of bonds from AAA to BB to C (non-rated) are issued with different interest rates and maturities. Commercial mortgages are originated by mortgage brokers, banks, investment banks, insurance companies, or other providers and sold into the CMBS pool. Once sold, the originator usually has nothing else to do with the mortgage. A mortgage servicing company is hired to collect the monthly mortgage payments and the trustee makes the payments to the bondholders. If there is a default on any of the loans, a special servicer takes over to resolve problems, or foreclose on the property.

REITs and any other commercial property owner can access the CMBS market for a loan on any property. Their reason to do so would be to receive a lower interest rate or more favorable terms than other financing options. The loan covenants on CMBS loans are usually standardized and not possible to negotiate (including prepayment terms). Also, there is no direct owner of the loan to talk to about issues, changes, or other problems that may arise. Therefore, most equity REITs to do not use CMBS loans on a regular basis and would only consider a CMBS loan if the interest rate on the loan were lower than other alternatives.

Mortgage REITs may invest in the different tranches (A, B, C) of CMBS bonds as they have the expertise to underwrite the pool of properties that back the bonds they purchase.

Senior Unsecured Notes

Similar to how lenders have priority of payment for interest and principal repayments over a company's preferred and common equity shareholders, a senior note is a bond whose repayment and receipt of interest payments takes priority over any and all other debt a company has outstanding. REITs that issue senior notes generally can issue them at low interest rates because the securities are investment grade rated; REITs that may have slipped below investment grade can still issue senior unsecured notes with non-investment-grade ratings or issue the notes in a private placement. In such cases, the REIT often will pursue a private placement of unsecured senior notes in order to negotiate a better rate and/or more advantageous terms than they could receive at that time in a public notes offering.

Preferred Stock

Preferred stock is often viewed as a hybrid security in that it shares characteristics of debt and equity. Like a bond, preferred shares are sold according to a face (or par) value, which, in the case of preferreds, is usually $25 per share. Unlike bonds, perpetual preferred stock has no maturity date. Typically, REITs that issue preferred shares have the right to redeem (or call) those shares at par after five years; if the REIT can issue new preferred shares or debt with a lower recurring payment than the old preferred shares, management will likely call those preferred shares and issue lower-cost capital to pay for the redemption. Similar to common stock, preferred shares pay investors a quarterly dividend. Like a bond, the preferred dividend is often a fixed amount based on par value, although sometimes the preferred shares contain a ratchet feature so that the preferred dividend increases by the same percentage as the common dividend in subsequent years.

There are three risks investors need to keep in mind when investing in preferred shares for dividend income, each of which involves liquidity or lack thereof. First, the secondary market for REIT preferred stock is not as liquid as the market for common stock in the same company. This means that investors may have a lag when selling (or even pricing) their preferred shares. This market has become more liquid over time.

Second, it is important to read and understand the term sheet in the prospectus of each preferred stock issuance before investing. Although the preceding paragraph detailed general terms that are typical for preferred stock issuances, there is no consistent underwriting standard to which issuers of preferred stock must conform. For example, a REIT that pays a $0.75 per share annualized common dividend may issue a preferred stock that pays $1.00 per share each year. If that preferred stock does not contain a ratchet feature or some other covenant to protect the preferred yield relative to that of the common shares, the management team legally could increase the annual common dividend to be greater than $1.00 per share. If that happens, the preferred issuance will become illiquid, making it extremely difficult (or impossible) to sell the securities anywhere close to par. The investors in the preferred stock in this example will likely have to sell their shares at a steep discount if they want to exit this investment.

The third level of liquidity risk relates to a change in control at a REIT, such as when a private equity firm or competing REIT buys a REIT that has preferred shares outstanding. In many instances, the preferred equity investors of the acquired (or target) REIT discover that the terms of their preferred stock allow an acquiring company to suspend their preferred dividend and/or that the acquiring entity may have no obligation to "cash out" the target REIT's preferred shareholders. As a result, acquiring companies often treat existing preferred stock as a form of mezzanine financing to increase their returns on the deal. The preferred stock investors become financially marginalized in the new entity and have no recourse. In contrast, common stock investors will receive cash, stock in the acquiring entity, or both as compensation for their investment.

However, it is important to note that preferred shares are senior to common shares in a bankruptcy or when a company incurs a severe liquidity event. Thus, companies must stop payment on the common dividends before stopping preferred dividend payments. Most REIT preferreds are "cumulative," meaning the REIT must pay back all of the past preferred dividends from the time they halted payment to date before reinstituting the common stock dividends.

Lastly, REITs that raise preferred equity capital typically do so by issuing the shares publicly. As noted in Chapter 4, at the end of 2019 there were less than $30 billion of preferred shares trading, so it remains a low-liquidity market. REITs can also place preferred shares directly with an investor or group of investors in a private placement, usually to lock in a better (lower) dividend rate than they could in a public issuance. Preferred stock is the most expensive form of capital that many REITs can access; thus it is usually issued when a REIT's equity shares are trading at a low value.

ANALYZING REIT DEBT AND PREFERREDS

As in other industries, REIT's corporate bonds and preferred shares are priced based upon the creditworthiness of the borrowing entity. There are major credit rating agencies that analyze companies and issue credit ratings on public companies (see Figure 9.1). Moody's and Standard & Poor's are the two largest along with Fitch. Ratings range from Aaa/AAA, Aa/AA, A/A for the best companies through Baa/BBB, Ba/BB, B/B, and C levels. The rate of interest the corporation pays increases as the credit rating slides down the scale

MOODY'S		S&P		FITCH		RATING DESCRIPTION	
LONG-TERM	SHORT-TERM	LONG-TERM	SHORT-TERM	LONG-TERM	SHORT-TERM		
Aaa	P-1	AAA	A-1+	AAA	F1+	PRIME	INVESTMENT GRADE
Aa1		AA+		AA+		HIGH GRADE	
Aa2		AA		AA			
Aa3		AA-		AA-			
A1		A+	A-1	A+	F1	UPPER MEDIUM GRADE	
A2		A		A			
A3	P-2	A-	A-2	A-	F2		
Baa1		BBB+		BBB+		LOWER MEDIUM GRADE	
Baa2	P-3	BBB	A-3	BBB	F3		
Baa3		BBB-		BBB-			
Ba1	Not Prime	BB+	B	BB+	B	NON-INVESTMENT GRADE SPECULATIVE	NON-INVESTMENT GRADE AKA HIGH-YIELD BONDS AKA JUNK BONDS
Ba2		BB		BB			
Ba3		BB-		BB-			
B1		B+		B+		HIGHLY SPECULATIVE	
B2		B		B			
B3		B-		B-			
Caa1		CCC+	C	CCC	C	SUBSTANTIAL RISKS	
Caa2		CCC				EXTREMELY SPECULATIVE	
Caa3		CCC-				DEFAULT IMMINENT; LITTLE PROSPECT FOR RECOVERY	
Ca		CC					
C		C					
/		D	/	DDD	/	IN DEFAULT	
				DD			
				D			

FIGURE 9.1 Credit Ratings

and risk increases. Most US REITs have ratings ranging from B up to single A, with the preponderance of the US-rated REITs in the Baa/BBB range. A lower rate of leverage garners a higher credit rating.

REITs receive a credit rating based upon numerous factors, such as a proven track record of operations including interest payments and loan repayments. The rating agencies have methodologies to help determine the ratings according to various metrics, such as fixed charge coverage, net debt/EBITDA, and secured debt. As explained in Chapters 4 and 11, REITs target to stay under 50% leverage in their portfolios and most attempt to remain in the 40 to 45% range, thus providing them financial flexibility so that they can take advantage of opportunities during distressed times. REIT unsecured bonds contain four major covenants that were required by the major REIT investors since they first started issuing bonds in the mid-1990s. These four covenants (see Figure 9.2) were modified by some REITs during the 2008 recession to include joint venture equity, but remain in all REIT bond issuances, except for some lodging and health-care REITs as they are typically structured differently due to the REIT requirements.

COVENANT	LIMIT	ADDITIONAL NOTES
TOTAL DEBT TO TOTAL ASSETS	Less than 60% (Incurrence Test)	Total assets definition typically has 1 of 2 valuation methods: 1. Consolidated undepreciated book less A/R and intangibles 2. Annualized consolidated EBITDA or NOI dividend by specific cap rate Some REITs have higher maximum (KIM, DDR, WRE and some EQR & SPG bonds at 65%)
SECURED DEBT TO TOTAL ASSETS	Less than 40% (Incurrence Test)	Some REITs have higher maximum, including BXP & VNO at 50%, while some SPG bonds have up to 55% max
FIXED CHARGE COVERAGE	Greater than 1.50x (Incurrence Test)	Some bonds have a higher minimum, including EPR, SKT, OHI & some VTR at 2x; some SPG bonds at 1.75x)
UNENCUMBERED ASSETS TO UNSECURED DEBT	Greater than 150% (Maintenance Test)	• Some REITs have higher maximum, including some HPT bonds at 200% • Some REITs have a lower minimum, including SKT & DDR at 135%, and some EQR & SPG bonds at 125%
NOTE: JOINT VENTURE EQUITY EXCLUSION	In 2009, several REITs began providing bondholders with additional protection-excluding JV equity from definition of unencumbered assets-strengthening unencumbered asset/unsecured debt covenant.	REITs that have issued bonds with new carve-out include WRE, EPR, SKT, O, DDR, REG, VTR, HCP, and UDR. For BXP, UAUD definition excludes equity in leveraged JVs, but includes equity in unleveraged JVs. Some REITs have started adding back some JV equity. This dichotomy shows why one must analyze how co's handle these metrics in order to compare apples-to-apples.

FIGURE 9.2 REIT Covenants to Access Bond Market

CONCLUSION

REITs have a major advantage over individual investors, due to the multiple financing options available to them. The most important financing tool is corporate bonds that have fewer restrictions than individual property mortgages and typically lower interest costs. Additionally, many credit agencies analyze and rate REIT financial health, which provides investors with risk ratings used to price REIT bonds. Investors also use a REIT's bond ratings as a comparative measure of financial stability, quality, and standing vis-à-vis its peer group. Lastly, most REITs have lines of credit that allow them instant access to cash for property purchases, making REITs preferred buyers that do not have to get a loan qualified before closing on a property. The bottom line is that private real estate investors have multiple options to finance projects, but public real estate companies have the additional option of accessing the public markets through the issuance of bonds, as well as public equity.

CHAPTER 10

REIT Performance in Various Market Conditions

HISTORICAL TOTAL RETURNS

Chapter 3 discussed real estate fundamentals, which are the dominant factor in determining REIT performance over the long term (defined as a hold period of three of more years). This chapter examines the market forces that influence demand for REIT shares in the short term, during which REIT share performance is still anchored to real estate fundamentals but also dependent on exogenous market factors such as interest rate changes (*are long-term rates rising or falling?*), geopolitical risks (*will there be a trade war with China or other significant global economy event?*), and investor risk preference for growth versus safety or yield (*have regulatory changes and or corporate tax cuts created a stronger earnings growth outlook for non-REIT companies?*). With an aggregate equity market capitalization of $1.3 trillion, REITs are an established asset class, but still represent a relatively small piece of the public stock investment world. For comparison, the market capitalization of Apple, Inc. (NASDAQ: AAPL) was approximately $1.4 trillion at the end of 2019 – larger than the entire publicly traded REIT industry. Incremental fund inflows or outflows represent nearly 1% of the REIT industry's outstanding common shares (also called *public float*) and influence short-term performance, especially among different property sectors. Understanding the various factors that influence REIT stock price performance in the short term should enable investors to make better buy, hold, or sell decisions among the various REITs that are publicly traded.

REITs were authorized by an act of Congress in 1960 and most of the original REITs were mREITs started by banks to allow them to make more real estate loans. The 1974 recession saw many mREITs forced to foreclose on their mortgages and become equity REITs. During this time, REITs were also removed from the S&P 500 Index. Equity REITs were mostly ignored in favor of tax-advantaged real estate structures (such as Real Estate Limited Partnerships, or RELPs) until 1986 and *The Tax Reform Act of 1986*, discussed later in this chapter.

Table 10.1 is an expansion of Table 2.1; the shaded areas show time periods during which REIT total returns exceeded those of major equity indices. Each time period of REIT outperformance – and underperformance – is associated with shorter term market factors that overpowered the effects of the real estate fundamentals taking place at the time. For instance:

- REITs delivered strong total returns in 1995–97, a period of time when the UPREIT structure and recent corporate governance improvements intersected and formed a real estate securitization boom in the US.
- The disappointing total returns in 1998–99 illustrate what can happen to REIT returns when fund flows rotate to higher growth sectors such as the NASDAQ during the dot-com technology boom.
- REITs outperformed 2000–06 during a prolonged investor flight-to-safety when the technology bubble burst, and again during 2009–12 when interest rates were declining, and REIT yields were more attractive than bonds.
- During the 2007–08 global financial crisis (GFC), REITs significantly underperformed other indexes in 2007, strongly rebounded (like other indexes) in 2009, and then significantly outperformed other indexes in 2010.

Understanding the emotions that drive the broader stock market in the short term and the evolution of the marketplace for REIT shares is instructive for predicting how individual companies may perform in future market circumstances. The following sections highlight major milestones in the evolution of the modern REIT market.

TABLE 10.1 Total Returns of REITs vs. Major Indices

	FTSE Nareit All REITs	S&P 500	Nasdaq	Russell 2000	10-Year US Treasury Yield[a]	10-Year BBB CMBS spread[b]
1990	−17.3%	−3.1%	−17.8%	**−19.5%**	8.1%	NA
1991	35.7%	30.5%	**56.9%**	46.0%	6.7%	NA
1992	12.2%	7.6%	15.5%	**18.4%**	6.7%	NA
1993	18.5%	10.1%	14.8%	**18.9%**	5.8%	NA
1994	0.8%	**1.3%**	−3.2%	−1.8%	7.8%	NA
1995	18.3%	37.6%	**39.9%**	28.5%	5.6%	NA
1996	**35.8%**	23.0%	22.7%	16.5%	6.4%	115
1997	18.9%	**33.4%**	22.2%	22.4%	5.8%	140
1998	−18.8%	28.6%	**39.6%**	−2.6%	4.7%	270
1999	−6.5%	21.0%	**85.6%**	21.3%	6.5%	210
2000	**25.9%**	−9.1%	−39.3%	−3.0%	5.1%	235
2001	**15.5%**	−11.9%	−21.1%	2.5%	5.0%	220
2002	**5.2%**	−22.1%	−31.5%	−20.5%	3.8%	181
2003	38.5%	28.7%	**50.0%**	47.3%	4.3%	129
2004	**30.4%**	10.9%	8.6%	18.3%	4.2%	127
2005	**8.3%**	4.9%	1.4%	4.6%	4.4%	180
2006	**34.4%**	15.8%	9.5%	18.4%	4.7%	123
2007	−17.8%	5.5%	**9.8%**	−1.6%	4.0%	790
2008	−37.3%	−37.0%	−40.5%	**−33.8%**	2.3%	5,362
2009	27.5%	26.5%	**45.3%**	27.2%	3.9%	7,315
2010	**27.6%**	15.1%	18.0%	26.9%	3.3%	388
2011	**7.3%**	2.1%	−0.8%	−4.2%	1.9%	742
2012	**20.1%**	16.0%	17.5%	16.4%	1.8%	405
2013	3.2%	32.4%	**40.1%**	38.8%	3.0%	377
2014	**27.2%**	13.7%	14.8%	4.9%	2.2%	367
2015	2.3%	1.4%	**7.0%**	−4.4%	2.3%	537
2016	9.3%	12.0%	8.9%	**21.3%**	2.5%	531
2017	9.3%	21.8%	**29.6%**	14.7%	2.4%	329
2018	−4.1%	−4.4%	−2.8%	−11.0%	**2.7%**	438
2019	28.1%	31.5%	**36.7%**	25.5%	1.9%	278
1994–2019, 25-year CAGR	10.6%	10.2%	10.4%	9.4%	–	–

[a] Represents the yield on ten-year US Treasury notes at the end of each year. *Source:* Yahoo!Finance.com.

[b] 10-year CMBS yield for BBB notes in excess of ten-year US Treasuries (CMBS "spreads"), in basis points. *Source:* Bloomberg & Wells Fargo Securities, LLC.

Shaded areas represent years in which REITs outperformed most (and sometimes all) major indexes. Bolded numbers represent the index with the highest total return that year.

Source: Nareit; S&P Global Market Intelligence.

DEMAND FOR REIT SHARES

A basic economic principle is that the price of something is driven by the demand for and supply of that product or investment. Demand for REIT shares plays a large and multi-faceted role in REIT performance. It can be measured by observing the weekly flow of funds into (or out of) real estate-dedicated mutual funds and exchange-traded funds (ETFs). (ETFs are similar to mutual funds in that they represent a basket of securities – such as REIT shares; ETFs differ from mutual funds in that they trade in real time throughout the day, like a company's listed shares, rather than trading once a day after the markets close, as do mutual funds.) In February 2020, Green Street Advisors (Green Street) published its semi-annual *FlowTracker* report. This latest study analyzed 179 equity REITs owned by more than 14,000 funds and nearly 6,000 institutions. The analysis revealed several important points:

- **REIT Ownership is Changing.** Real estate-dedicated fund flows ebb and flow from year to year, and from the mid-1990s up until the GFC of 2007–08 the REIT industry enjoyed gradual increases in fund flows. As shown in Figure 10.1, at the end of the third quarter, 2019, REIT-dedicated investors owned 36% of REIT shares: 23% in active funds, and 13% in passive funds.

  While dedicated ownership is down from 50% ownership in 2011, Green Street found that changes in REIT-dedicated active ownership are loosely correlated with outsized returns. Active REIT-dedicated fund managers, while owning a smaller percentage of the industry than before, continue to influence REIT performance, especially among REIT sectors.
- **Generalist Active Investors Crowded Out by REIT-Dedicated Funds.** Green Street also found that generalist active managers have generally maintained their market share, despite the steady rise of generalist passive funds (which includes index funds and ETFs). Green Street found that generalist active investors continue to be unable to meet their full REIT allocations because of the large positions owned by REIT-dedicated investors. This implies REITs can issue more shares (provided valuations support share issuance), and that generalists would likely absorb the new supply to get closer to their optimum allocation to REITs.
- **Pension Funds Still Prefer Direct Real Estate.** Green Street also determined that while US pension fund allocations to real estate have

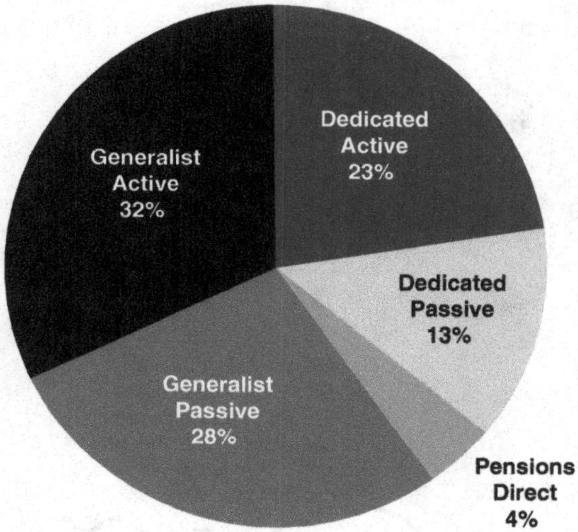

FIGURE 10.1 Breakdown of REIT Ownership at September 30, 2019
Source: Green Street Advisors, *FlowTracker* report dated February 3, 2020.

nearly doubled since 2000, their ownership of REIT shares has "barely budged" (Figure 10.2), most likely due to their preference to avoid the short-term volatility of share price movements on a day-to-day basis.

Events That Increased Demand for REIT Shares

Larger, More Liquid REIT Market

REITs existed for three-and-a half decades, from 1960 through 1995, before the industry gained meaningful traction with investors. Until the mid-1990s, the percent of real estate assets as a percent of total mutual fund assets was less than 25 basis points. Prior to 1990, the supply of REIT shares was too small and the marketplace for REITs was too illiquid to attract meaningful institutional investor interest. Though REITs offered attractive yields and strong portfolio diversification benefits, as discussed in Chapter 2, their thin average daily trading volumes (see Figure 10.3) relegated them to a subset of income-seeking individual investors. In 1990, for example, there were 58 equity REITs with a combined average trading volume of $114 million, implying an average trading dollar volume per REIT of less than $2 million. By contrast, in 1990, The Walt Disney Company (NYSE: DIS) average daily dollar trading volume was $58 million (*Source:* NYSE).

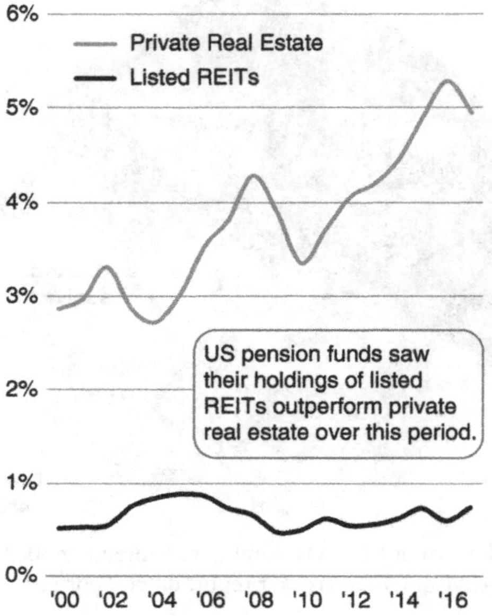

FIGURE 10.2 Pension Fund Allocations to Commercial Real Estate
Source: Green Street Advisors, *FlowTracker* report dated February 3, 2020.

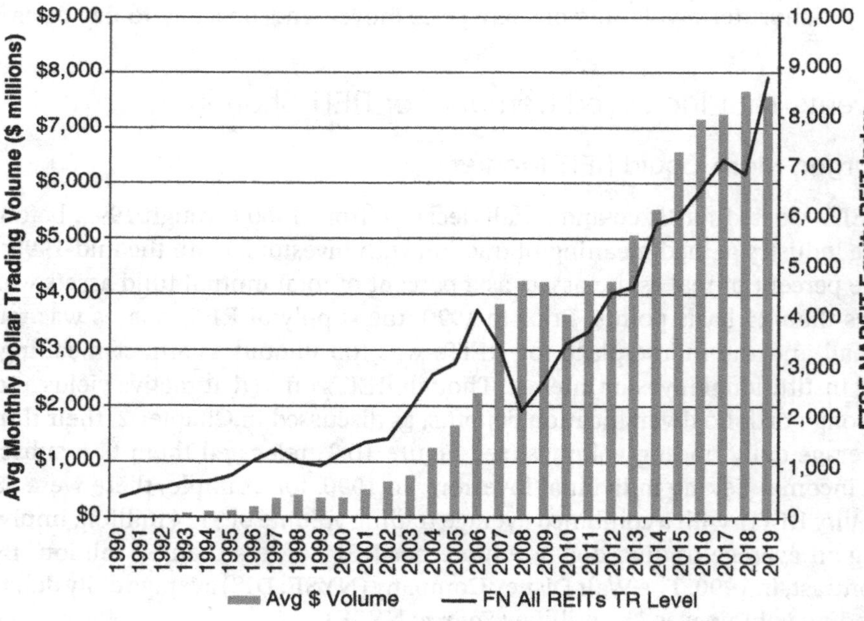

FIGURE 10.3 Average Dollar Trading Volume of the FTSE Nareit All REITs 1990–2019
Source: Nareit.

Since 1995, the REIT industry has grown dramatically. In the 1990s and due in part to the advent of the UPREIT structure discussed in Chapter 8, the REIT industry went through a period of tremendous growth, both in terms of the number of REITs that became public and in terms of the market capitalization of the REIT industry itself. Referring to Table 1.1 in Chapter 1 – which summarizes the industry's growth since the early 1970s – in 1990, there were 58 equity REITs, 43 mortgage REITs, and 18 hybrid REITs, for a total of 119 companies with a combined equity market capitalization of $8.7 billion. At the end of 2019, there were 186 equity REITs and 40 mortgage REITs, for a total of 226 companies with a combined equity market capitalization of $1.3 trillion.

As important, the market for REIT shares grew and became more liquid. Since 2005, for example, the industry's average daily dollar trading volume has compounded at an 11% average annual rate, increasing from $1.6 billion in 2005 to $7.6 billion in 2019 (*Source:* Nareit). As the marketplace for REIT shares became more liquid, more institutional fund managers were able to invest. Several distinct events supported the REIT industry's rapid growth since 1990. The following pages address the major milestones that punctuated the REIT industry's growth.

S&L Crisis of 1980s Was a Unique Buying Opportunity

During the savings-and-loan crisis in the 1980s (the S&L crisis), approximately one-third of the 3,234 savings-and-loan associations in the United States failed between 1986 and 1995. Two government organizations were created to close or otherwise resolve the failed associations: The Federal Savings and Loan Insurance Corporation (FSLIC) and the Resolution Trust Corporation (RTC). A major tactic used by these organizations was to sell the commercial real estate holdings of S&Ls, often for pennies on the dollar. Real estate companies and REITs purchased high-quality assets from the RTC for deeply discounted prices, a rare buying opportunity that positioned the REIT industry for tremendous growth in the 1990s. As the US economy and commercial real estate markets recovered, REITs began leasing up vacancy and capturing higher market rents in their RTC properties. As a result, REITs were able to generate average annual total returns of 17% from 1992 through 1996, which significantly outperformed the returns of other investments (refer back to Table 10.1).

REIT Returns Attract Tsunami of New Capital, 1992–96

The REIT industry's strong performance from 1992–96 attracted significant amounts of new capital. Taking advantage of the strong demand for REIT shares, dozens of private companies and portfolios were able to complete the initial public offering (IPO) process, swelling the ranks of publicly traded REITs from 138 companies at the end of 1991 to 199 at the end of 1996. By the same token, the size of the REIT industry also expanded rapidly. According to Nareit, REITs issued $49.7 billion in equity (both through IPOs and follow-on stock offerings) from 1990 through 1996. The industry's equity market capitalization increased from $13.0 billion at the end of 1991 to $88.8 billion at the end of 1996, representing a compound annual increase of 37.7%.

Professional Money Managers Discover REITs

The advent of professional money managers into the REIT market was a critical component of the industry's growth and evolution. In 1985, Cohen & Steers, Inc. (NYSE: CNS) created the first real estate-dedicated mutual fund and was the sole real estate-dedicated mutual fund until 1989. As Figure 10.1 demonstrated earlier in this chapter, investors have increased their allocations to real estate-dedicated mutual funds dramatically since the late 1980s. Today, hundreds of institutional money managers invest in a vast array of over 40 REIT-dedicated mutual funds.

Improvements to the REIT Structure Aligned Management with Shareholders

REITs were small and micro-cap companies prior to the 1990s, as Real Estate Limited Partnerships (RELPs) gave investors a tax shelter by passing depreciation through to the investor, who could shelter other income from taxes. *The Tax Reform Act of 1986* (the 1986 Tax Act) eliminated the use of real estate depreciation tax deductions from regular earned income, thus requiring all real estate investments to be economically viable first. Also prior to the 1986 Tax Act, REITs were externally advised and managed by third parties, just as all mutual funds still are today. Managers were paid a percent of the book value of assets owned by the REIT, rather than according to profitability. The 1986 Tax Act allowed REITs to hire employees and self-manage, self-advise, and provide basic "landlord" services to tenants. Accordingly, REIT management teams became active managers of their assets, enabling companies to differentiate themselves from other REITs by motivating management with stock ownership.

The REIT Simplification Act of 1994 further streamlined the REIT structure so that companies could operate as fully integrated businesses run by professional managers who were compensated for creating shareholder value, rather than just amassing large portfolios. *The REIT Modernization Act of 1999* (the RMA) became effective January 1, 2001, and further increased REITs' ability to provide tenant services through the use of taxable REIT subsidiaries (TRSs). The result of these Acts was to align the economic interests of REIT management teams with those of the shareholders, making REITs more appealing investments.

Inclusion in Major Stock Indexes Boosted Market Capitalizations and Liquidity

The structural improvements to REITs discussed in the preceding paragraphs, combined with the sector's attractive total returns, continued to attract an increasing level of capital to the REIT industry in the 1990s. As the average market capitalization of REITs and trading volumes increased, it became cost efficient for a broader array of money managers and pension funds to build and maintain a position in REITs as part of their portfolios. Then in 2001, Standard & Poor's (S&P) admitted the first equity REIT into its 500 Index. During the past 19 years, several REITs have been added and, at the end of 2019, the S&P 500 Index included 30 equity REITs (see Table 1.2 in Chapter 1 for more detail). The inclusion of an increasing number of REITs to broader market indexes that money managers use as benchmarks, combined with a strong investor appetite for the safety and yield offered by REITs, sparked a second sustained inflow of funds into REIT-dedicated mutual funds, from 2000 to 2006. REITs generally outperformed other indexes again from 2009 to 2015, years of slow economic growth and lackluster performance from the broader stock market that followed the Great Recession of 2008–09.

Creation of Real Estate GICS Sector in 2016 Increased Demand for REITs

On September 1, 2016, S&P and MSCI created a new Global Industry Classification Standard (GICS) sector called *Real Estate*, which has precipitated a steady increase in demand for REIT shares, especially among generalist fund managers (please refer back to Figure 10.1). In the industry's initial decades, mREITs outnumbered equity REITs. First impressions linger and, while the number of equity REITs and their combined market capitalizations have been greater than those of mREITs since the 1970s, many investors viewed REITs as being a type of financial institution. In 1999, when S&P established its ten GICS classifications, they formally categorized REITs into the *Financials* code, cementing this impression. Now *Real Estate* is the eleventh such investment sector, and its formation is slowly but surely increasing investor awareness of REITs – as real estate stocks, rather than as finance vehicles – and broadening the industry's appeal to individual and institutional investors. (Note that mREITs remained in S&P's *Financials* sector.)

REITS VERSUS THE ATTRACTIVENESS OF OTHER INVESTMENTS (LESSONS FROM HISTORY)

Demand for REIT shares is also affected by the availability of alternative investments that investors think may offer better returns. REITs periodically have underperformed other investments during certain time periods, not so much because of real estate fundamentals, but because of market forces that drove investor dollars into growth stocks (1998–99), into US Treasuries (2004–05), and into people's mattresses (2007–08). Conversely, when returns on the S&P 500 Index are uncertain, REITs generally outperform because investors tend to look for investments that offer safety (or certainty) and yield. The annual total returns presented in Table 10.1 at the beginning of this chapter illustrate these distinct trading periods.

Growth Stocks and a *Risk-On* Environment versus REITs, 1998–99

REIT share prices have been and will continue to be vulnerable to shifts in investor sentiment toward higher-growth sectors. As shown in Table 10.1, from 1993 through 1997 REITs delivered average annual total returns of 18.5%, which kept pace with the similarly strong returns in both the S&P 500 Index and the NASDAQ (also see area A of Figure 10.4). Investor sentiment – and their funds – quickly shifted away from REITs in 1998, however, when the dot-com and tech frenzy accelerated. During this rotation-to-growth, which is also called a *risk-on* trade, investors pulled funds out of defensive investments, like bonds and REITs, and plowed them into the tech-heavy NASDAQ. As Area B in Figure 10.4 shows, REIT returns simply could not compete for investor dollars against the NASDAQ's 40% returns in 1998 and their eye-popping 86% total return in 1999. Even though fundamental demand for commercial real estate in 1998 and 1999 was strong across all property types, REITs delivered negative total returns of 18.8%

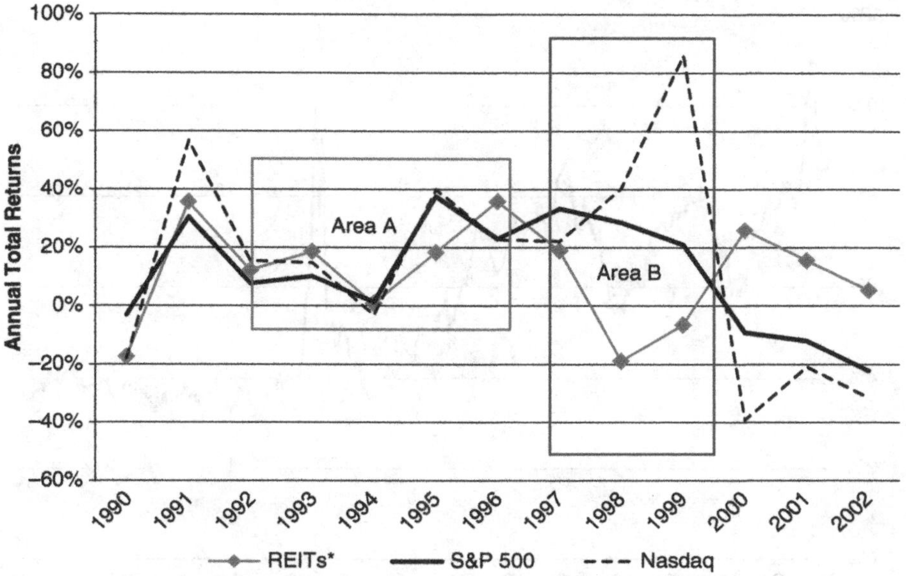

FIGURE 10.4 REIT Performance versus S&P 500 and NASDAQ, 1990–2002
*Annual total returns on the FTSE Nareit All REITs Index.
Source: Nareit; S&P Global Market Intelligence.

and 6.5% in those respective years. Note that in the spring of 2000, when the dot-com investment bubble burst, investors rotated out of the NASDAQ. This *risk-off* trade by investors is reflected in the NASDAQ's negative 39.2% return in 2000 and the REIT industry's positive 25.9% total return that same year.

Treasury Yield versus REITs, 2004–06

Although REITs outperformed the S&P 500 and the NASDAQ handily from 2004 to 2006, their returns were muted for several months from yield investors opting out of REITs in favor of US government bonds. Because REITs offer attractive dividend income, investors have (and should) always compare REIT yields to those of fixed-income investments. Historically, REIT yields have been compared against the yield on ten-year US Treasury notes (see Figure 10.5). From March 2004 through June 2006, notable increases in the yield on ten-year US Treasuries precipitated equally distinct declines in REIT valuations. The valuation decline was short term and

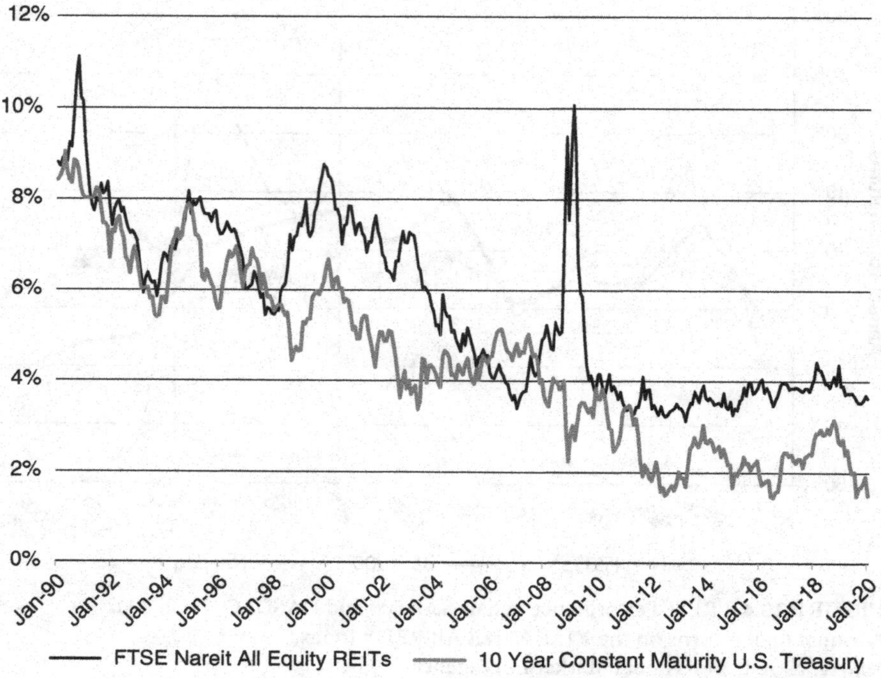

FIGURE 10.5 REIT Dividend Yields vs. Ten-Year US Treasury Yields January 1990–December 2019

Source: Reproduced by permission of the National Association of Real Estate Investment Trusts® (Nareit) and is used subject to the Terms and Conditions of Use set forth on the Nareit website, including, but not limited to, Section 9 thereof.

sporadic. Typically, a decline in REIT valuations in reaction to rising interest rates or Treasury yields turns out to be a compelling buying opportunity for REIT investors, especially those that are patient. (Please refer to *REIT Performance When Interest Rates Change* later in this chapter for a more detailed discussion of this topic.)

Safety and Yield, and the Big League of Benchmarks, 2000–06

The bursting of the technology bubble in spring 2000; the accounting scandals at high-profile companies like Enron (formerly NYSE: ENE) in 2001 and 2002; the tragedy associated with events in the United States on September 11, 2001 (9/11). Each event shook investor confidence and negatively affected the broader stock market. Each event also helped fuel a seven-year rally in REITs, as investors increasingly looked to the group as a source of stable, more visible income. As Table 10.1 illustrated earlier in this chapter, REITs outperformed the broader markets from 2000 through 2006. As previously discussed, investors already were rotating from the NASDAQ into investments, like REITs, that offered safety and yield. From 2000 through 2006, REITs issued $200 billion of equity, preferred stock, and debt capital, $65.3 billion of which was common equity. The industry's market capitalization increased approximately 250%, from $124 billion at the beginning of 2000 to $438 billion at the end of 2006 (see Figure 10.6). The strong demand for REIT shares was driven both by the fundamental investor appetite for safer, higher-yielding investments, such as REITs, and also by a watershed event for REITs: the addition of the first equity REIT, Equity Office Properties (former NYSE: EOP) to the S&P 500 Index. REITs had made it back to the big league of benchmarks, and the added visibility from inclusion in the S&P 500 Index supercharged market dynamics that already favored REIT investment.

Note that investor preference for safety and yield from 2000 through 2006 was different than a broad-based, *risk-off* market environment that prevailed during the global financial crisis of 2007–08 (discussed next) or during the first few months of the COVID-19 pandemic in 2020, where investors categorically sold equities in favor of bonds, gold, and cash.

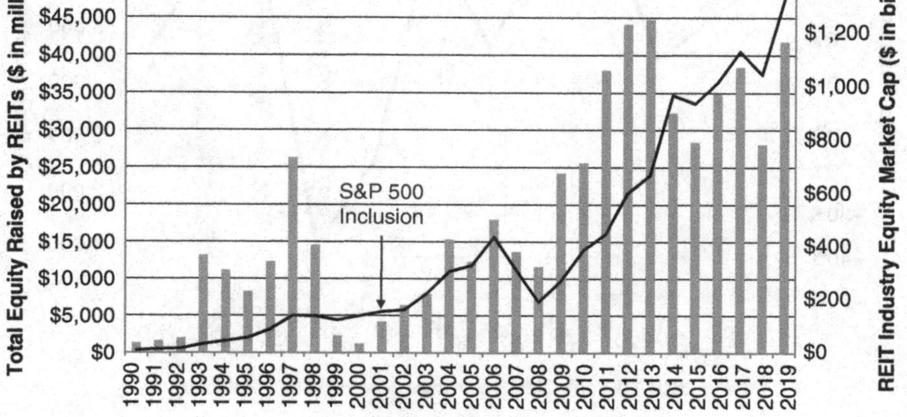

FIGURE 10.6 REIT Common Stock Issuance and Growth in Industry Market Cap, 1990–2019

* FTSE Nareit All REITs Index.

Source: Nareit.

Risk-Off: REITs During the Financial Crisis of 2007–08

One of the most reliable ways investors can gauge market risk is to observe the weekly rate of change in BBB ten-year commercial mortgage-backed security (CMBS) spreads. (If investors do not have access to a Bloomberg terminal, they can request this information from their financial advisors.) When CMBS spreads increase (or *widen*) over the prior week's level, then the market is factoring in more risk, such as the risk of recession or other events that would affect the broader markets.

Changes in BBB ten-year CMBS spreads have proven to be a highly accurate predictor of short-term returns in the REIT market. For example, the BBB ten-year CMBS spreads, which are expressed as a number of basis points above the yield on ten-year US Treasury notes, dramatically widened by 667 basis points during 2007, from 123 basis points at the beginning of the year, to 790 basis points. By the end of 2008, BBB ten-year CMBS spreads had *exploded* to 5,362 basis points over Treasuries. As Figure 10.7 and Table 10.1 show, REIT share prices declined commensurately as the BBB CMBS spreads increased. Even though the Global Financial Crisis of 2007–08 (GFC) began

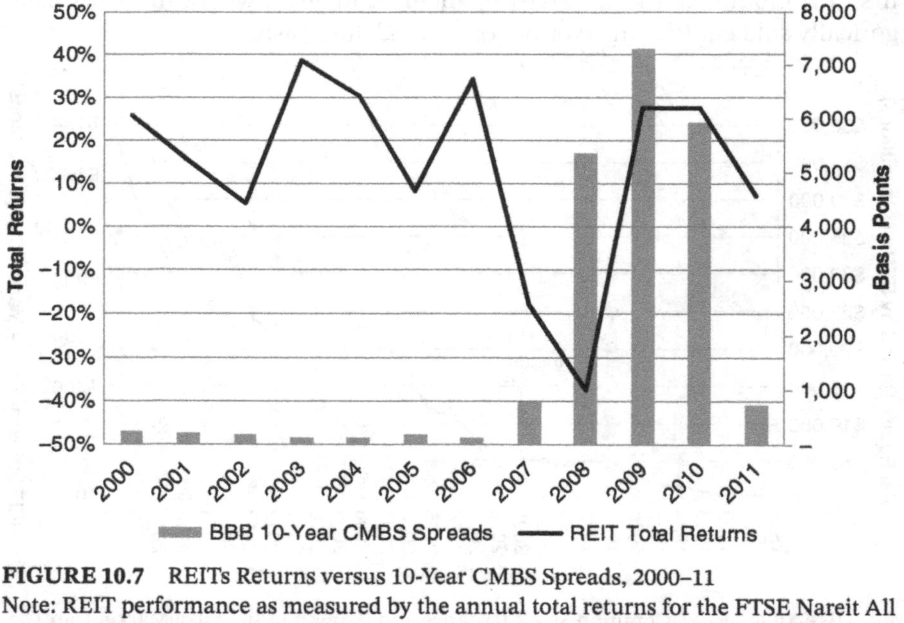

FIGURE 10.7 REITs Returns versus 10-Year CMBS Spreads, 2000–11
Note: REIT performance as measured by the annual total returns for the FTSE Nareit All REITs Index. CMBS Spreads are for ten-year, BBB notes at year-end, in basis points.
Source: Nareit; Bloomberg & Wells Fargo Securities, LLC.

in the overleveraged housing market, rather than in the commercial property markets, REITs delivered total returns of negative 17.8% in 2007 and negative 37.3% in 2008.

Investors feared that all companies, including REITs, would either refinance maturing debt at abnormally high interest rates or, worse, that they might not be able to refinance debt "at any price," in which case management may choose to dilute existing shareholders with an "emergency" equity issuance to raise capital. Any of these pricey refinancing alternatives would dampen future REIT profitability. As discussed in Chapter 4, during the GFC and the year that followed it, only one publicly traded equity REIT entered bankruptcy to restructure its debt, but nearly two-thirds cut or suspended their dividends to preserve capital during these highly uncertain market conditions. Once REITs began issuing new equity – at low stock prices that were highly dilutive to existing shareholders and to future earnings – it became clear that the industry and its constituents would survive. REIT valuations recovered fairly rapidly in 2009, as a result.

Investment Tip

If a credit crisis is possible, stocks associated with real estate, such as REITs, are likely to underperform the broader market due to investor fears – real and imagined – about the sustainability of common dividends and the risk of defaulting on loans scheduled to mature in the near term.

THREE PRIMARY DRIVERS OF REIT PERFORMANCE

The REIT industry comprises an increasingly wide array of commercial real estate. Each REIT in every property sector is governed by three broad forces that affect their performance, both on an absolute basis and relative to other REITs: real estate fundamentals (discussed in Chapter 3), lease structure (including duration), and cost of capital. Real estate fundamentals, and especially the consistency (or *inelasticity*) of demand for a property type, strongly affects REIT performance and profitability over the long term. A property sector like industrial warehousing and distribution, for example, benefits from steady demand for its product; regardless of the state of the economy, goods need to be distributed to end consumers. Consistent demand translates into steady occupancy levels, which should translate into a consistently profitable REIT. Different lease structures and durations discussed in Chapter 5 result in different operating margins, which also affect operating profits. Lastly, how a management team finances its operations is an increasingly important factor in determining long-term total returns. When the economy slows or goes into recession, the profitability of any real estate usually declines. But stock performance across property sectors and among companies can differ widely due to these three basic extrinsic and intrinsic factors, which the next several pages explain in more detail.

Real Estate Fundamentals: "Defensive" Property Types Enjoy Steady Demand

Some types of property are less sensitive to changes in the economy because they serve a critical function and therefore are always in demand. The more essential the function a property type supports in the economy, the more durable (or *inelastic*) the demand for that property type. The magnitude of demand may ebb and flow, but it does not (and cannot) evaporate completely. REITs that own durable demand properties, such as industrial warehouses and apartments, generate consistent earnings and/or maintain fairly high

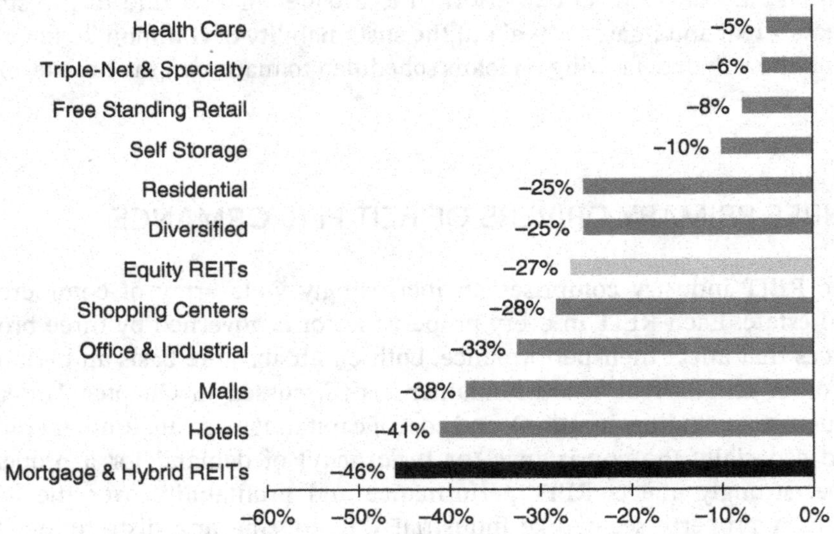

FIGURE 10.8 Total Returns of Different Property Types During the 2007–08 Global Financial Crisis
Source: Nareit; S&P Global Market Intelligence.

occupancy rates regardless of the economic or business cycle and, accordingly, tend to trade with lower volatility, especially during economic downturns.

If the economy has a high probability of slipping into recession, property sector returns from the recent global financial crisis are instructive. As Figure 10.8 demonstrates, the more defensive property sectors (net-lease REITs, health-care, self-storage, and industrial REITs) significantly outperformed less defensive asset types (malls, office, apartments, and hotels).

More generally, Table 10.2 summarizes how demand for different commercial property types typically changes in light of economic statistics that are in the daily news. The table oversimplifies, but investors can still use the information to observe how different property types have performed in past economic recessions and recoveries, and perhaps anticipate future performance.

In summary, investors may enhance their returns by accurately assessing the direction of the economy and aligning that view with REIT investments in property sectors that are likely to benefit from current and expected economic conditions.

> *"There are three things that matter in property: location, location, location."*
>
> Lord Harold Samuel (1912–87)

Within Each Property Type, Location and Efficiency Matter. As Chapter 3 discussed, demand for a property is measured by how fully occupied a building is, especially when compared to similar, competing buildings in a market. If office building A is 90% occupied and office building B is only 80% occupied, it is likely that office building A is both more modern and functionally efficient for office tenants than building B, and/or building A may be in a better location than B. The average rents in place at a building also help investors gauge how desirable a property is, as better locations almost always garner higher rental rates. Regardless of whether the underlying economy is expanding or contracting, office building A has the competitive advantages of functionality and location, and should benefit from higher tenant demand throughout the economic cycle than building B. To quote Lord Harold Samuel, a British real estate tycoon who founded Land Securities: "There are three things that matter in property: location, location, location."

TABLE 10.2 Economic Drivers of Demand for Real Estate

	Impact on Demand for Space		
Economic Indicator	**Direct**	**Indirect**	**None**
Rising Unemployment	Office (–) Apartments (–)(+)[a]	Industrial (–) Retail (–) Hotels (–) Self-Storage (+)	Health Care
Decreased Corporate Spending	Hotels (–) Office (–)	Industrial (+)[b] Apartments (–)	Health Care Retail Self-Storage
Decreased Consumer Spending	Industrial (–) Hotels (–) Retail (–)	Apartments (–) Office (–) Self-Storage (–)	Health Care
Rising Interest Rates	Mortgage REITs (–)[c]	Apartments (+)(–)[d,e] Industrial (–)[e] Hotels (–)[e] Health Care (–)[e] Office (–)[e] Retail (–)[e] Self-Storage (–)[e]	

[a] If unemployment is high for an extended period of time, demand for apartments may increase as some homeowners will need to sell their homes (or be foreclosed upon) and become renters.

[b] While a prolonged recession likely would result in decreased demand for industrial space to accommodate a smaller volume of goods flowing to market, in the short term, inventories typically accumulate, causing a modest, short-lived increase in demand for industrial space.

[c] Rising interest rates would lower the positive spreads most mREITs could lock in on investments. The 'spread' is the difference between where a REIT can invest capital versus its cost of that capital.

[d] A rise in long-term interest rates would make home buying less affordable, which would generate incremental demand for apartments.

[e] An increase in interest rates would negatively affect any REIT that needed to refinance debt, provided that the interest rate on new debt is higher than the rate on the debt that is maturing. However, any such dilution to future cash flow would be limited to specific debt maturities that need to be refinanced, rather than the REIT's entire debt profile.

How Lease Length and Structure Affect REIT Returns

Most investors have heard or read that real estate is a lagging indicator. Whatever the economy is doing, it takes a number of months or years for an office building or shopping mall to reflect economic changes in the form of higher/lower rents and occupancy levels. The longer the leases the landlord has negotiated with tenants, the longer it will take a property's cash flows to reflect a change – good or bad – in the local economy. In other words, real estate lags because it has leases.

Real estate performance lags economic conditions, depending on the leases in place. The longer the lease length, the longer the property's cash flow takes to reflect what's happening in the economy. Knowing the average lease length and the type of lease structure a REIT employs helps predict how a REIT's shares may trade during times of economic expansion and contraction.

Existing leases generate revenues even when there is no new leasing or demand for property in the market. It takes varying amounts of time for changes in the economy to trickle through and affect the cash flows of different property types. Knowing the average lease length and type of lease used by a REIT, therefore, is helpful in determining when to buy or sell its stock.

For example, the longer average lease term associated with office space is the main reason why office REITs often outperform in the early phases of a recession. Their multi-year average lease term delays the effects of current employment trends from manifesting in their rents and occupancies for several years. Assuming the landlord prudently staggers lease expirations throughout the portfolio, five-year leases would translate into approximately one-fifth, or 20% of leases expiring each year. Office landlords mark the expiring leases to current market rents, and they try to lease any vacancy their portfolio contains. During the early phase of an economic decline, office REIT returns are buffered by the existence of in-place leases, and the sector tends to outperform the average REIT. Conversely, office REITs tend to underperform the REIT industry during the early stages of an economic recovery, as rents that were negotiated in better economic times expire and roll to potentially lower market rents.

REITs with Shorter Lease Durations Tend to Trade with Higher Trading Volatility. As a general rule, REITs that own commercial properties with shorter initial lease lengths tend to trade with more volatility – meaning they experience greater percentage change in their daily stock price – than REITs that employ longer leases. For example, REITs that employ long-term triple-net leases (see Chapters 5 and 6) provide fairly predictable cash flow streams that, due to their long lease durations, can bridge over adverse economic periods. The only disruptions to the landlord's cash flows tend to be when a tenant goes bankrupt or does not renew a lease that expires. Neighborhood or community shopping centers also tend to be defensive assets because they usually are anchored by a grocery or drug store, both of which enjoy fairly inelastic demand for their goods. In contrast, hotels have no leases with their customers, and experience higher vacancies when consumers cut back business and leisure travel when the economy slows. Understanding the structure and duration of leases used by a REIT can help investors make opportunistic investments.

> Shares of REITs that own properties with shorter-term leases tend to trade with more volatility than those with longer lease lengths.

Hotel REITs' Higher Volatility Can Be an Investment Opportunity. The cyclical nature of demand for lodging combined with hotels' lack of leases are the main reasons hotel REITs trade with greater levels of volatility than the average REIT. This volatility lends itself to greater risks for would-be investors but also to greater potential returns. As Table 10.3 illustrates, hotel REIT annual total returns tend to diverge from that of the broader REIT industry. For example, in 2008 when the US economy was sliding into recession, the average REIT declined 41% and hotel REITs fell 63%. Conversely, in 2009, when the economy stabilized and started to recover, the average REIT rebounded 27%, which was impressive but still paled in comparison to the 63% price appreciation enjoyed by hotel REITs.

Because they trade with greater volatility, hotel REITs are one of the few property types investors may want to buy opportunistically when they are at depressed levels and sell when the stocks – and the underlying economy – are recovered. There is an old expression that the only people who can time the stock market are fools and/or liars. However, using a contrarian trading strategy with hotel REITs, over time, does seem to be possible and should help investors avoid "buying high and selling low."

TABLE 10.3 Hotel REIT Performance versus US GDP

	1990	1991	1992	1993	1994	1995	1996	1997	1998	1999	2000	2001	2002	2003	2004	2005	2006	2007	2008	2009	2010
Hotel REIT[a]	−74%	−14%	−9%	105%	−4%	21%	43%	25%	−54%	−29%	31%	−13%	−5%	25%	29%	6%	23%	−27%	−63%	63%	38%
All Equity REITs[b]	−26%	25%	6%	13%	−4%	7%	26%	13%	−22%	−12%	17%	6%	−3%	28%	24%	7%	30%	−19%	−41%	21%	23%
US GDP[c]	2%	0%	3%	3%	4%	3%	4%	5%	4%	5%	4%	1%	2%	3%	4%	3%	3%	2%	0%	−3%	3%

[a]*Source: S&P Global Market Intelligence; Price-only hotel REIT performance.*

[b]*Source: FTSE Nareit Equity REITs Index; Price-only.*

[c]*Source: Bureau of Economic Analysis.*

Recession years are shaded.

Weighted Average Cost of Capital and REIT Performance

Chapter 1 highlighted the fact that REITs with above-average leverage do not have as much financial flexibility as REITs that operate with lower levels of debt. As a result, the more highly leveraged REITs often are not able to take advantage of opportunistic investments. Research has demonstrated that REIT management teams who operate with more leverage typically underperform their lower-leveraged peers. This section discusses the possible perils of debt and the overall importance of a REIT's cost of capital.

Debt as a Four-Letter Word. The Global Financial Crisis of 2007–08 illustrated somewhat dramatically that balance sheets matter. According to an analysis by S&P Global Market Intelligence, of the 128 REITs that were paying a dividend in 2007, 84 – or roughly two-thirds – cut their dividend over the following two years. The portfolio of 44 REITs that did not cut their dividends (*Keepers* in Figure 10.9) delivered a 135% return from the beginning of 2008 through 2015, whereas the *Cutters* portfolio returned only 78%. Figure 10.9 plots the performance of these Keeper versus Cutter REITs. Furthermore, studies by numerous, reputable firms such as Green Street Advisors have demonstrated how REITs that operate their business with lower levels of debt tend to outperform other, more leveraged REITs.

The 44 Keeper REITs were those that had relatively lower levels of debt going into 2007, before the crisis took hold of the markets. Specifically, the median 2007 debt-to-EBITDA multiples of Keepers was 5.67 times, and for the Cutters it was 7.23 times, clearly demonstrating how higher leverage levels lead to dividend cuts during the global financial crisis. (Debt-to-EBITDA is defined and discussed in Chapters 4 and 11.)

Competitive Advantage or Disadvantage – Why Cost of Capital Matters. One of the main reasons why REITs with more highly leveraged balance sheets tend to underperform is that they miss opportunities to acquire assets at deeply discounted prices during times of market dislocation, such as we saw during the GFC and through 2010 as property markets were still recovering. REITs with too much debt going into a recession or market crisis simply don't have the financial flexibility to capitalize on market opportunities. By contrast, REITs with lower leverage can and do, thereby meriting a higher relative valuation from investors.

Even in normal market conditions, a REIT's weighted average cost of capital (WACC) affects stock price performance. As Chapter 11 discusses in more detail, WACC is calculated by adding up a company's debt, preferred stock, and common equity costs, weighting each portion of capital by the average cost of each piece. Using an oversimplified example, if KKM REIT (introduced in Chapter 4) has $50 million of debt outstanding with

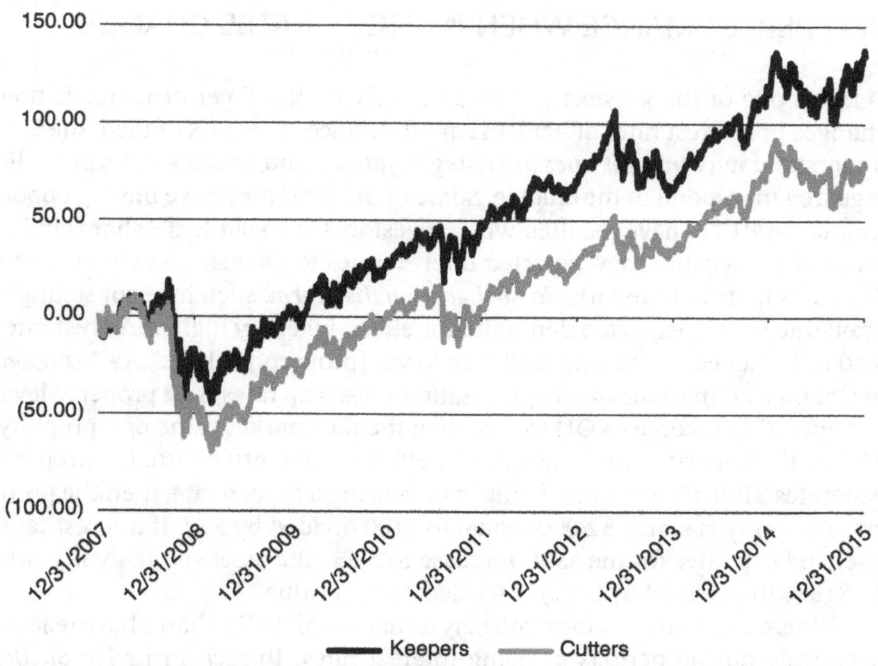

FIGURE 10.9 Total Returns of REITs That Cut versus Those That Did Not Cut Dividends, 2007–09
Source: S&P Global Market Intelligence.

a weighted average interest rate of 5%, $10 million of preferred stock with a 6.5% coupon rate, and $100 million of common equity with an estimated cost of 9% (dividend yield plus expected earnings growth), then KKM REIT's WACC is 7.6%, which essentially is this company's cost of doing business. In order to make a profit on new investments, KKM REIT needs to invest its capital into opportunities that return more than 7.6%. When competing for an acquisition property or development opportunity, REITs that have a WACC that is less than 7.6% will have a competitive advantage over KKM REIT by being able to pay a higher price. Lastly, KKM REIT's management, if they feel they are under pressure to grow, may commit "unforced errors," such as investing in high-yielding but low-quality assets. Ultimately, a poor allocation of capital into subpar assets will translate into a lower stock valuation for KKM REIT. Rather than chase growth through questionable investments, KKM REIT's management would serve shareholders better by paying down debt, which will help lower its WACC to more competitive levels.

REIT PERFORMANCE WHEN INTEREST RATES CHANGE

Perhaps one of the greatest nuances underlying REIT performance is how changes in interest rates affect REIT performance. The crux of the issue is to understand ***why** interest rates are rising or falling*, and how a REIT's portfolio is geared to respond to the change. Some of the most attractive buying opportunities in REITs have resulted when investors have sold REIT shares indiscriminately because they expected interest rates to increase. As Green Street discusses in its 2018 report, *No Shelter from the Storm*, such investor selling is often due to "the expected denominator effect, whereby higher interest rates lead to higher cap rates, and therefore lower [property] values." As discussed in Chapter 11, investors use capitalization rates (cap rates) and property-level net operating income (NOI) to calculate the fair market value of a property. The math supporting the denominator effect is straightforward. If a property generates $100 of NOI and is being valued using a 5% cap rate, then the property currently is worth $2,000 (equal to $100 divided by 5%). If interest rates rise, and cap rates for the asset increase to 5.5%, the asset suddenly is worth $1,818 ($100 divided by 5.5%), a 9% decrease in value.

Where the nuance comes into play is that not all REIT shares have reacted negatively during periods of rising interest rates. In fact, in its *No Shelter from the Storm* report Green Street found that REITs that own properties in low cap rate (i.e., high value) markets, such as major urban locations, have actually outperformed more frequently when interest rates rise. Their conclusion was that "a powerful numerator effect is at play" that mitigates or even completely offsets the denominator effect. The numerator effect Green Street identified has to do with demand elasticity for properties (discussed earlier in this chapter) as well as what factors are driving interest rates higher. If the rate increases are in anticipation of higher GDP growth, then office, apartment, hotel, and other commercial property demand (and future cash flows) should increase as well, and especially for the assets that have the best locations.

Green Street also found that REIT industry performance in relation to interest rate changes has shifted dramatically in recent year, and that REIT shares behave differently today than they did in the past. In its 2018 report, *Perception Becomes Reality*, Green Street analyzed a 30-year period during which there were multiple interest rate spikes and found that, from 1998 through 2011, there was no statistical relationship between changes in US Treasury rates and REIT performance; they also showed that since 2012, REIT short-term performance has become much more sensitive to interest rate movements. This change in REIT share sensitivity to interest rates is demonstrated in Figure 10.10.

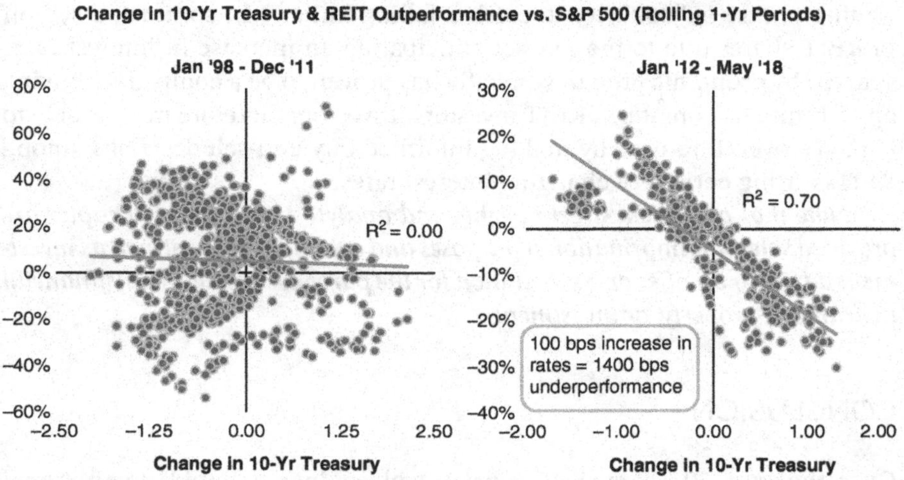

FIGURE 10.10 REIT Performance Has Become Sensitivity to Interest Rate Changes
Source: Green Street Advisors, *Perception Becomes Reality* report dated June 13, 2018.

This same Green Street analysis also found that "the sensitivity of a given property sector changes in interest rates and/or outlook is a function of its economic sensitivity and the duration of leases. Lodging stands out as performing well when rates rise, while health care and net leases are among the most negatively impacted by increasing rates," as investors trade them as "bond proxies."

"Don't try to catch a falling knife": When the stock market is in an extreme risk-off mode due to widespread uncertainty regarding future economic growth (e.g., COVID-19 pandemic of 2020 or the GFC of 2007–08), most companies' stock prices will decline for a period of time. Investors should be patient and not buy stocks too early, as what may look "cheap" can become cheaper before the market stabilizes and recovers.

Lastly, Green Street found that "today's extreme linage between rates and REITs is an overreaction." In other words, the market for REIT shares is sometimes inefficient, especially in the short term. If a broad-based economic uncertainty causes all equities – including REITs – to decline (a *risk-off* environment), investors considering a new investment in REITs should be patient and let share prices find a bottom before buying. (An old Wall Street trading phrase is "don't try to catch a falling knife!") In contrast, a sell-off in REIT shares due to the market anticipating an increase in interest rates spurred by economic growth generally has proven to be a compelling buying opportunity for long-term REIT investors. Investors therefore may be able to enhance overall returns by making informed buy-and-sell decisions among REITs during periods of changing interest rates.

Note that all Green Street insights and analytics cited in this chapter are provided solely for informational purposes and are not to be construed as investment advice or an offer or a solicitation for the purchase or sale of any financial instrument, property, or investment.

CONCLUSION

Over the past 30 years, REITs have evolved into a liquid, institutional investment class vehicle available to all investors. With greater liquidity comes greater volatility, which when understood and interpreted appropriately, can lead to greater returns. As the industry has evolved, real estate fundamentals and company-specific characteristics, rather than broad-brush industry trends, increasingly have driven REIT stock performance. Property type demand and supply, market locations, lease structure, and financial flexibility collectively determine individual company returns in different economic environments, with property type (that is, fundamental demand) being the dominant factor. Moreover, REITs that own properties for which tenant demand is relatively inelastic and that are in the best locations, tend to outperform during periods of rising interest rates. Investors should choose REITs based on their outlook for economic trends and in accordance with their individual tolerance for risk.

CHAPTER 11

Analyzing REITs

This chapter is designed to provide investors with an understanding of the performance and valuation metrics required to evaluate REITs. When used in combination, these measurements provide insight into companies' financial flexibility, dividend safety, long-term growth prospects, and current valuations.

One of the more enduring challenges in analyzing REITs – individually and for comparison purposes – is the lack of standardized reporting. Each publicly traded REIT files quarterly Form 10-Q and annual Form 10-K reports with the SEC (10-Qs and 10-Ks, respectively). These reports provide information about a company's history and summarize its latest financial performance and capital allocation actions (e.g., acquisitions, dispositions, capital raises). Although REITs report results in accordance with GAAP, the fundamental profitability metric used to analyze REITs is a non-GAAP, supplemental metric known as funds from operations (FFO). In its most basic form, FFO is calculated as a REIT's net income (calculated in accordance with GAAP) plus the depreciation and amortization related to real estate (non-cash expenses). Both net income and the depreciation adjustment can be found on a REIT's consolidated income statement in its 10-Qs and 10-Ks. The confusion sets in because even REITs within the same property sector have slightly (or greatly) different strategies and tactics they follow to grow their businesses and attract shareholders. Some REITs develop new buildings from scratch, some do not; others opportunistically prune their portfolio by selling buildings, while others may not. Some US-based REITs operate in other countries, while most do not. These differences create unique risks and disclosure variances. The result is that nearly all REITs report FFO as defined by Nareit; however, nearly as many also provide a "core" FFO calculation (or some other nomenclature) that management believes more accurately reflects their profitability; core FFO and Nareit FFO disclosure is most easily found in each company's quarterly supplemental information package.

Accordingly, in addition to reading a company's earnings releases, and SEC filings, investors should obtain the **supplemental information package** that most REITs provide (often filed as a Form 8-K with the SEC). REITs provide non-GAAP, supplemental calculations and metrics that may or may not be in accordance with GAAP, but which are helpful for understanding and forecasting their businesses. Most companies post all their SEC filings, along with their press releases, on their company websites; Appendix C provides website addresses for the REITs in the FTSE Nareit All REITs Index as of December 31, 2019.

OPERATING METRICS

There are a number of metrics used to assess the relative strength of a REIT's operations. The following pages provide key operating metrics that are germane to understanding REITs.

Net Operating Income (NOI)

Net operating income (NOI) is similar to a non-REIT C-corporation's gross profit in that a REIT's NOI is comparable to revenues less the cost of goods sold, where the latter equals the direct costs associated with operating a building. As shown in Table 11.1, NOI equals the sum of rental revenues from properties, less all property operating expenses, including property management costs, maintenance, taxes, and insurance. (Please refer to Chapter 5 for an overview of leasing terminology and recent changes to REIT disclosure related to ASC 842, the New Lease Accounting Standard.) Said another way, NOI measures the property-level profit on a stand-alone basis, excluding the REIT's corporate overhead or the effects of financing.

NOI Margin. Like a gross margin for a non-REIT company, a REIT's gross margin shows the percent of revenues that exceed the property operating costs. If a REIT's NOI margin increases over time, then the REIT is enjoying better rental rate growth (through escalations and/or negotiating higher rents on renewing leases) or has implemented cost savings and better expense control measures at the property level – or a combination of the two. Bottom line is that a higher NOI margin equates to higher property-level

TABLE 11.1 Calculating Net Operating Income (NOI)

Revenues from real estate operations		$40.00
+	Other revenue (e.g., monthly parking)	5.00
Total lease revenues		45.00
–	Property operating expenses (includes property management fee)	(15.00)
–	Taxes & insurance	(5.00)
Net operating income (NOI)		$25.00

profitability. The example below calculates the NOI margin using numbers from Table 11.1:

$$\text{NOI margin} = \frac{\text{NOI}}{\text{Total lease revenues}} = \frac{\$25.00}{\$45.00} = 56\%$$

Lastly, NOI may not be comparable among REITs owing to differences in the amounts, if any, of corporate overhead expenses included in property operating expenses.

Same-Store NOI (*Organic NOI*)

Borrowed from the retail industry, the term *same-store* generally refers to revenues, operating expenses, and net operating income from assets a REIT has owned and operated for 12 or more months. Isolating the profitability of assets owned for at least 12 months from results generated by recently acquired or developed properties enables investors to gauge how competent the REIT management team is at operating their properties. Increases in same-store NOI is also referred to as "organic" or "internal" growth (though these descriptions are not technically precise), whereas increases generated from newly acquired or developed buildings are often referred to as "external growth." Each company may have slight variations about how they classify properties into (or out of) their same-store portfolio; generally, once a company has owned and operated an asset for 12 months as of January first of a given year, that asset is added to the same-store portfolio.

Growth in a REIT's same-store NOI measures a REIT management team's ability to grow earnings internally, or "organically" – without buying or building new assets. Contractual increases built into tenants' cash rents, the expiration and re-leasing of space at higher (or lower) market rents, and changes in occupancy levels generate increases or decreases in same-store

NOI. Among these variables, a change in occupancy is the dominant driver of fluctuations in same-store NOI because, in addition to no longer receiving rental revenue on the vacated space, the landlord also has to pay the basic operating expenses that no longer get reimbursed by a tenant. These expenses are basic electricity to keep the space's temperature ambient (too cold, and drywall cracks and/or pipes burst; too hot or moist and mold can infiltrate), plus property taxes and insurance. The basic operating costs are not as high as the full expenses incurred when the space is occupied, but the inability to pass them through to a tenant significantly impedes a landlord's operating margin on the building. The one-two combination-punch that vacancy has on landlord's operating margins – the loss of revenue, plus increased operating expenses – is why the demand profile for a property sector is a dominant factor in determining long-term performance. (Please also refer to Chapters 3 and 10.) In short, vacancy is not profitable, and property sectors for which demand remains steady during economic downturns tend to outperform other sectors.

The one-two combination-punch that vacancy has on landlord's operating margins – the loss of revenue, plus increased operating expenses – is why the demand profile for a property sector is a dominant factor in determining long-term performance.

"Earnings Growth" for REITs is "FFO Growth"

REITs calculate earnings growth like any company: as the percentage change in earnings for the most current reporting period, versus results from the prior year's comparable period. Non-REIT C-corporations measure growth as a change in earnings per share (EPS); REITs measure growth as the year-over-year change in funds from operations (FFO).

Nareit created FFO in 1991 as a supplemental measure of REIT operating performance. In 2003, the SEC officially recognized Nareit's definition of FFO as a supplemental earnings measure. When referring to a REIT's "earnings," analysts and investors are referring to FFO and FFO per share, not Net Income or EPS. Accordingly, REIT earnings growth is called FFO growth, calculated as follows:

$$\text{REIT FFO growth} = \left[\left(\frac{\text{Current period FFO per share}}{\text{FFO per share for same period a year ago}}\right) - 1\right] \times 100$$

A REIT increases its FFO by combining same-store growth with external growth derived from acquiring or developing properties, less the FFO associated with any properties sold, net of the equity and debt costs used to finance operations. Many REITs also have "other income" that is separate from the profit generated by their buildings. Since the *REIT Modernization Act of 1999*, REITs have had more flexibility to provide tenant services or property management to others through taxable REIT subsidiaries (TRSs). (Please refer to Chapters 8 and 10 for more information.) Since that legislation went into effect, many REITs now also derive small amounts of additional income from real estate-related services and businesses. FFO also includes the REIT's general and administrative (G&A) costs. Comparing the G&A as a percent of real estate revenues across different REITs in the same property type is a quick way to compare the relative efficiency with which respective management teams operate their real estate. Lastly and similar to EPS, FFO per share also accounts for the effects of any changes to a REIT's capital structure in the form of higher (or lower) interest expense and/or a different diluted share count.

As with any industry, higher earnings growth generally merits a higher valuation, provided that the quality of earnings is sound. For REITs, investors typically ascribe a higher multiple to "better quality" earnings, namely those derived from the business of owning and leasing real estate. Investors generally ascribe a lower valuation to earnings generated from areas of the business that are less predictable, such as income from merchant development or third-party property management activities.

Management's Track Record as a Screening Tool

There is no hard-and-fast way to quantify and compare one REIT's management team against another. Over time, however, better senior-management teams should generate above-average same-store NOI growth and superior annual total returns for shareholders. Assessing management's performance by comparing the last five or more years of reported same-store NOI growth and annual total returns against peer companies' results should help investors quickly assess if the REIT they are evaluating tends to perform on-, below-, or above-par versus similar REITs. S&P Global Market Intelligence, whose website is listed in the Further Resources section of this book's conclusion, has one of the more robust databases of historical same-store and other data on individual REITs dating back to the mid-1990s. Nareit's website, www.reit.com, also provides a host of historical company data, including annual total returns.

PROFITABILITY METRICS

Like other C-corporations, REITs report net income and EPS calculated in accordance with GAAP. According to GAAP, however, REITs must depreciate the cost of their properties (excluding the amount allocated to the cost of land) over the useful life of an asset. Since equity REITs invest primarily in real property, depreciation can be a very large, non-cash expense, even greater than NOI; as a result, instead of earnings per share, a REIT may report a *loss per share* on its income statement. Additionally, well located properties tend to *appreciate* in value over time.

In 1991, to address the discrepancy between GAAP rules and current market values for real estate and to provide a uniform, widely accepted supplemental industry standard for measuring equity REIT performance, the REIT community adopted FFO as a supplemental measure of operating performance. FFO and two additional supplemental performance metrics – adjusted FFO (AFFO) and cash (or funds) available for distribution (CAD or FAD) – are described in the paragraphs that follow, and Table 11.2 illustrates the major adjustments that need to be made to reconcile "Net income available to shareholders" to an estimate of CAD. (Depending on the REIT's operations, there can be many more adjustments, and investors should consult each REIT's supplemental information packages to ensure they are accounting for things correctly.)

Funds from Operations

Funds from operations is a supplemental though more broadly used measurement of REIT earnings, created by the REIT industry in 1991 and recognized by the SEC in 2003. According to Nareit's latest (December 2018) White Paper on the topic, FFO equals:

Net income, as computed in accordance with GAAP, excluding:

- Depreciation and amortization related to real estate.
- Gains and losses on real estate assets.
- Gains and losses from change in control.
- Impairment write-downs of certain real estate assets and investments in entities when the impairment is directly attributable to decreases in the value of depreciable real estate held by the entity.

TABLE 11.2 Reconciliation of GAAP Net Income to CAD

Net income (loss) available to common shareholders[a]	
+	Preferred stock dividends paid to preferred share & unitholders
Net income[a]	
+	Real estate depreciation and amortization
–	Gains on the sale of real estate assets sold, net of income taxes
+	Impairment write-downs on real estate assets
±	Reconciling FFO related to non-controlling interests[b]
Funds from Operations (FFO) attributable to the Company, per Nareit	
–	Recurring capital expenditures[c]
±	Adjustment for straight-lining of rents[d]
+	Amortization of stock compensation
+	Amortization of deferred financing costs
±	One-time items, such as the losses on the early extinguishment of debt
Adjusted FFO (AFFO)	
–	Capitalized interest expense
–	Scheduled principal amortization payments on debt[e]
Cash Available for Distribution (CAD)	

[a]If starting with net income available to common shareholders, adjust back to "net income" before calculating FFO and Adjusted FFO. Like interest payments on debt, preferred share dividends and preferred unit distributions are allocations of net income and FFO to parties other than shareholders and, as such, are deducted from net income available to common shareholders and FFO available to common shareholders. When calculating diluted FFO available to common share and unitholders (see Table 11.3), subtract preferred dividends and distributions from Nareit-defined FFO.

[b]These generally are partnerships and joint ventures in which the REIT owns less than a controlling interest.

[c]Also called "replacement capex," recurring capex includes monies spent on leasing space (e.g., tenant improvements and leasing commissions paid to leasing agents) and replacing certain elements of the building that are non-structural, such as mechanicals and HVAC units. Non-recurring capital expenditures add value to or extend the life of a property and include major structural items, such as expanding a property or constructing a parking deck. Both recurring and non-recurring items are generally capitalized, which increases the building's basis, and are then depreciated. However, *only recurring capital expenditures are deducted in calculating AFFO*.

[d]In accordance with GAAP "accrual accounting" and as discussed in Chapter 5, REITs "straight-line" the rental income they are contractually entitled to receive for each lease.

[e]Excludes balloon or maturing principal payments.

Many REITs also report a "core" FFO that better reflects their specific operations than Nareit's White Paper definition. When comparing companies, investors need to be aware of (and adjust for) major differences. S&P Global calculates a "normalized FFO" for each REIT in an attempt to make them more comparable.

The reconciling items include amounts to adjust earnings from consolidated partially-owned entities and equity in earnings of unconsolidated affiliates to FFO. Alternatively, these adjustments could be presented on a single-line item. In either case, the FFO of partially-owned entities should be calculated in accordance with the Nareit FFO White Paper.

While the great majority of equity REITs measure FFO in accordance with Nareit's definition, there are variations in the securities to which the reported Nareit-defined FFO applies (e.g., all equity securities, all common shares, all common shares less shares held by non-controlling interests). Though each of these metrics may represent FFO as defined by Nareit, accurate labeling with respect to applicable securities is important. Therefore, care should be taken in labeling the FFO metric, as well as the GAAP earnings metric in all FFO reporting. This is particularly so in the GAAP earnings to Nareit FFO reconciliation required by the SEC.

REITs can report Nareit FFO attributable to the company, as well as Nareit FFO attributable to common shareholders. Both are reported in accordance with the White Paper definition of FFO, so long as the measure is accurately labeled. If a REIT has preferred stock or preferred OP units outstanding, its Net Income will be higher than its Net Income Available to Common Share and Unit Holders. In such instances, subtract the preferred dividends and distributions paid to these investors in order to calculate the numerator used to compute diluted FFO per share, as shown in Table 11.3. (The denominator will include the REIT's common shares and common OP units outstanding at the end of the reporting period.)

Adjusted Funds from Operations (AFFO)

Adjusted funds from operations (AFFO) is a better metric for determining a REIT's ability to pay dividends than FFO because it adjusts for non-cash GAAP accounting conventions such as straight-lining of rents, and for recurring capitalized expenditures (see footnotes *c* and *d* for Table 11.2, as well as the Glossary). AFFO is calculated by adding any amortized

TABLE 11.3 Calculating Diluted FFO per Nareit (Adjusting for Preferred Equity Investors)

Net income[a]	
+	Depreciation and amortization related to real estate
±	(Gains) Losses from the sale of certain real estate assets
±	(Gains) Losses from changes in control
+	Impairment write-downs of certain real estate assets and investments in entities when the impairment is directly attributable to decreases in the value of depreciable real estate held by the entity
±	Reconciling FFO related to non-controlling interests[b]
Funds from Operations (FFO) attributable to the Company, per Nareit	
–	Dividends and distributions paid to preferred shareholders and preferred unitholders
Diluted FFO available to common share and common OP unit holders[c]	

[a]As defined by GAAP, and before payment of dividends to preferred shareholders and distributions to preferred unitholders.
[b]These generally are partnerships and joint ventures in which the REIT owns less than a controlling interest. These may be reported as part of the other reconciling items or disclosed on a separate line item, as shown in this table.
[c]This will be the numerator for calculating diluted FFO per share.

expenses (which are non-cash items) to FFO, then subtracting a "normalized level" of recurring (or *replacement*) capital expenditures and adjusting for straight-lined rents.

Examples of recurring capital expenditures include leasing commissions and tenant improvement paid to lease a space, both of which are capitalized and then amortized (that is, *averaged*) over the life of the lease. Observing the last three to five years of historical data is helpful in estimating what is a reasonable level of recurring capital expenditures for each REIT. Recurring capital expenditure information typically can be found in the AFFO reconciliations REITs provide in the quarterly supplemental packages. To estimate future spending, divide the average annual recurring capital expenditures by the average occupied square feet in each year, then multiply the resulting "CapEx per square foot" number by the amount of occupied square feet forecasted for future years. Note that square feet in this calculation should only include space associated with a REIT's in-service portfolio. Development square footage and costs (including tenant improvements and leasing commissions committed to in leasing the developments) should not be included.

Lastly, the effects of any one-time items should be reversed. For example, it is customary to add back charges that get written off when REITs redeem preferred shares. These charges are the original underwriting costs incurred when the REIT issued the preferred stock. They are non-cash expenses associated with the redemption and are non-recurring. Therefore, it makes sense to exclude them when calculating AFFO.

Cash Available for Distribution (CAD)

While many investors and analysts refer to AFFO as a measure of a REIT's free cash flow, cash available for distribution (CAD) is a more precise metric and provides a better measure of the cash a REIT has available to pay dividends. CAD is calculated by subtracting capitalized interest expense and principal amortization payments due on secured debt – excluding any principal amounts that are maturating; these "balloon payments" are accounted for in the financing activities section of a company's Statement of Cash Flows and typically get refinanced with new debt when they mature. (See the *Debt Maturity Schedule* discussion later in this chapter for more information.) Not every analyst or investor goes the extra mile to calculate CAD, however, and Nareit currently offers no opinion on it. As a result, the investment community uses AFFO to assess the safety of a REIT's dividend.

BALANCE SHEET METRICS AND ANALYSIS

A REIT's balance sheet can also provide important information about dividend safety or a REIT's ability to grow FFO. The following metrics enable investors to assess a REIT's financial flexibility.

Leverage

Leverage is the use of debt to fund part of a property purchase. The REIT industry has progressively de-levered over the decades. Prior to 1990, it was not unusual for real estate companies to finance 80% or more of their property values with debt. Using large amounts of leverage (*leveraging up*) to acquire or develop buildings results in higher return on equity and impressive FFO per share growth; however, it also adds significant risk and, historically, when combined with an economic slowdown, has been the root cause of many private real estate company bankruptcies. In the 2000s, leverage came back in vogue, only to end poorly for many overleveraged private landlords when the Global Financial Crisis began to unfold in 2007.

When assessing the financial health of any real estate company or REIT, investors may want to remember one truism:

"More Debt = More Risk"

In contrast to the private property market, REITs historically have maintained a more disciplined, conservative approach to financing operations with debt. To wit, as of December 31, 2006, the REIT industry's average debt-to-gross book ratio was 57%. Out of the 130 REITs that composed the FTSE Nareit All REITs Index going into 2007 and the global financial crisis, only one REIT, General Growth Properties (formerly NYSE: GGP), ended up reorganizing under Chapter 11 bankruptcy law. As discussed in Chapter 4, General Growth's debt-to-tangible book ratio at the end of 2006 was 74%, or 17 percentage points greater than the industry average.

Debt-to-Total Market Capitalization Ratio

As of December 31, 2019, and according to Nareit, equity REITs' average debt-to-total market capitalization ratio was 27.5%. This ratio is calculated by dividing a company's total debt outstanding by its total market capitalization, the latter of which is the sum of the following:

- Total debt outstanding.
- The liquidation value of any preferred equity outstanding, calculated as the liquidation value per share or unit (typically $25) times the number of preferred shares and units outstanding. A company's supplemental package and/or the footnotes to its periodic SEC filings typically contain the liquidation values of preferred shares and units.
- The REIT's Equity Market Capitalization (EMC or *equity market cap*), calculated as the current stock price times the sum of all common shares and OP units outstanding:

$$\text{EMC} = (\text{Common shares} + \text{OP units}) \times \text{current stock price}$$

The combined formula for calculating debt-to-total market capitalization is as follows:

$$\text{Debt-to-total market capitalization} = \frac{\text{total debt outstanding}}{\left[\begin{array}{c}\text{total debt + preferred equity at} \\ \text{liquidation value} \\ \text{+ equity market capitalization}\end{array}\right]}$$

As discussed in Chapter 4, a debt-to-total capitalization ratio changes daily depending on a REIT's current stock price, resulting in leverage being over- or understated. To obtain a more accurate idea about how leveraged a REIT is, calculate its debt-to-gross book value ratio.

Debt-to-Tangible Book Value Ratio

Tangible book value can be calculated by taking total assets listed on the balance sheet of the REIT's financial statements, less any goodwill or intangibles, plus any accumulated depreciation and amortization (generally listed in the footnotes to the financial statements), as shown in the following equation.

$$\text{Debt-to-tangible book value} = \frac{\text{total debt outstanding}}{\text{(total assets-intangibles) + accumulated depreciation}}$$

According to S&P Global, at September 30, 2019, the average debt-to-tangible book ratio of REITs in the FTSE Nareit All REITs index was 44%.

The one caveat to using debt-to-tangible book to assess a REIT's leverage is that it is not as transparent a number as investors may think because the GAAP rules regarding the treatment of fully depreciated tenant improvements (TIs) are not definitive. While GAAP requires a REIT to depreciate tenant improvement dollars spent on leasing or renewing tenant spaces, it does not require a company to write-off (that is, eliminate) the fully depreciated TIs at the end of the lease terms. Companies that choose to keep fully depreciated TIs on their books, therefore, are able to inflate their tangible book values and, by extension, understate their leverage ratios. The accounting community is becoming more attuned to such legal, but unethical, accounting practices and may address them in the future. Until then, investors should not rely solely on debt-to-tangible book values to determine a company's leverage and dividend safety.

Debt-to-EBITDA Ratio

One of the most critical ratios the investment community focuses on is a REIT's debt-to-EBITDA, which measures how many years it would take a company, in theory, to pay off its leverage using the most recent quarter's earnings before interest, taxes, depreciation, and amortization (EBITDA). REITs that are investment-grade rated have to operate their businesses within the leverage limits (or *covenants*) imposed on them by their lenders and rating agencies. The largest three rating agencies in the United States are Standard & Poor's, Moody's, and Fitch. For example, a debt-to-EBITDA ratio of 4.5× implies it would take the REIT four-and-a-half years to repay its debt, assuming the most recent quarter's EBITDA is recurring. As shown in Table 4.2 in Chapter 4, REITs with investment-grade rated securities outstanding at September 30, 2019, had an average debt-to-EBITDA ratio of 5.8×, which is down from an average ratio of 7.7× at the end of 2010.

Calculating a REIT's debt-to-EBITDA sounds straightforward: divide total debt outstanding by the most recent quarter's recurring EBITDA, annualized. However, in practice, there are many adjustments that need to be made to the denominator to ensure the EBITDA is *recurring*. Many (but not all) REITs that issue investment-grade-rated securities disclose their debt-to-EBITDA ratio in the "debt analysis" pages of their quarterly supplemental information packages. A lower ratio equates to lower levels of debt and, implicitly, a more secure common dividend.

Weighted Average Cost of Capital (WACC)

Often referred to as a company's "cost of capital," the weighted average cost of capital (WACC) is the average return a company expects to pay its lenders and equity investors. WACC is calculated by proportionately weighting the cost of each of the three types of capital – debt, preferred, and common equity – as a percentage of the company's total market capitalization (defined earlier in this chapter). The formula for calculating WACC is as follows:

$$\text{WACC} = \frac{D}{TMC} \times D_c + \frac{P}{TMC} \times P_c + \frac{E}{TMC} \times E_c$$

or simply:

$$\text{WACC} = \frac{(D \times D_C) + (P \times P_c) + (E \times E_c)}{TMC}$$

where:

D is the total amount of debt outstanding
D_c is the average interest rate on total
P is the liquidation value of all preferred shares and units*
P_c is the average dividend rate on all preferred equity
E is the equity market capitalization*
E_c is the cost of common equity
TMC is the total market capitalization*

*These calculations are also discussed in Chapter 10.

Determining the cost of equity for the preceding calculation is not as easy as looking something up in the company's SEC filings or supplemental package. Technically, common stock does not have an explicit cost associated with it the way that loans and preferred equity issuances do with their respective interest rates and dividend coupon rates. One accepted method is to use the long-term (25-year) average total return for the industry, which for REITs is 10–12% (please refer to Table 2.1 in Chapter 2). To be more precise, an investor can look up the average annual returns associated with each type of REIT, based on the type of commercial property they own. (See the "REIT Data" section of Nareit's website, www.reit.com, for current and historical information.) Another method for calculating a company's cost of equity is to use the following formula:

$$E_c = \frac{\text{Current Dividend, Annualized}}{\text{Current Share Price}} + \text{Average Dividend Growth}$$

There are other methods for calculating the cost of equity, some of which are more scientific, some of which are more subjective. As long as the approach for estimating the cost of equity is consistently applied, then the relative WACCs should be meaningful for comparing across different REITs.

A higher WACC could signal a company's capital allocation is out-of-whack.

Companies with a higher WACC implicitly are riskier than companies with lower costs of capital. Before investing, be sure to understand if a company's WACC is higher than its peers because the company is newer to the public market and, as a result, perhaps has a less institutional quality balance sheet. Provided investors and analysts believe management is allocating capital wisely, a company can lower its WACC over time by refinancing maturing debt with new debt that has a lower interest rate, or by redeeming existing preferred stock by issuing new, lower-cost preferred stock, and also by increasing its common share price. Each of these tactics will lower a company's WACC, but they are only possible if management consistently executes a growth strategy that investors deem to be a good balance between risks and returns.

Alternatively, a company may have a higher WACC than its peers because its management team does not allocate capital well. A company that grows FFO by levering up its balance sheet with short-term, variable rate debt – which carries a lower interest rate than long-term debt – may fool investors for a little while; ultimately, when that company has to refinance debt at higher rates, or, more likely, if investors choose to sell their shares because they are uncomfortable with the increased leverage, the REIT's stock price will decline, further increasing the company's WACC.

Variable versus Fixed Rate Debt; Secured versus Unsecured Debt

As discussed in Chapter 9, REITs have a wide array of ways they can raise debt capital. Table 11.4 shows KKM REIT's debt schedule from its fictitious supplemental disclosure.

REITs generally have a line of credit and/or construction line(s), where the former can be either secured or unsecured by properties, and the latter is secured by the development project(s) it is funding. KKM REIT has fixed-rate debt and variable-rate debt outstanding; the interest expense on variable-rate (or *floating rate*) debt fluctuates with the benchmark rate to which it is tied – in this case, to 30-day LIBOR. (LIBOR is the London Inter-Bank Offered Rate, and will likely be replaced by the Secured Overnight Financing Rate (SOFR) or another broadly used index in the near future.) REITs that have less variable-rate debt than fixed-rate debt tend to have less risk embedded in their balance sheets because a sudden increase in benchmark interest rates would not materially affect their future interest rate payment obligations. (Conversely, if rates drop, the REIT is not able to take advantage of possibly lower debt costs, at least not without incurring early termination fees from its lender.) As such, it is helpful to show a quick comparison of a REIT's fixed versus variable interest rate debt outstanding, as shown in Figure 11.1.

TABLE 11.4 KKM REIT's Summary of Outstanding Debt

Unsecured Debt	Interest Rate	Amount Outstanding	Balloon Payment due Upon Maturity	Maturity Date
Revolving credit facility	L + 1.0%	$50,000	N/A	Mar-Yr 3
Senior unsecured notes:				
3.5% due Year 1	3.50%	$350,000	N/A	Nov-Yr 1
3.75% due Year 2	3.75%	$500,000	N/A	Jun-Yr 2
5.0% due Year 3	5.00%	$350,000	N/A	May Yr 3
3.25% due Year 5	5.00%	$500,000	N/A	Sep-Yr 5
Subtotal - Senior unsecured notes				
Unsecured bank term loans:				
2022 Maturity	L + .9%	$100,000	N/A	Sep-Yr 2
2024 Maturity	L + .75%	$150,000	N/A	Oct-Yr 4
Total unsecured debt		**$2,000,000**		
Secured Debt				
Mortgage on property A	L + 1.75%	$16,500	$15,000	Yr 1
Mortgage on property B	4.00%	$25,000	$19,000	Yr 3
Mortgage on property C	4.50%	$30,000	$15,000	Yr 4
Mortgage on property D	5.00%	$25,000	$12,500	Yr 5
Total secured debt		**$96,500**	$61,500	
Total debt outstanding	**3.71%***	**$2,096,500**		

*Weighted average interest rate for total debt outstanding, assuming 30-day LIBOR rate of 0.5% (or 50 basis points).

From the information in Table 11.4, investors can also calculate the percent of KKM's debt that is secured by assets versus unsecured (see Figure 11.2). A REIT with a greater percentage of unsecured debt is able to make more nimble assets management decisions, as its management team can sell unencumbered properties without consulting a lender like they have to do before selling assets that are collateralizing a loan.

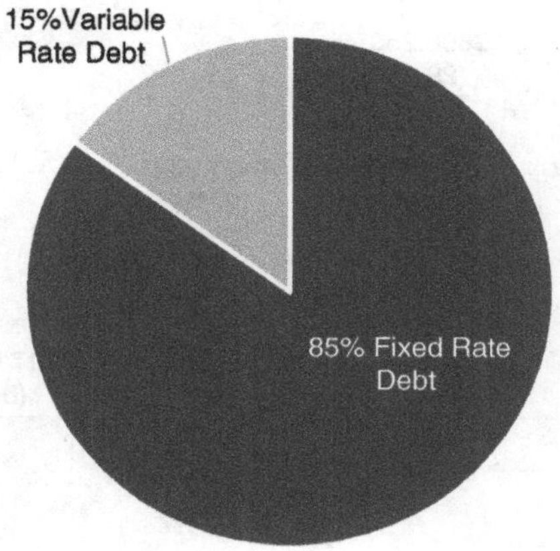

FIGURE 11.1 KKM REIT's Percent of Fixed-Rate vs. Variable Rate Debt

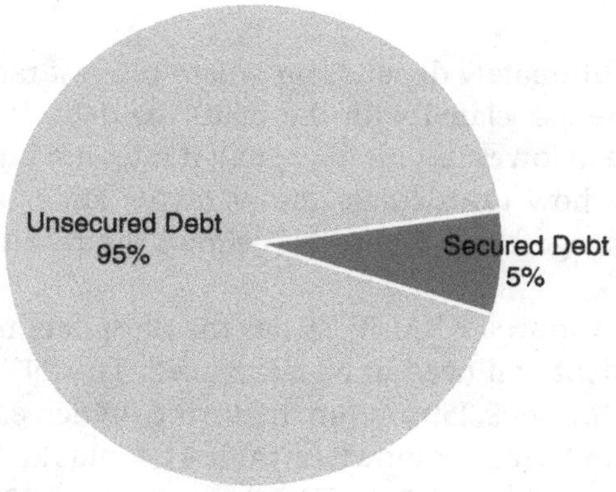

FIGURE 11.2 KKM REIT's Percent of Secured vs. Unsecured Debt

Debt Maturity Schedule

Additionally, investors can use the information in Table 11.4 to analyze KKM REIT's debt maturity ladder. By graphing the principle amounts maturing in each year, as well as any principal amortization payments scheduled, investors can quickly see if a REIT has any year(s) in which the management team will need to refinance a disproportionate amount of debt.

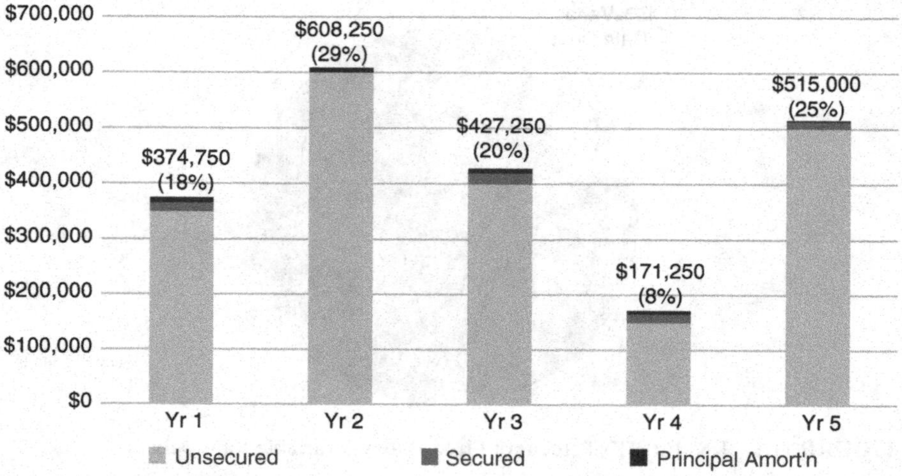

FIGURE 11.3 Debt Maturity Schedule for KKM REIT

Refinancing risk ultimately depends on where interest rates will be relative to the interest rate associated with the maturing debt. If rates are lower, a REIT may be able to lower its cost of capital; if rates are higher, the opposite. Table 11.5 shows how to calculate the principal amortizations associated with KKM's mortgages, and Figure 11.3 shows the resulting debt maturity schedule.

As Figure 11.3 shows, KKM REIT has the most debt maturing in Year 2 when 29% of its debt will need to be refinanced. The 29% number is calculated by dividing the $608,250 amount maturing (which equals $600 million of debt maturing in Year 2, as shown in Table 11.4, plus $8.25 million of principal amortization in Table 11.5) by KKM's total debt of $2,096,500 shown in Table 11.4. The average interest rate associated with those maturing loans is 3.36%, calculated as follows:

- 3.75% × $500,000 for the senior unsecured notes due Year 2
- Plus LIBOR + 0.9% (or 1.4%) × $100,000 unsecured bank term loans also due in Year 2
- Divide that sum by the total debt outstanding to arrive at an average interest rate of 3.36%

TABLE 11.5 KKM REIT's Principal Amortization Schedule

Annual Principal Amortization	Amount Outstanding	Balloon at Maturity	Total Amortization	Yrs Left	Annual Amortization	Yr 1	Yr 2	Yr 3	Yr 4	Yr 5
Mortgage on property A	$16,500	$15,000	$1,500	1	$1,500	$1,500	$0	$0	$0	$0
Mortgage on property B	$25,000	$19,000	$6,000	3	$2,000	$2,000	$2,000	$2,000	$0	$0
Mortgage on property C	$30,000	$15,000	$15,000	4	$3,750	$3,750	$3,750	$3,750	$3,750	$0
Mortgage on property D	$25,000	$12,500	$12,500	5	$2,500	$2,500	$2,500	$2,500	$2,500	$2,500
Total	$96,500	$61,500	$35,000		$9,750	$9,750	$8,250	$8,250	$6,250	$2,500

PORTFOLIO ANALYSIS

The best way to assess a REIT's portfolio – the quality and actual location of its assets relative to competing supply – is to drive the markets and see for oneself. Most investors don't have the time or may not want to allocate resources for such diligence and can, instead, use four approaches that use a company's regular disclosures to assess the relative strengths of a REIT's portfolio.

Analyze the Geographic Concentration (or Diversification) of Owned Assets

The degree to which a REIT is diversified across many geographic locations or, conversely, concentrated in strong markets can also affect its long-term performance. (Please refer also to the Real Estate Cycle analysis in Chapter 3.) Table 11.6 shows KKM REIT's geographic locations by state, as well as information about how well-leased the portfolio is, in total and by state. An investor can see the percent of square feet KKM has invested in each state (also called *market exposure* or *market penetration*), and the percent of revenues generated from each state. If the economic prospects of Delaware, for example, are expected to decline because a recent merger between the state's two largest employers is going to cause job reductions (elimination of redundant facilities between the merged companies), investors can see that KKM REIT derives 10% of its revenues from Delaware. Because any number over 3% is meaningful, investors should investigate further as to what KKM REIT owns in Delaware and whether its buildings are leased to either employer – and ultimately if they are at risk of becoming vacant in the future.

Read Local Real Estate Broker Reports on Markets

After determining the major markets in which a REIT operates, one of the first steps an investor should take is to look for current market reports from the major commercial real estate service companies. Firms such as JLL, Cushman & Wakefield, and CBRE Group provide research on major markets, and often have regional and national research reports available on their websites for free.

TABLE 11.6 KKM REIT's Geographic Diversification

Location	Total Square Feet Owned (000s)	% Leased	Rental Revenues	% of Total Rents
Alabama	8,000	94%	$33,994	10%
Colorado	9,000	92%	$38,243	12%
Delaware	7,500	93%	$31,869	10%
Florida	6,500	100%	$27,620	8%
Georgia	5,000	100%	$21,246	6%
Kentucky	7,500	97%	$31,869	10%
Maryland	2,500	90%	$10,623	3%
Michigan	2,750	82%	$11,685	4%
Missouri	5,000	100%	$21,246	6%
Pennsylvania	7,500	100%	$31,869	10%
South Carolina	5,000	90%	$21,246	6%
Texas	12,000	100%	$50,990	15%
Total	78,250	96%	$332,500	100%

Tenant Quality Metrics

Table 11.7 shows the Top 20 Tenant List from KKM REIT's supplemental information package.

The information presented here provides several ways investors can assess the quality of KKM's tenant list and associated rental revenues. This example shows that KKM REIT derives nearly 56% of its rents from its top 20 tenants. Should one of the more sizeable tenants file for bankruptcy, KKM's common shares are likely to be negatively affected, at least in the near term, until that tenant's operating future becomes clear again. (Recall from Chapter 4 that, unless a bankruptcy court allows a tenant to "reject a lease," the REIT/landlord continues to receive rent when a tenant is in bankruptcy. While a REIT may not incur a cash flow disruption from a tenant going through bankruptcy, investors may still sell the REIT's shares anyway. When a company's share price reacts negatively to news, even though that news does not affect its bottom line, this is called *headline risk*.) One way to see

TABLE 11.7 KKM REIT's Top 20 Tenant List

Tenant	Leased Square Feet (000s)	% of Annualized Rents	Weighted Average Remaining Lease Term (in years)	Tenant Credit Ratings*	Industry
Tenant 1	4,500	8.00%	15.0	BBB/Baa2/BBB	Grocery Store
Tenant 2	3,275	7.00%	15.0	AA-/Baa1/-	Fast Food
Tenant 3	3,500	6.00%	12.0	BBB/Baa2/-	Health & Fitness
Tenant 4	2,500	4.75%	5.0	—	Entertainment
Tenant 5	3,700	4.00%	7.5	—	Home Improvement
Tenant 6	2,780	3.50%	6.0	BBB-/Baa3/-	Child Care
Tenant 7	3,591	3.00%	4.2	—	Home Improvement
Tenant 8	2,870	2.75%	3.5	BBB/Baa2/BBB	Grocery Store
Tenant 9	1,998	2.50%	8.4	BBB/Baa2/BBB	Grocery Store
Tenant 10	1,850	2.25%	1.5	—	Child Care
Tenant 11	1,687	2.00%	3.5	AA-/Baa1/-	Grocery Store
Tenant 12	1,250	1.88%	4.5	BBB/Baa2/BBB	Fast Food
Tenant 13	1,400	1.75%	7.5	BBB/Baa2/BBB	Fast Food
Tenant 14	1,000	1.50%	2.5	AA-/Baa1/-	Fast Food
Tenant 15	950	1.25%	2.8	—	Fast Food
Tenant 16	925	1.00%	3.0	AA-/Baa1/-	Health & Fitness
Tenant 17	800	0.75%	3.5	—	Child Care
Tenant 18	875	0.75%	4.0	BBB/Baa2/BBB	Grocery Store
Tenant 19	765	0.50%	2.0	AA-/Baa1/-	Grocery Store
Tenant 20	425	0.43%	1.0	BBB/Baa2/BBB	Home Improvement
Subtotal Top 20 Tenants	40,641	55.55%	7.3		
All remaining tenants	34,359	44.45%	6.7		
Total/Weighted Average	75,000	100.00%	7.0		

*Investment-grade tenants are those with a credit rating of Baa3/BBB- or higher from one of the three major ratings agencies (Moody's/S&P/Fitch, respectively).

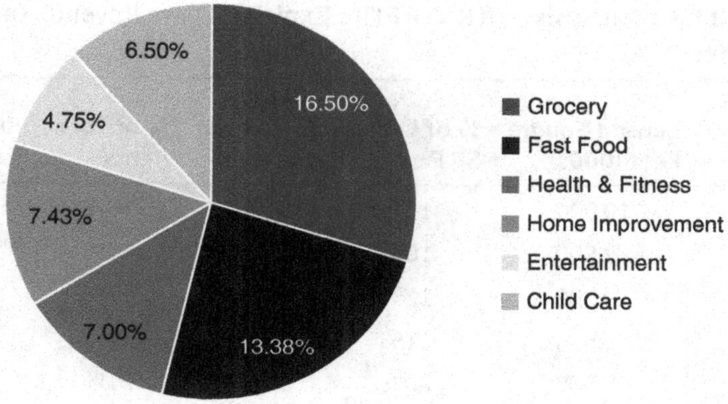

FIGURE 11.4 Analysis of KKM REIT's Expiring Lease Revenue (and/or Square Feet)

how potentially at-risk tenants are is to calculate the percentage of tenants with investment-grade ratings.

A third analysis to assess how well diversified a REIT's rental revenues may be is to calculate which industry types are generating what percent of a REIT's revenues. In Table 11.7, by adding together the two largest "slices", an investor can quickly determine that KKM REIT derives 30% of its revenues from tenants in the grocery business and fast-food chains - both fairly resilient industries. Depicting the revenues derived from industry groups in a pie graph, like Figure 11.4, is a helpful way to assess the industry concentration strengths and risks in a REIT's portfolio.

Lease Expiration Schedule

Table 11.8 shows KKM REIT's lease expiration schedule for the next five years. By charting the square feet and/or lease revenues scheduled to expire in each year, investors can assess the relative safety – or risk – of associated rental revenues. Similar to the debt maturity ladder, if a REIT has a year in which a disproportionate percent of its leased square feet or rental revenues are scheduled to expire, that year carries disproportionate operating risk to the REIT – and its shareholders – than other years. Investors should also compare the rents per square foot (PSF) scheduled to expire versus current market rents. If a REIT's expiring leases have rents that are above current market rates, there is the risk the renewing rents (assuming the tenants renew, rather than vacate) could be below current rents, in which case the REIT may generate lower future FFO and AFFO.

TABLE 11.8 Analysis of KKM REIT's Expiring Lease Revenue (and/or Square Feet)

Tenant	Leased Square Feet (000s)	% of Leased SF Expiring	Rental Revenues Expiring	% of Total Rents	Rent PSF Expiring
Year 1	10,000	13%	$50,000	15%	$5.00
Year 2	7,500	10%	$35,000	11%	$4.67
Year 3	9,000	12%	$40,000	12%	$4.44
Year 4	8,500	11%	$37,500	11%	$4.41
Year 5	15,000	20%	$70,000	21%	$4.67
Thereafter	25,000	33%	$100,000	30%	$4.00
Total	75,000	100%	$332,500	100%	$4.43

VALUATION METRICS

Valuation is a critical step in selecting which REITs to buy, hold, or sell. The following metrics provide different ways to measure a REIT's relative value versus a group of peer companies or on an absolute basis.

Price/Earnings Multiple

As was discussed at the beginning of this chapter, REITs tradeoff expected FFO per share estimates rather than EPS. Accordingly, REIT earnings multiples are expressed as FFO multiples, calculated simply as the current stock price divided by current or next year's FFO per-share estimates, depending on how forward looking the analysis. The equation to calculate price/earnings (P/E) is:

$$\text{A REIT's "P/E"} = \frac{\text{current stock price}}{\text{the current or next year's estimate of FFO per share}}$$

A lower FFO multiple may indicate a REIT is trading at a bargain price. Assume KKM REIT trades at 10.0× next year's estimate FFO, and REIT ABC with a similar portfolio of assets trades at 12.5×. If there appears to be no fundamental problem with KKM REIT's markets and operations, then its shares probably represent good value relative to REIT ABC. Alternatively,

KKM REIT may have operational, portfolio, balance sheet, or executive management problems that cause its shares to trade at a lower multiple than its peers. Looking at other metrics discussed in the chapter should help determine the answer.

PEG Ratios

Investors look at FFO multiples as a simple calculation of the relative valuation of REITs within their sectors. Although FFO multiples are helpful indicators for assessing relative value, price multiple-to-earnings growth, or PEG ratios, are a better indicator of how much an investor is paying today for a company's expected earnings growth. PEG ratios for REITs are calculated by dividing the price/FFO multiple by expected future growth in FFO. For example, if KKM REIT's FFO multiple on next year's estimated FFO is 9.5×, and its FFO per share is expected to increase 8% next year, the PEG ratio for KKM REIT is 9.5 divided by 8, or 1.2×. This can be calculated using the following equation:

$$\text{KKM REIT's PEG ratio} = \frac{\text{next year's FFO multiple}}{\text{next year's expected growth in FFO per share}}$$

Because PEG ratios isolate the growth component of value, they provide investors with a clearer understanding of how much they are paying today for future earnings. Assuming comparable risk profiles among companies, lower PEG ratios represent better relative values to investors. One caveat regarding PEG ratios is that in years when companies are expected to deliver flat or modestly negative earnings growth, PEG ratios should be calculated using a longer-term (three-to-five-year) estimate of earnings potential for each company.

Selecting Stocks Based upon FFO Multiple to FFO Growth

Basic stock analysis states that companies with higher earnings growth deserve a higher price and, therefore, a higher earnings multiple (P/E) than lower growth companies. The same is true of REIT stocks, but earnings are best analyzed by a REIT's FFO instead of GAAP earnings, as described earlier in this chapter. Table 11.9 shows 12 REITs with their current FFO multiple and the projected one-year growth for each. FFO multiples range between 12.2× and 13.8×; thus one might assume REIT 11's 12.2× multiple is cheap and a good buy. FFO Growth ranges from 6.5% to 23.9% and one

TABLE 11.9 FFO Multiple-to-FFO Growth Analysis

REIT	Projected FFO Growth	Current FFO Multiple
R1	18.24%	13.58 x
R2	12.00%	12.70 x
R3	23.90%	13.80 x
R4	17.01%	13.20 x
R5	14.87%	13.46 x
R6	12.70%	12.47 x
R7	13.12%	12.90 x
R8	16.39%	12.84 x
R9	15.31%	13.20 x
R10	21.11%	13.22 x
R11	6.50%	12.20 x
R12	13.34%	13.32 x
R13	15.37%	13.07 x

might assume REIT 3 is the best buy with the highest growth. By placing all the REITs on an Excel graph (Figure 11.5), investors can calculate a regression line and the regression equation that shows that, for each unit increase in FFO growth, the FFO multiple should be higher by 8.36%. The R^2 tells investors that FFO growth explains 65.15% of the FFO multiple – which is a large percentage and the most dominant factor affecting price.

If all other factors were equal – and the market was 100% rational – all the REITs would trade on the line. Any REIT trading below the line would be considered undervalued, so REIT 6 with 12.70% FFO growth should trade at a 12.85x FFO multiple (thus it would trade on the line) or 3% higher than its current multiple. (Take REIT 6's projected growth of 12.70% times regression equation 0.0836 + 11.79 = 12.85.) Thus, any REIT trading below the line would be a BUY (REITs 2, 6, 8, 10, and 11) and any REIT trading above the line would be a SELL (REITs 1, 5, 9, and 12), and any REIT trading on the line would be a HOLD (REITs 3, 4, and 7) all other factors being equal.

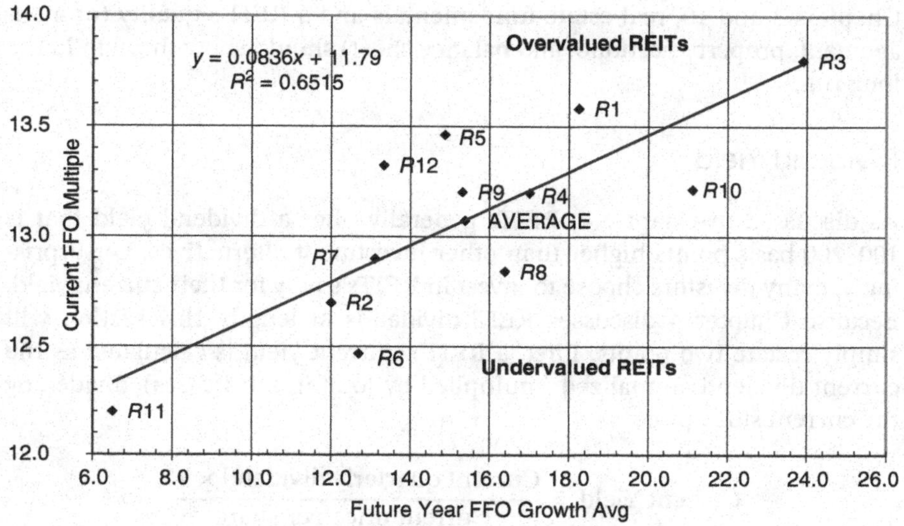

FIGURE 11.5 FFO Multiple-to-FFO Growth Regression Analysis
Source: Mueller.

However, there may be reasons for premiums or discounts. REIT 6 may be overleveraged and thus the stock price is depressed with a lower multiple because of the high debt risk. REIT 8 may have management turnover problems or an impending lawsuit that put uncertainty into the future earnings growth estimate. On the other side, REIT 1 may have a majority of properties in good markets in the growth phase of the cycle. REIT 5 may have high-quality class A properties with credit-rated tenants, thus reducing its earnings risk.

This analysis allows investors to see graphically how far away from average the any REIT's pricing is compared to its peers, as well as calculate the price premium or discount with the regression equation. Then investors can focus their analysis on the reasons for that premium or discount pricing to make better investment decisions.

FFO Multiple-to-Growth quickly identifies the pricing of growth, allowing investors to focus their fundamental analysis on the REITs they believe have the best upside potential. There is no right answer in stock selection and the market may or may not price the REIT industry, individual REIT property sectors, or companies correctly in the short term – but as discussed in

Chapters 3 and 10, real estate fundamentals and a REIT's quality (of management, property portfolio, and balance sheet) should show through in the long run.[1]

Dividend Yield

As discussed in Chapter 4, REITs generally offer a dividend yield that is 100–200 basis points higher than other investment alternatives. Unsurprisingly, many investors choose to invest in REITs solely for their current yield. Because Chapter 4 discusses REIT dividends at length, this section will simply restate two points. First, a REIT's current yield is calculated as the current dividend annualized (multiplied by four, in most cases), divided by the current stock price:

$$\text{Current Yield} = \frac{\text{Current quarterly dividend} \times 4^{\dagger}}{\text{Current price per share}}$$

Second, because many investors hold investments for several years, it is also important to understand the concept of yield on cost, which is calculated by dividing the current dividend annualized by the investor's cost basis in the REIT's stock:

$$\text{Yield on Cost} = \frac{\text{Current quarterly dividend} \times 4^{\dagger}}{\text{Shareholder's per} - \text{share cost basis}}$$

Dividend Safety

Chapter 4 addresses dividend safety, but the point bears repeating. Although the contractual nature of leases makes most property sector dividends reasonably secure, REITs have cut or suspended their dividends in times of financial crisis – both in the wake of the S&L crisis of the late 1980s/early 1990s, and more recently in response to the Global Financial Crisis of 2007–08 and, to a lesser degree thus far, in response to the COVID-19 pandemic of 2020.

Putting aside such extreme economic times, REIT dividends tend to be sustainable. By calculating a REIT's dividend payout ratio, discussed next, investors can assess how secure the dividend is, at least in the near term.

[1] *Special thanks to Glenn R. Mueller, Ph.D., for contributing the FFO Multiple-to-FFO Growth analysis.*

† *If the REIT pays a monthly dividend, multiply by 12.*

Three General Rules about Dividend Safety

1. REITs that own property types with short-term lease revenues carry more risk of cutting their dividends during a financial crisis than those with longer-term leases.
2. Dividends tend to be more at-risk in companies whose management teams incur too much leverage. A debt-to-gross asset value of 45% generally should be the absolute maximum amount of leverage (and even that level may prove to be too high, depending on the property sector).
3. REITs with dividend yields that materially exceed the industry's average tend to be companies with significantly more corporate risk and less secure dividends.

Bottom line: If a REIT's yield looks too good to be true, it probably is.

Dividend Coverage, or Payout Ratios

FFO, AFFO, and CAD payout ratios are a common means of evaluating the relative security of a company's dividend. FFO is quoted more broadly because stock analysts provide Thomson First Call, Bloomberg, and S&P Global Market Intelligence with their estimates of FFO per share for companies. Increasingly, analysts are also furnishing AFFO per-share estimates on REITs they analyze, but the practice is not yet uniform. As discussed in Chapter 4, FFO payout ratios indicate the relative ability of a REIT to meet its dividend obligation, in that, if the payout ratio is less than 1.0, the dividend is reasonably secure:

$$\text{Dividend payout ratio} = \frac{\text{current quarterly dividend}^{*} \times 4}{\text{next year's FFO}^{\dagger}\text{per} - \text{share estimate}}$$

Dividing the annualized dividend by the next year's estimate of AFFO or CAD per share is a better method for gauging dividend safety than using FFO estimates; however, investors may need to do the spadework to create their own estimates of both metrics, if stock analysts providing research on the REIT do not provide them.

---

*Note: If the REIT pays a monthly dividend, multiply the most recent dividend by 12.
†Use AFFO or CAD per-share estimates, if available, instead of FFO.

Dividend Discount Model

Investors who are interested in owning REITs primarily for dividend income should also employ the dividend discount model to evaluate whether a REIT's shares are fairly priced. The following formula will calculate the present value of a REIT's expected future dividends, using a discount rate and a reasonable expected annual growth rate for the current dividend. If the fair value for a REIT calculated using the dividend discount model is higher than the price at which the stock is trading, then the stock most likely is a good value.

$$\text{Fair stock price} = \frac{\text{Annualized dividend per share}}{\text{Discount Rate} - \text{Dividend Growth Rate}}$$

In terms of the inputs, investors can use a company's historical annualized growth rate in its dividend, which often is cited in an annual report to shareholders or company presentation posted on the company's website. Determining which discount rate, or cost of equity, to use is more difficult. In addition to the methods discussed earlier in this chapter related to WACC, some investors simply add an equity risk premium of 500 basis points to the ten-year US Treasury bond rate (the *risk-free* rate).

Dividend Discount Model Example

To illustrate the dividend discount model with a practical example, assume that KKM REIT:

- Pays a dividend of $0.25 per share per quarter.
- Has increased its annualized dividend 3%, on average, for the past five years.
- Has a cost of equity (or discount rate) of 12%.

Based on the dividend discount model, $11.11 is a fair value for KKM REIT's shares:

$$\$11.11 = (\$0.25 \times 4) \div [12\% - 3\%]$$

If KKM REIT's shares are trading below $11.11, then the stock most likely is a good investment from a valuation standpoint.

Net Asset Valuation (NAV)

Net asset value (NAV) estimates the current private market (or liquidation) value of a REIT's properties, net of other non-real estate assets and liabilities.

Investors prefer NAV per share over gross book value per share because the latter does not account for changes in the value of the underlying land on which properties are built, or the future earnings potential (and associated change in market value) of real estate assets. One way to assess if the managers of a REIT are prudent allocators of shareholder capital is to observe the investment tactics they use when their stock is trading significantly above or below NAV.

REITs whose shares trade at a premium to NAV have a cost of capital advantage and should continue buying and/or developing to grow their portfolios (assuming they issue enough common stock to maintain their prior debt ratios, discussed earlier). In contrast, if a REIT's shares are trading at a significant discount to NAV, management should shrink its portfolio by selling assets and use the proceeds to pay down debt (or redeem any callable preferred shares) or buy back the low-price stock. If the discount persists for several quarters, management should also consider buying back common stock – but only if they can do so without increasing their total debt.

Stock Price Above NAV = Green Light on Growth

Stock Price Below NAV = Red Light on Growth

REITs whose stocks trade at premiums to estimated NAV per share might have some specific reason, such as their property sector or markets may be in favor with investors. Alternatively, the premium may indicate the shares are overvalued. Conversely, if a stock is trading at a steep discount to NAV per share, then either the market is undervaluing the business, in which case investors can buy shares at an attractive sale price; or the investment community believes management is destroying shareholder value, in which case the shares are cheap for a reason and should be avoided.

Historically, REITs have traded at a modest premium to NAV per share most of the time, as the market generally prescribes some premium for liquidity and an even greater premium to REITs with management teams that have consistently added value through rigorous property management, asset allocation tactics, and prudent capital structure. That said, according to an analysis provided by S&P Global Market Intelligence, REITs traded at an average 2.8% discount to NAV at the end of 2019 (see Figure 11.6). Because NAV is one of the two main valuation metrics investors use to make buy-and-sell decisions (the other being FFO or AFFO per-share growth), the remainder of this chapter demonstrates how individuals may calculate it.

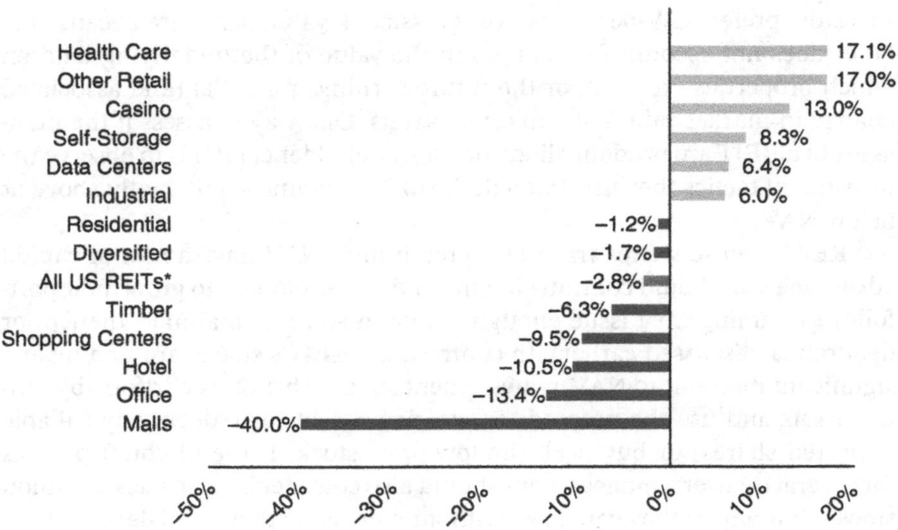

FIGURE 11.6 REIT's Average Premium (Discount) to NAV at December 31, 2019
Includes publicly traded US equity REITs that trade on the Nasdaq, NYSE, or NYSE American with market capitalizations of at least $200 million.
"Other retail" includes outlet centers, single tenant and other retail; residential includes multifamily, single-family, student housing, and manufactured homes.
* Includes two additional specialty REITs that are not reflected in a property type category.
Source: S&P Global Market Intelligence; data compiled on January 2, 2020.

Calculating NAV

Although there are several calculations involved in estimating a REIT's NAV, the basic concept is simple: estimate the current private market liquidation value of the REIT's portfolio, then add any other tangible assets, subtract all liabilities, and divide the sum by the common shares and OP units outstanding. Table 11.10 provides a simplified example for calculating NAV, after which the five major components of NAV are broken down and explained in more detail. One critical point investors should note is that private market cap rates are the *most* influential variable when calculating NAV. (Cap rates are discussed as part of Step #4.) As Table 11.10 shows, a cap rate range of 100 basis points – from 5.0% to 6.0% – equates to nearly a $5.50 per-share difference in NAV per-share values. It is important for investors to determine what they believe to be "the correct" cap rate for NAV, but also to look at a range to understand a span of values that are reasonable.

TABLE 11.10 Basic Calculation of NAV per Share

Cash NOI "run rate" for recent quarter	$10,000	$10,000	$10,000	$10,000	$10,000
x 4 to annualize	x 4	x 4	x 4	x 4	x 4
Annualized adjusted cash NOI	$40,000	$40,000	$40,000	$40,000	$40,000
x (1 + 3% annual same store growth assumption)	x 1.03	x 1.03	x 1.03	x 1.03	x 1.03
Annualized adjusted cash NOI	$41,200	$41,200	$41,200	$41,200	$41,200
÷ Cap rate	**5.00%**	**5.25%**	**5.50%**	**5.75%**	**6.00%**
Fair market value of a REIT's in-service properties	$824,000	$784,762	$749,091	$716,522	$686,667
Adjusted for:					
+ Accounts receivable, cash, and other tangible assets, net of current liabilities	1,500	1,500	1,500	1,500	1,500
+ Fair value of properties held for sale[1]	NA	NA	NA	NA	NA
+ Properties under development at costs invested to-date	20,000	20,000	20,000	20,000	20,000
– Total debt	(250,000)	(250,000)	(250,000)	(250,000)	(250,000)
– Preferred stock, at liquidation value	(150,000)	(150,000)	(150,000)	(150,000)	(150,000)
Net asset value (NAV)	$445,500	$406,262	$370,591	$338,022	$308,167
Common shares & OP units outstanding at the end of the quarter	25,000	25,000	25,000	25,000	25,000
NAV per share	$17.82	$16.25	$14.82	$13.52	$12.33

1. The NOI from assets held for sale (HFS) is included in continuing operations, so their book value does not need to be added.

Step 1: Estimating "Cash" NOI

The first step in calculating NAV is to convert a REIT's GAAP NOI, as reported in its most recent SEC filing, into its billable NOI. Note that billable (or *contractual*) NOI is often referred to as "cash" NOI. The goal of Step 1 is to isolate the cash NOI due to a REIT from its in-service portfolio. Then the cash NOI needs to be adjusted for any assets bought, sold, or placed into service during the most recent reporting period (quarter). In-service properties are ones that are not under development. Other assets, such as income from a business services TRS or properties still under construction, are valued in a later step.

Cash NOI Estimation

Estimate Cash NOI for most recently reported quarter:	**First Approach**	**Second Approach**	**Likely Source**
Total rental revenues reported for Q	$15,000	--	Income statement
– Property operating expenses for Q	(6,500)	---	Income statement
Net operating income (NOI) reported for Q	8,500	---	
± Straight-lined rent adjustment	(1,000)	--	AFFO calculation (supplemental)
Cash NOI for Q	$7,500	$7,500	

The *First Approach* represents financial results of a REIT that does not disclose cash NOI in its supplemental information package, in which case investors need to calculate it using line items from the income statement and the straight-lined rent adjustment disclosed in the reconciliation from FFO to AFFO. (Refer to Chapter 5, Leases, for a discussion of straight-lining of rents.) The *Second Approach* shows the short cut investors can take advantage of when a REIT reports cash NOI in its supplemental information package available. Note that Step #2 through Step #5 will only show one method as there are no further disclosure differences to highlight. Also, NAV cannot directly value properties that are in-service but not collecting rent (i.e., vacant properties). One of the fastest ways a REIT can grow its NAV per share is to lease-up vacant space.

Step 2: Estimating a "Quarterly Run Rate" for Cash NOI

Very few REITs provide good disclosure on what their quarterly cash NOI "run rate" is from in-service properties. Run rate cash NOI is the cash NOI calculated in Step 1, adjusted for the estimated addition (or deletion) of cash NOI in the period related to the REIT's investment activity. The following example demonstrates how to adjust a REIT's cash NOI to a run rate that can serve as the basis of the NAV calculation:

Adjustments to Cash NOI to estimate "run rate" for the in-service portfolio

	Run Rate Adjustments	
Cash NOI for Q, calculated in Step #1		$7,500
± Unaccounted NOI from:		
• Acquisitions made during Q	(A)	17
• Developments placed into service in the Q	(B)	58
– NOI from assets sold during the Q	(C), (D)	(20)
Net adjustment to cash NOI from investment activity in the Q		55
Cash NOI "run rate" for Q		$7,555

Run Rate Adjustments - note that the numbers presented are rounded:

A. The company acquired a building in the middle of the quarter. The purchase price was $2,500 and the property has a stabilized return (or "yield") of 5.5%. Accordingly, only half of the asset's NOI was included in the most recent reported quarter.
B. The company developed a building for $5,000 that has a stabilized yield on cost of 7.0%. The building was placed into service at on the 60th day of the 90-day quarter. Therefore, only one month (30 days) of NOI was in the latest quarter's NOI.
C. On the 30th day of the 90-day quarter, the company sold a low-growth asset for $3,000. The cap rate (discussed in Step #4) based on the property's cash NOI in place was 8.0%. One month of NOI from this asset was in the most recent quarter's NOI.

The table below calculates the amount of cash NOI that needs to be added to or subtracted from cash NOI to get to a run rate:

Adjustment	Total Cost	Cap Rate	Total NOI*	Qtly NOI	Months of NOI to Adjust	Adjustment to Cash NOI
A - Acquisition	$2,500	5.5%	$138	$34	+ 45/90 = ½	$17
B - Development	$5,000	7.0%	$350	$88	+ 60/90 = ⅔	$58
C - Asset sold	($3,000)	8.0%	($240)	($60)	−30/90 = (⅓)	($20)
Total estimated adjustments from investment activity in the Q						$55

D. **Held for Sale (HFS) versus Discontinued Operations.** If a company sold an asset that was held for sale (HFS) or sold an asset quickly and therefore without classifying it as being HFS, the asset's NOI is reported in the continuing operations, and needs to be adjusted out of NOI. If the REIT sells an asset that qualified for Discontinued Operations accounting, the asset's NOI will not be included in the REIT's continuing operations and does not need to be adjusted out of cash NOI. Its income will be listed as a separate line item in the income statement, and the cash proceeds will have been used to pay down the REIT's line of credit balance and will be reflected as an increase in the REIT's cash balance. Again, no adjustment needs to be made for such an asset sale.

Step 3: Annualize the Quarterly Run Rate for Cash NOI & Adjust for Same-Store Growth

The third step is to annualize the cash NOI run rate calculated in Step 2 and make a reasonable assumption about what degree these earnings will grow (or contract) over the next 12 months:

Cash NOI Run Rate for Q (Step #2) × 4	$30,220
× 2% same-store growth assumption	× 1.02
Annualized cash NOI	$30,824

Same-Store Growth Assumption. As Table 11.11 shows, each property sector exhibits certain growth or contraction during times of economic

TABLE 11.11 Historical Same-Store NOI Growth Rates for Major Property Types

	1999–2008	2009–10	2011–15	2016–3Q19
Apartments	2.4%	−2.8%	6.0%	3.4%
Industrial	2.0%	−4.4%	3.2%	4.6%
Malls	3.3%	−0.6%	3.0%	2.1%
Office	0.0%	−1.1%	1.5%	3.8%
Self-Storage	3.8%	−1.4%	8.3%	3.8%
Shopping Centers	2.3%	−2.3%	2.9%	2.2%

Source: S&P Global Market Intelligence.

expansion or decline. Investors should make a reasonable assumption, based on the historical same-store growth a company has achieved, tempered by the investors' outlook on the broader economy. Apart from pulling years' worth of same-store NOI growth data from individual companies and market cap weighting them, the fastest way to determine the correct same-store growth for a REIT is to download same-store data from S&P Global Market Intelligence.

Step 4: Calculate Fair Market Value of the In-Service Portfolio

The fourth step uses the annualized cash NOI calculated in Step 3 to estimate the fair market value of the REIT's in-service properties. As the example below shows, divide the annualized cash NOI calculated in Step 3 by an appropriate cap rate.

Annualized cash NOI (from Step #3)	$30,824
÷ Cap rate	6.00%
Fair market value of in-service properties	$513,733

Fair market value is the price a buyer would pay today for the REIT's assets, before taking into consideration the assumption of any debt, preferred shares and other liabilities the REIT has outstanding. In an actual transaction, the buyer would analyze each property and calculate the present value of expected cash NOI from the portfolio over five or ten years. A shorthand way of expressing the resulting value is to use a capitalization rate, or *cap rate*.

The cap rate is expressed as the quotient of the portfolio's annualized adjusted cash NOI divided by the purchase price a buyer is willing to pay. In the analytical world, there always is a lot of debate about which cap rate is appropriate for calculating a REIT's NAV. Although there is no "right answer," knowledge of the debate should help investors adopt one that is defensible.

Capitalization Rates. Capitalization rates (or more commonly, *cap rates*) are a measure of the expected unleveraged return on assets. Another way to think about cap rates is that they are the inverse of a P/E ratio, where "price" is the fair market value (a.k.a., purchase price) of the asset, and "earnings" are the property's cash NOI. Cap rates for the same type of property may differ vastly based on the general quality of the physical assets, as well as the quality of its locations (based on the relative strength of the markets' supply-and-demand fundamentals), and buyer or seller motivation to complete the trade.

$$\text{Cap rate} = \frac{\text{"Earnings"}}{\text{"Price"}} = \frac{\text{Property's Cash NOI}}{\text{Market value or price paid for a property}}$$

In theory, the cap rate should approximate a price at which the assets of the REIT could be sold in the direct property markets. Investors can estimate which cap rates to use for their NAV calculations by looking at the cap rates at which similar assets (or portfolios of assets) have traded recently. The national average cap rate may be 6%, while a portfolio of class A properties in top markets may trade for a 5% cap rate and class A properties in secondary markets may trade at a 5.5% cap rate.

Ultimately, however, cap rates are subjective. If a seller is motivated by some extenuating circumstance, such as the inability to refinance debt on the property that may be maturing, the seller may be willing to sell the asset below fair market value. The lower the price, the higher the cap rate. The amount of money one buyer is willing to pay for an asset may differ widely from what another buyer would pay. Differences among buyers' bids are a function of multiple factors, including divergent views on the economic outlook, or tenant relationships that a buyer possesses and the seller lacks, or differing plans to redevelop the asset over time. It is important to be aware of any "distressed seller" situation that may be affecting the cap rate at which an asset sold. Obtaining a reasonable cap rate is the key to good NAV analysis, so it is important to exclude any recent transactions that could distort current average cap rates.

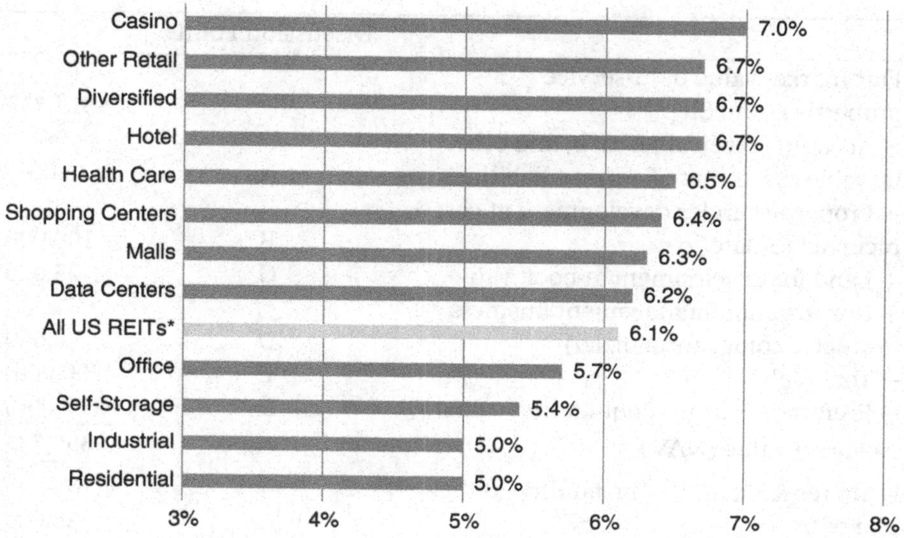

FIGURE 11.7 Median Cap Rate Estimates for Different Property Types
Includes publicly traded US equity REITs that trade on the Nasdaq, NYSE, or NYSE American with market capitalizations of at least $200 million.
"Other retail" includes outlet centers, single tenant and other retail; residential includes multifamily, single-family, student housing, and manufactured homes.
* Includes three additional specialty REITs that are not reflected in a property type category.
Source: S&P Global Market Intelligence; data compiled on January 2, 2020.

Apart from looking up comparable asset sale trades on Real Capital Analytics (rcanalytics.com) or CoStar and/or speaking about recent cap rates with a commercial real estate broker, looking up cap rate in S&P Global Market Intelligence is one of the best ways to determine a relevant range of cap rates for calculating NAV. Figure 11.7 provides median cap rate estimates at the end of 2019 for many of the property types.

Step 5: Adjust Fair Market Value for Other Investments and Financing

The final step in calculating NAV is to adjust the fair market value calculated in Step 4 to include values for assets that are not currently generating NOI, and to subtract the REIT's total debt and preferred equity outstanding:

	Discussion Points	
Fair market value of in-service properties from Step #4		$513,733
± Accounts receivable, cash, and other tangible assets, net of current liabilities	A	(15,000)
+ Properties under development at cost incurred to-date	B	100,000
+ Land for development at book value	C	25,000
+ Construction management business (5× net income, annualized)	D	4,000
– Total debt	E	(200,000)
– Preferred equity, at liquidation value	E	(75,000)
Net asset value (NAV)		$352,733
÷ Shares & OP units outstanding at the end of Q		25,000
NAV per share		$14.11
- vs. -		
Closing current stock price		$15.00
Premium (discount) to NAV per share		6.3%

Discussion Points to Step #5

A. Using information from the REIT's balance sheet, add tangible assets not accounted for as in-service properties, such as cash and restricted cash, accounts receivable, and prepaid expenses. Tangible assets do not include deferred items, such as deferred leasing and financing costs or deferred rent receivable. Note also that the *Property operating (or financing) "right-of-use" asset(s)* and, by the same token, the *Property operating lease liability(s)* are excluded from current assets and current liabilities, respectively. These line items resulted from the New Lease Accounting Standard (ASC 842) discussed in Chapter 5, and for NAV purposes are not tangible assets or liabilities.

B. If a REIT has properties under development, they most likely are not accounted for in NOI. (Some REITs place partially completed projects into service before the entire building is in-service, though most do not.) The industry values developments two ways. First, if the REIT's disclosure is adequate, investors can project the estimated cash flows from the development projects and calculate their net present value. However, this calculation is complicated and usually not materially better than the more simplified method of adding the costs incurred to-date for any development or redevelopment project, including land being used in the development. If the developments appear to be low risk in nature (e.g., they are preleased), a premium of 10% (or more) can be added.

C. Add land at book value (generally listed on the balance sheet or in a schedule in the supplement or footnotes to the financial statements in the most recent 10-Q or 10-K).

D. Value business services by adding their last four quarters of net income, and multiply the sum by five, which is the equivalent of applying a 20% cap rate. Such services are viewed as being variable, so a high cap rate typically is appropriate.

E. Next, subtract all debt outstanding and the liquidation value of any preferred stock or preferred units at the OP level. (See Chapters 4 and 9 for additional information on preferred shares.) This resulting sum is the REIT's NAV. Divide the NAV by the sum of the REIT's total common shares and OP units outstanding to calculate NAV per share.

Implied Capitalization Rate

A REIT's implied capitalization rate (implied cap rate) is analogous to an unlevered internal rate of return (IRR) in that it is the unleveraged return an investor locks-in if he or she buys the REIT at the current price. Since a cap rate is equal to the inverse of a company's earnings multiple, a REIT with a higher implied cap rate generally is considered a better relative value than a comparable REIT trading at a lower implied cap rate, especially if similar quality properties have recently been sold in similar markets at lower cap rates.

A second way to apply implied cap rates in analyzing REITs is to compare them to cap rates being paid for similar assets in the direct property markets. For example, if the implied cap rate of an industrial REIT is higher than cap rates on recent, comparable industrial assets that recently traded owners, then buying the industrial REIT's shares is the better value.

If a REIT's implied cap rate > cap rates on similar assets in the direct property market, the REIT's shares are likely an attractive value.

TABLE 11.12 Implied Cap Rate Calculation

Step # 1:	REIT's current share price	$15.00
	x Common shares & OP units outstanding	25,000
	Implied net asset value	$375,000
Step # 2:	Adjust for non-income-producing items & financing:	
	Implied net value	$375,000
	+ Preferred equity, at liquidation value	75,000
	+ Total debt	200,000
	– Construction management business	(4,000)
	– Land for development at book value	(25,000)
	– Properties under development	(100,000)
	± Accounts receivable, cash, and other tangible assets, net of current liabilities	15,000
	Implied fair market value	$536,000
Step # 3:	Divide the annualized cash NOI by the implied fair market value:	
	Annualized adjusted cash NOI	$30,824
	÷ Implied fair market value	$536,000
	Implied Cap Rate	**5.8%**

To calculate the implied cap rate at which a REIT is trading, enter the current stock price as the REIT's NAV per share and solve for the cap rate. Table 11.12 illustrates these steps, which are simply the reverse of the major steps used to calculate NAV.

Conclusion

REITs are C-corporations and can be analyzed using some of the methods employed to evaluate non-REIT C-corporations' shares. However, REITs are not like regular companies as they generate revenues from owning and leasing hard assets rather than manufacturing products to sell; as a result, investors must apply a unique set of metrics to evaluate them properly. By employing the calculations and techniques detailed in this chapter, investors can determine a REIT's operating strength, profitability, portfolio attractiveness, balance sheet flexibility, and pricing in order to evaluate their suitability for investment purposes.

Conclusion

Many investors make the mistake of buying a REIT because they "like the buildings" or know someone who works at a certain REIT. Those are easy emotional reasons that may or may not work and involve higher risk than analyzing stocks and building a diversified portfolio. This book provides the means to select REITs that have superior properties, conservative financials, and management teams with proven track records of investing capital prudently. Buying "cheap" may mean higher risk and lower long-term returns. Buying quality and future earnings growth has proven over time to be the superior investment strategy.

> Buying a REIT because you "like the buildings" may not work and involves higher risk than analyzing stocks and building a diversified portfolio.

Most investors do not have the opportunity to assess the character of REIT management teams directly. They also may not be skilled at gauging the direction in which the US economy is headed in the long run. But when the economy grows, demand for real estate has always increased. REIT investors should understand the risks and rewards inherent in the different REIT property types, their lease structures, their tenants, as well as the durability of demand for a property type in times of economic growth or contraction.

Longer leases typically generate steady, more predictable earnings, whereas earnings from shorter leases can be more volatile. REIT share prices and, by extension, P/FFO multiples (see Chapter 11) reflect this fundamental difference in earnings volatility. Table C.1 summarizes typical lease durations used by each property type and ranks the property sectors by their *betas*.

Investopedia.com, defines beta as a measure of a stock's volatility in relation to the stock market, where the stock market has a beta of 1.0. A "high-beta stock" is one that exhibits price swings greater than the market over time and has a beta above 1.0. Conversely, lower volatility stocks ("low-beta stocks") have a beta that is less than 1.0. Stocks with higher betas

TABLE C.1 Lease Length and Stock Beta by Property Type

Property Sector	Typical Lease Duration	Average of Beta	
		1 Year (2019)	3 Years (2017-2019)
Regional Mall	3–7 years	1.03	0.82
Hotel	N/A	0.83	0.76
Specialty	Varies by Company	0.56	0.59
Shopping Center	3–7 years	0.50	0.58
Industrial	3–7 years	0.57	0.56
Office	3–7 years	0.58	0.53
Diversified	Varies by Company	0.46	0.47
Multifamily	1 year	0.38	0.44
Health Care	10-plus years	0.36	0.44
Other Retail (triple-net)	10-plus years	0.33	0.42
Manufactured Home	Monthly	0.32	0.37
Self-Storage	Monthly	0.16	0.28

Source: S&P Global Market Intelligence.

carry more risk but can also deliver higher returns. Table C.1 shows the one-year and three-year average betas for REITs based on which property type they own. Sorting by the three-year average betas, from highest to lowest, all REIT sectors have a beta of less than 1.0, meaning the REIT industry trades with less volatility than the overall market. Hotel REITs, which have no leases, trade with greater volatility than those that own properties associated with longer-term leases; as expected, REITs that own more essential property types – for which demand is relatively inelastic – have the lowest betas. Investors should understand which REITs are appropriate, given their personal tolerances for risk.

WHICH REITS ARE IN YOUR PORTFOLIO?

Understanding how REIT property sectors have traded in the past is instructive for setting expectations as to how they may perform in similar trading environments in the future. Nareit provides total return data by property sector from 1994–present. However, developing a sense of *when* to buy *which* REITs is complicated by the fact that real estate fundamentals lag the economy, but REIT shares (as stocks) reflect future expectations.

Predicting REIT returns is more complicated than for other industries. The difficulty arises from the fact that commercial property is a defensive, lagging indicator for the economy. However, stock prices represent investors' present value of future earnings. As a result, REIT stock prices rarely reflect what investors physically see as they go to work, shop, or enjoy recreational activities.

Real estate fundamentals lag the general economy; by how much depends on the type of property (office, industrial, retail, etc.), the structure and average lease length in place in existing buildings, and how balanced the demand for commercial space is with the supply. There is no hard-and-fast rule to determine when the time is right to buy or sell which property sectors. Each economic cycle is different in length and magnitude and no one but God knows when it will turn. There is an adage about investing that still holds true:

People who say they can time the market are either fools or liars.

The point being: there is not a best time to buy or sell any stocks, including REIT shares. Applying the guidelines, data, and historical information, as well as the analytical tools provided in this book, will help investors choose REITs that are appropriate for their portfolios. Reading the information that is available on company websites will also yield a wealth of information that an investor and financial advisors can use to decide if a REIT fits the investor's tolerance for risk and return goals. Investors who do not like to see the prices of their stocks gyrate wildly may want to avoid investing in hotel or office REITs. If investors are more interested in buying REITs for the dividend income, they should focus on REITs that use long-term triple-net leases, such as the freestanding retail REITs, most health-care REITs, and many of the specialty REITs.

Investors should discuss the appropriateness of their investment with a licensed and informed financial advisor – preferably one who has also read this book! Ultimately, the most-sound investment strategy for investing in REITs is to go for quality: quality real estate, quality balance sheet, and quality management. Identifying REITs whose senior management teams have successfully navigated their companies through at least one recession is a good screening technique, though there are many skilled teams running newly formed REITs. Assess the strength of the balance sheet and the safety of the dividend using the simple equations provided in Chapters 4 and 11 and read about the quality of their properties in research reports and in the REIT's public information. *Educated REIT Investing* provides the tools and guidelines needed to choose the higher quality REITs, and to avoid or reduce risks. REITs are a complex but rewarding investment opportunity vehicle that allow individual investors access to large real estate properties with professional management and public market oversight that investors could never buy on their own. We hope this book has been helpful in your investing education.

FURTHER RESOURCES

Educated REIT Investing can be used in several ways. Individuals who simply want to have more informed discussions about REITs with their financial advisors should focus on Chapters 1–7. Chapters 8–11 are more technical in nature and are geared for professional money managers and analysts who may be investing other people's money in the sector. Financial advisors, depending on the quality of REIT research they have access to within their firms, may want to read every chapter, even if their firm employs a research team to analyze REITs.

REIT.com is NAREIT's website and contains news, articles, and data on REITs and the industry. Investors can download nearly all information for free, including the basics of REIT investment in real estate, lists of REIT funds, detailed company-specific information, and detailed industry research. They also put out a free daily email with current REIT industry news.

SPGlobal.com is the website for S&P Global Market Intelligence, an organization that provides the information that's essential for companies, governments, and individuals to make decisions with conviction. Previously known as SNL Financial, S&P Global Market Intelligence has provided specialized data and news on the REIT industry since 1994.

GreenStreetAdvisors.com is the website for Green Street Advisors. Founded in 1985, Green Street Advisors is the pre-eminent independent research and advisory firm concentrating on the commercial real estate industry in North America and Europe. The company is a leading provider of real estate analytics, research, and data on both the listed and private

REIT markets. Green Street also offers investment research on Real Estate Investment Trusts (REITs) and trading services to equity investors.

RASTANGER.com is the website for Robert A. Stanger & Co. (Stanger), which is well known for its flagship publication, *The Stanger Report,* a nationally recognized newsletter focused on direct participation program and PNLR investing. Stanger also publishes *The Stanger Market Pulse, The Stanger Interval Fund Report, The Stanger Digest,* and *The IPA/Stanger Monitor.*

The following two books provide deeper historical accounts of the REIT market's evolution:

- *Watch that Rat Hole: And Witness the REIT Revolution* by Kenneth D. Campbell, 2016.
- *Investing in REITs: Real Estate Investment Trusts* (4th edition) by Ralph L. Block, 2011.

APPENDIX A

REITs Listed Alphabetically by Company Name

Company Name	Ticker Symbol	Type
Acadia Realty Trust	AKR	Equity
AG Mortgage Investment Trust	MITT	mREIT
AGNC Investment Corp.	AGNC	mREIT
Agree Realty Corp.	ADC	Equity
Aimco	AIV	Equity
Alexander & Baldwin Inc.	ALEX	Equity
Alexander's Inc.	ALX	Equity
Alexandria Real Estate	ARE	Equity
Alpine Income Property Trust	PINE	Equity
American Assets Trust Inc.	AAT	Equity
American Campus Communities	ACC	Equity
American Finance Trust	AFIN	Equity
American Homes 4 Rent	AMH	Equity
American Tower Corp. (REIT)	AMT.REIT	Equity
Americold Realty Trust	COLD	Equity
Annaly Capital Management	NLY	mREIT
Anworth Mortgage Asset Corporation	ANH	mREIT
Apollo Commercial Real Estate Finance	ARI	mREIT

Company Name	Ticker Symbol	Type
Apple Hospitality REIT Inc.	APLE	Equity
Arbor Realty Trust, Inc.	ABR	mREIT
Ares Commercial Real Estate Corp.	ACRE	mREIT
Arlington Asset Investment Corp.-Class A	AI	mREIT
Armada Hoffler Properties Inc.	AHH	Equity
ARMOUR Residential REIT	ARR	mREIT
Ashford Hospitality Trust	AHT	Equity
AvalonBay Communities Inc.	AVB	Equity
Blackstone Mortgage Trust, Inc. - Class A	BXMT	mREIT
Bluerock Residential Growth	BRG	Equity
Boston Properties Inc.	BXP	Equity
Braemar Hotels & Resorts	BHR	Equity
Brandywine Realty Trust	BDN	Equity
Brixmor Property Group Inc.	BRX	Equity
Brookfield Property REIT Inc.[1]	BPYU	Equity
BRT Apartments Corp.	BRT	Equity
Camden Property Trust	CPT	Equity
Capstead Mortgage Corp.	CMO	mREIT
CareTrust REIT Inc.	CTRE	Equity
CatchMark Timber Trust Inc.	CTT	Equity
CBL & Associates Properties	CBL	Equity
Cedar Realty Trust Inc.	CDR	Equity
Chatham Lodging Trust	CLDT	Equity
Cherry Hill Mortgage Investment Corp.	CHMI	mREIT
Chimera Investment Corp.	CIM	mREIT
CIM Commercial Trust Corp.	CMCT	Equity
City Office REIT Inc.	CIO	Equity
Clipper Realty Inc.	CLPR	Equity
Colony Capital, Inc.	CLNY	Equity
Colony Credit Real Estate, Inc. - Class A	CLNC	mREIT
Columbia Property Trust	CXP	Equity
Community Healthcare Trust Inc.	CHCT	Equity
Condor Hospitality Trust Inc.	CDOR	Equity
CoreCivic Inc.	CXW	Equity
CorEnergy Infrastructure Trust	CORR	Equity
CorePoint Lodging Inc.	CPLG	Equity
CoreSite Realty Corp.	COR	Equity

Company Name	Ticker Symbol	Type
Corporate Office Properties Trust	OFC	Equity
Cousins Properties Inc.	CUZ	Equity
Crown Castle International	CCI.REIT	Equity
CubeSmart	CUBE	Equity
CyrusOne Inc.	CONE	Equity
DiamondRock Hospitality Co.	DRH	Equity
Digital Realty Trust Inc.	DLR	Equity
Diversified Healthcare Trust[2]	DHC	Equity
Douglas Emmett Inc.	DEI	Equity
Duke Realty Corp.	DRE	Equity
Dynex Capital, Inc.	DX	mREIT
Easterly Government Ppts Inc.	DEA	Equity
EastGroup Properties Inc.	EGP	Equity
Ellington Financial, Inc.	EFC	mREIT
Ellington Residential Mortgage REIT	EARN	mREIT
Empire State Realty Trust Inc.	ESRT	Equity
EPR Properties	EPR	Equity
Equinix Inc. (REIT)	EQIX.REIT	Equity
Equity Commonwealth	EQC	Equity
Equity Life Style Properties	ELS	Equity
Equity Residential	EQR	Equity
Essential Properties Realty Tr	EPRT	Equity
Essex Property Trust Inc.	ESS	Equity
Exantas Capital Corp.	XAN	mREIT
Extra Space Storage Inc.	EXR	Equity
Farmland Partners Inc.	FPI	Equity
Federal Realty Investment	FRT	Equity
First Industrial Realty Trust	FR	Equity
Four Corners Property Trust	FCPT	Equity
Franklin Street Properties	FSP	Equity
Front Yard Residential Corp.	RESI	Equity
Gaming and Leisure Properties	GLPI	Equity
GEO Group Inc.	GEO	Equity
Getty Realty Corp.	GTY	Equity
Gladstone Commercial Corp.	GOOD	Equity
Gladstone Land Corp.	LAND	Equity
Global Medical REIT	GMRE	Equity

Company Name	Ticker Symbol	Type
Global Net Lease	GNL	Equity
Global Self Storage	SELF	Equity
Granite Point Mortgage Trust	GPMT	mREIT
Great Ajax Corp.	AJX	mREIT
Hannon Armstrong Sustainable Infra. Cap'l	HASI	mREIT
Healthcare Realty Trust Inc.	HR	Equity
Healthcare Trust of America	HTA	Equity
Healthpeak Properties[3]	PEAK	Equity
Hersha Hospitality Trust	HT	Equity
Highwoods Properties Inc.	HIW	Equity
HMG/Courtland Properties Inc.	HMG	Equity
Host Hotels & Resorts	HST	Equity
Hudson Pacific Properties Inc.	HPP	Equity
Hunt Companies Finance Trust	HCFT	mREIT
Independence Realty Trust Inc.	IRT	Equity
Industrial Logistics Ppts	ILPT	Equity
Innovative Industrial Ppts Inc.	IIPR	Equity
InnSuites Hospitality Trust	IHT	Equity
Invesco Mortgage Capital	IVR	mREIT
Investors Real Estate Trust	IRET	Equity
Invitation Homes Inc.	INVH	Equity
Iron Mountain Inc.	IRM	Equity
iStar Inc.	STAR	mREIT
JBG SMITH Properties	JBGS	Equity
Jernigan Capital, Inc.	JCAP	mREIT
Kilroy Realty Corp.	KRC	Equity
Kimco Realty Corp.	KIM	Equity
Kite Realty Group Trust	KRG	Equity
KKR Real Estate Finance Trust	KREF	mREIT
Ladder Capital Corp. - Class A	LADR	mREIT
Lamar Advertising Co. (REIT)	LAMR.REIT	Equity
Lexington Realty Trust	LXP	Equity
Liberty Property Trust[4]	LPT	Equity
Life Storage Inc.	LSI	Equity
LTC Properties Inc.	LTC	Equity
MAA	MAA	Equity
Macerich Co.	MAC	Equity

Company Name	Ticker Symbol	Type
Mack-Cali Realty Corp.	CLI	Equity
Medalist Diversified REIT	MDRR	Equity
Medical Properties Trust Inc.	MPW	Equity
MFA Financial, Inc.	MFA	mREIT
Monmouth Real Estate	MNR	Equity
National Health Investors Inc.	NHI	Equity
National Retail Properties	NNN	Equity
National Storage Affiliates Trust	NSA	Equity
New Residential Investment Corp	NRZ	mREIT
New Senior Investment Group	SNR	Equity
New York Mortgage Trust	NYMT	mREIT
NexPoint Residential Trust Inc.	NXRT	Equity
Office Properties Income Trust	OPI	Equity
Omega Healthcare Investors	OHI	Equity
One Liberty Properties Inc.	OLP	Equity
Orchid Island Capital	ORC	mREIT
OUTFRONT Media Inc. (REIT)	OUT.REIT	Equity
Paramount Group Inc.	PGRE	Equity
Park Hotels & Resorts Inc.	PK	Equity
Pebblebrook Hotel Trust	PEB	Equity
Pennsylvania REIT	PEI	Equity
PennyMac Mortgage Investment Tr	PMT	mREIT
Physicians Realty Trust	DOC	Equity
Piedmont Office Realty Trust	PDM	Equity
Plymouth Industrial REIT Inc.	PLYM	Equity
Postal Realty Trust	PSTL	Equity
PotlatchDeltic Corp.	PCH	Equity
Power REIT	PW	Equity
Preferred Apartment Comm.	APTS	Equity
Prologis Inc.[4]	PLD	Equity
PS Business Parks Inc.	PSB	Equity
Public Storage	PSA	Equity
QTS Realty Trust Inc.	QTS	Equity
Rayonier Inc.	RYN	Equity
Ready Capital Corp	RC	mREIT
Realty Income Corp.	O	Equity
Redwood Trust	RWT	mREIT

Company Name	Ticker Symbol	Type
Regency Centers Corp.	REG	Equity
Retail Opportunity Investments	ROIC	Equity
Retail Properties of America	RPAI	Equity
Retail Value Inc.	RVI	Equity
Rexford Industrial Realty Inc.	REXR	Equity
RLJ Lodging Trust	RLJ	Equity
RPT Realty	RPT	Equity
Ryman Hospitality Properties	RHP	Equity
Sabra Health Care REIT	SBRA	Equity
Sachem Capital Corp.	SACH	mREIT
Safehold Inc.	SAFE	Equity
Saul Centers Inc.	BFS	Equity
SBA Communications - class A	SBAC.REIT	Equity
Seritage Growth Properties	SRG	Equity
Service Properties Trust[5]	SVC	Equity
Simon Property Group	SPG	Equity
SITE Centers Corp.	SITC	Equity
SL Green Realty Corp.	SLG	Equity
Sotherly Hotels Inc.	SOHO	Equity
Spirit Realty Capital Inc.	SRC	Equity
STAG Industrial Inc.	STAG	Equity
Starwood Property Trust	STWD	mREIT
STORE Capital Corp.	STOR	Equity
Summit Hotel Properties Inc.	INN	Equity
Sun Communities Inc.	SUI	Equity
Sunstone Hotel Investors Inc.	SHO	Equity
Tanger Factory Outlet Centers	SKT	Equity
Taubman Centers Inc.	TCO	Equity
Terreno Realty Corp.	TRNO	Equity
TPG RE Finance Trust	TRTX	mREIT
Tremont Mortgage Trust	TRMT	mREIT
Two Harbors Investment Corp.	TWO	mREIT
UDR Inc.	UDR	Equity
UMH Properties Inc.	UMH	Equity
Uniti Group Inc.	UNIT	Equity
Universal Health Realty Trust	UHT	Equity
Urban Edge Properties	UE	Equity

Company Name	Ticker Symbol	Type
Urstadt Biddle Properties - class A	UBA	Equity
Ventas Inc.	VTR	Equity
VEREIT Inc.[6]	VER	Equity
VICI Properties Inc.	VICI	Equity
Vornado Realty Trust	VNO	Equity
W. P. Carey Inc.	WPC	Equity
Washington Prime Group Inc.	WPG	Equity
Washington REIT	WRE	Equity
Weingarten Realty Investors	WRI	Equity
Welltower Inc.	WELL	Equity
Western Asset Mortage Cap'l Corp.	WMC	mREIT
Weyerhaeuser Co.	WY	Equity
Wheeler REIT Inc.	WHLR	Equity
Whitestone REIT	WSR	Equity
Xenia Hotels & Resorts Inc.	XHR	Equity

[1] In March 2020, Brookfield Property REIT changed its ticker symbol from BPR to BPYU.

[2] During 2019, Diversified Healthcare Trust (NASDAQ: DHC) changed its name and ticker symbol from Senior Housing Properties Trust (NASDAQ: SNH).

[3] During 2019, Healthpeak Properties (NYSE: PEAK) changed its name and ticker symbol from HCP, Inc. (NYSE: HCP).

[4] In the first quarter of 2020, Prologis (PLD) acquired Liberty Property Trust (LPT).

[5] During 2019, Service Properties Trust (NASDAQ: SVC) changed its name and ticker symbol from Hospitalities Properties Trust (NASDAQ: HPT).

[6] Former name: American Realty Capital Properties (NYSE: ARCP).

APPENDIX B

REITs Listed Alphabetically by Ticker Symbol

Ticker Symbol	Company Name	Type
AAT	American Assets Trust Inc.	Equity
ABR	Arbor Realty Trust, Inc.	mREIT
ACC	American Campus Communities	Equity
ACRE	Ares Commercial Real Estate Corp.	mREIT
ADC	Agree Realty Corp.	Equity
AFIN	American Finance Trust	Equity
AGNC	AGNC Investment Corp.	mREIT
AHH	Armada Hoffler Properties Inc.	Equity
AHT	Ashford Hospitality Trust	Equity
AI	Arlington Asset Investment Corp.-Class A	mREIT
AIV	Aimco	Equity
AJX	Great Ajax Corp.	mREIT
AKR	Acadia Realty Trust	Equity
ALEX	Alexander & Baldwin Inc.	Equity
ALX	Alexander's Inc.	Equity

Ticker Symbol	Company Name	Type
AMH	American Homes 4 Rent	Equity
AMT.REIT	American Tower Corp. (REIT)	Equity
ANH	Anworth Mortgage Asset Corporation	mREIT
APLE	Apple Hospitality REIT Inc.	Equity
APTS	Preferred Apartment Comm.	Equity
ARE	Alexandria Real Estate	Equity
ARI	Apollo Commercial Real Estate Finance	mREIT
ARR	ARMOUR Residential REIT	mREIT
AVB	AvalonBay Communities Inc.	Equity
BDN	Brandywine Realty Trust	Equity
BFS	Saul Centers Inc.	Equity
BHR	Braemar Hotels & Resorts	Equity
BPYU[1]	Brookfield Property REIT Inc.	Equity
BRG	Bluerock Residential Growth	Equity
BRT	BRT Apartments Corp.	Equity
BRX	Brixmor Property Group Inc.	Equity
BXMT	Blackstone Mortgage Trust, Inc - Class A	mREIT
BXP	Boston Properties Inc.	Equity
CBL	CBL & Associates Properties	Equity
CCI.REIT	Crown Castle International	Equity
CDOR	Condor Hospitality Trust Inc.	Equity
CDR	Cedar Realty Trust Inc.	Equity
CHCT	Community Healthcare Trust Inc.	Equity
CHMI	Cherry Hill Mortgage Investment Corp.	mREIT
CIM	Chimera Investment Corp.	mREIT
CIO	City Office REIT Inc.	Equity
CLDT	Chatham Lodging Trust	Equity
CLI	Mack-Cali Realty Corp.	Equity
CLNC	Colony Credit Real Estate, Inc. - Class A	mREIT
CLNY	Colony Capital, Inc.	Equity
CLPR	Clipper Realty Inc.	Equity
CMCT	CIM Commercial Trust Corp.	Equity
CMO	Capstead Mortgage Corp	mREIT
COLD	Americold Realty Trust	Equity
CONE	CyrusOne Inc.	Equity
COR	CoreSite Realty Corp.	Equity
CORR	CorEnergy Infrastructure Trust	Equity

Ticker Symbol	Company Name	Type
CPLG	CorePoint Lodging Inc.	Equity
CPT	Camden Property Trust	Equity
CTRE	CareTrust REIT Inc.	Equity
CTT	CatchMark Timber Trust Inc.	Equity
CUBE	CubeSmart	Equity
CUZ	Cousins Properties Inc.	Equity
CXP	Columbia Property Trust	Equity
CXW	CoreCivic Inc.	Equity
DEA	Easterly Government Ppts Inc.	Equity
DEI	Douglas Emmett Inc.	Equity
DHC[2]	Diversified Health-care Trust	Equity
DLR	Digital Realty Trust Inc.	Equity
DOC	Physicians Realty Trust	Equity
DRE	Duke Realty Corp.	Equity
DRH	DiamondRock Hospitality Co.	Equity
DX	Dynex Capital, Inc.	mREIT
EARN	Ellington Residential Mortgage REIT	mREIT
EFC	Ellington Financial, Inc.	mREIT
EGP	EastGroup Properties Inc.	Equity
ELS	Equity LifeStyle Properties	Equity
EPR	EPR Properties	Equity
EPRT	Essential Properties Realty Tr	Equity
EQC	Equity Commonwealth	Equity
EQIX.REIT	Equinix Inc. (REIT)	Equity
EQR	Equity Residential	Equity
ESRT	Empire State Realty Trust Inc.	Equity
ESS	Essex Property Trust Inc.	Equity
EXR	Extra Space Storage Inc.	Equity
FCPT	Four Corners Property Trust	Equity
FPI	Farmland Partners Inc.	Equity
FR	First Industrial Realty Trust	Equity
FRT	Federal Realty Investment	Equity
FSP	Franklin Street Properties	Equity
GEO	GEO Group Inc.	Equity
GLPI	Gaming and Leisure Properties	Equity
GMRE	Global Medical REIT	Equity
GNL	Global Net Lease	Equity
GOOD	Gladstone Commercial Corp.	Equity

Ticker Symbol	Company Name	Type
GPMT	Granite Point Mortgage Trust	mREIT
GTY	Getty Realty Corp.	Equity
HASI	Hannon Armstrong Sustainable Infra. Cap'l	mREIT
HCFT	Hunt Companies Finance Trust	mREIT
HIW	Highwoods Properties Inc.	Equity
HMG	HMG/Courtland Properties Inc.	Equity
HPP	Hudson Pacific Properties Inc.	Equity
HR	Healthcare Realty Trust Inc.	Equity
HST	Host Hotels & Resorts	Equity
HT	Hersha Hospitality Trust	Equity
HTA	Healthcare Trust of America	Equity
IHT	InnSuites Hospitality Trust	Equity
IIPR	Innovative Industrial Ppts Inc.	Equity
ILPT	Industrial Logistics Ppts	Equity
INN	Summit Hotel Properties Inc.	Equity
INVH	Invitation Homes Inc.	Equity
IRET	Investors Real Estate Trust	Equity
IRM	Iron Mountain Inc.	Equity
IRT	Independence Realty Trust Inc.	Equity
IVR	Invesco Mortgage Capital	mREIT
JBGS	JBG SMITH Properties	Equity
JCAP	Jernigan Capital, Inc.	mREIT
KIM	Kimco Realty Corp.	Equity
KRC	Kilroy Realty Corp.	Equity
KREF	KKR Real Estate Finance Trust	mREIT
KRG	Kite Realty Group Trust	Equity
LADR	Ladder Capital Corp. - Class A	mREIT
LAMR.REIT	Lamar Advertising Co. (REIT)	Equity
LAND	Gladstone Land Corp.	Equity
LPT[3]	Liberty Property Trust	Equity
LSI	Life Storage Inc.	Equity
LTC	LTC Properties Inc.	Equity
LXP	Lexington Realty Trust	Equity
MAA	MAA	Equity
MAC	Macerich Co.	Equity
MDRR	Medalist Diversified REIT	Equity
MFA	MFA Financial, Inc.	mREIT
MITT	AG Mortgage Investment Trust	mREIT

Ticker Symbol	Company Name	Type
MNR	Monmouth Real Estate	Equity
MPW	Medical Properties Trust Inc.	Equity
NHI	National Health Investors Inc.	Equity
NLY	Annaly Capital Management	mREIT
NNN	National Retail Properties	Equity
NRZ	New Residential Investment Corp.	mREIT
NSA	National Storage Affiliates Trust	Equity
NXRT	NexPoint Residential Trust Inc.	Equity
NYMT	New York Mortgage Trust	mREIT
O	Realty Income Corp.	Equity
OFC	Corporate Office Properties Trust	Equity
OHI	Omega Healthcare Investors	Equity
OLP	One Liberty Properties Inc.	Equity
OPI	Office Properties Income Trust	Equity
ORC	Orchid Island Capital	mREIT
OUT.REIT	OUTFRONT Media Inc. (REIT)	Equity
PCH	PotlatchDeltic Corp.	Equity
PDM	Piedmont Office Realty Trust	Equity
PEAK[4]	Healthpeak Properties	Equity
PEB	Pebblebrook Hotel Trust	Equity
PEI	Pennsylvania REIT	Equity
PGRE	Paramount Group Inc.	Equity
PINE	Alpine Income Property Trust	Equity
PK	Park Hotels & Resorts Inc.	Equity
PLD[3]	Prologis Inc.	Equity
PLYM	Plymouth Industrial REIT Inc.	Equity
PMT	PennyMac Mortgage Investment Tr	mREIT
PSA	Public Storage	Equity
PSB	PS Business Parks Inc.	Equity
PSTL	Postal Realty Trust	Equity
PW	Power REIT	Equity
QTS	QTS Realty Trust Inc.	Equity
RC	Ready Capital Corp.	mREIT
REG	Regency Centers Corp.	Equity
RESI	Front Yard Residential Corp.	Equity
REXR	Rexford Industrial Realty Inc.	Equity
RHP	Ryman Hospitality Properties	Equity
RLJ	RLJ Lodging Trust	Equity

Ticker Symbol	Company Name	Type
ROIC	Retail Opportunity Investments	Equity
RPAI	Retail Properties of America	Equity
RPT	RPT Realty	Equity
RVI	Retail Value Inc.	Equity
RWT	Redwood Trust	mREIT
RYN	Rayonier Inc.	Equity
SACH	Sachem Capital Corp.	mREIT
SAFE	Safehold Inc.	Equity
SBAC.REIT	SBA Communications - class A	Equity
SBRA	Sabra Health Care REIT	Equity
SELF	Global Self Storage	Equity
SHO	Sunstone Hotel Investors Inc.	Equity
SITC	SITE Centers Corp.	Equity
SKT	Tanger Factory Outlet Centers	Equity
SLG	SL Green Realty Corp.	Equity
SNR	New Senior Investment Group	Equity
SOHO	Sotherly Hotels Inc.	Equity
SPG	Simon Property Group	Equity
SRC	Spirit Realty Capital Inc.	Equity
SRG	Seritage Growth Properties	Equity
STAG	STAG Industrial Inc.	Equity
STAR	iStar Inc.	mREIT
STOR	STORE Capital Corp.	Equity
STWD	Starwood Property Trust	mREIT
SUI	Sun Communities Inc.	Equity
SVC[5]	Service Properties Trust	Equity
TCO	Taubman Centers Inc.	Equity
TRMT	Tremont Mortgage Trust	mREIT
TRNO	Terreno Realty Corp.	Equity
TRTX	TPG RE Finance Trust	mREIT
TWO	Two Harbors Investment Corp.	mREIT
UBA	Urstadt Biddle Properties Inc.	Equity
UDR	UDR Inc.	Equity
UE	Urban Edge Properties	Equity
UHT	Universal Health Realty Trust	Equity
UMH	UMH Properties Inc.	Equity
UNIT	Uniti Group Inc.	Equity
VER[6]	VEREIT Inc.	Equity

Ticker Symbol	Company Name	Type
VICI	VICI Properties Inc.	Equity
VNO	Vornado Realty Trust	Equity
VTR	Ventas Inc.	Equity
WELL	Welltower Inc.	Equity
WHLR	Wheeler REIT Inc.	Equity
WMC	Western Asset Mortage Cap'l Corp.	mREIT
WPC	W. P. Carey Inc.	Equity
WPG	Washington Prime Group Inc.	Equity
WRE	Washington REIT	Equity
WRI	Weingarten Realty Investors	Equity
WSR	Whitestone REIT	Equity
WY	Weyerhaeuser Co.	Equity
XAN	Exantas Capital Corp.	mREIT
XHR	Xenia Hotels & Resorts Inc.	Equity

[1] In March 2020, Brookfield Property REIT changed its ticker symbol from BPR to BPYU.
[2] During 2019, Diversified Healthcare Trust (NASDAQ: DHC) changed its name and ticker symbol from Senior Housing Properties Trust (NASDAQ: SNH).
[3] In the first quarter of 2020, Prologis (PLD) acquired Liberty Property Trust (LPT).
[4] During 2019, Healthpeak Properties (NYSE: PEAK) changed its name and ticker symbol from HCP, Inc. (NYSE: HCP).
[5] During 2019, Service Properties Trust (NASDAQ: SVC) changed its name and ticker symbol from Hospitalities Properties Trust (NASDAQ: HPT).
[6] Former name: American Realty Capital Properties (NYSE: ARCP)

APPENDIX C

REITs by Sector

TABLE C.1 Diversified REITs

Company Name	Ticker Symbol	Headquarters City, State	Website Address
Alexander & Baldwin	ALEX	Honolulu, HI	www.alexanderbaldwin.com
Alexander's Inc.	ALX	Paramus, NJ	www.alx-inc.com
American Assets Trust	AAT	San Diego, CA	www.americanassetstrust.com
Armada Hoffler Properties Inc.	AHH	Virginia Beach, VA	www.armadahoffler.com
Colony Capital, Inc.	CLNY	Los Angeles, CA	www.clny.com
Gladstone Commercial	GOOD	McLean, VA	www.GladstoneCommercial.com
Global Net Lease	GNL	New York, NY	www.globalnetlease.com
HMG/Courtland Properties Inc.	HMG	Coconut Grove, FL	www.hmgcourtland.com
JBG SMITH Properties	JBGS	Bethesda, MD	www.jbgsmith.com
Lexington Realty Trust	LXP	New York, NY	www.lxp.com
Mack-Cali Realty Corp.	CLI	Jersey City, NJ	www.mack-cali.com

TABLE C.1 *(continued)*

Company Name	Ticker Symbol	Headquarters City, State	Website Address
Medalist Diversified REIT	MDRR	Richmond, VA	www.medalistreit.com
One Liberty Properties	OLP	Great Neck, NY	www.onelibertyproperties.com
VEREIT Inc.[a]	VER	Phoenix, AZ	www.vereit.com
Vornado Realty Trust	VNO	New York, NY	www.vno.com
W. P. Carey Inc.	WPC	New York, NY	www.wpcarey.com
Washington REIT	WRE	Washington, DC	www.washreit.com
Whitestone REIT	WSR	Houston, TX	www.whitestonereit.com

[a]Former name: American Realty Capital Properties (NYSE: ARCP).
Sources: Nareit, S&P Global Market Intelligence.

TABLE C.2 Specialty REITs

Company Name	Ticker Symbol	Nareit Sub-Property Type	Headquarters City, State	Website Address
CoreCivic Inc.	CXW	Prison	Nashville, TN	www.corecivic.com
EPR Properties	EPR	Diversified	Kansas City, MO	www.eprkc.com
Farmland Partners	FPI	Land	Denver, CO	www.farmlandpartners.com
Gaming and Leisure Properties	GLPI	Casino	Wyomissing, PA	www.glpropinc.com
GEO Group Inc.	GEO	Prison	Boca Raton, FL	www.geogroup.com
Gladstone Land Corp.	LAND	Land	McLean, VA	www.gladstonefarms.com
Iron Mountain Inc.	IRM	Specialty	Boston, MA	www.ironmountain.com
Lamar Advertising Co. (REIT)	LAMR.REIT	Advertising	Baton Rouge, LA	www.lamar.com
OUTFRONT Media Inc. (REIT)	OUT.REIT	Advertising	New York, NY	www.outfrontmedia.com
Safehold Inc.	SAFE	Diversified	New York, NY	www.safeholdinc.com
VICI Properties Inc.	VICI	Casino	New York, NY	www.viciproperties.com

Sources: Nareit, S&P Global Market Intelligence.

TABLE C.3 Data Center REITs

Company Name	Ticker Symbol	Headquarters City, State	Website Address
CoreSite Realty Corp.	COR	Denver, CO	www.CoreSite.com
CyrusOne Inc.	CONE	Dallas, TX	www.cyrusone.com
Digital Realty Trust Inc.	DLR	San Francisco, CA	www.digitalrealty.com
Equinix Inc. (REIT)	EQIX.REIT	Redwood City, CA	www.equinix.com
QTS Realty Trust Inc.	QTS	Overland Park, KS	www.qtsdatacenters.com

Sources: Nareit, S&P Global Market Intelligence.

TABLE C.4 Infrastructure REITs

Company Name	Ticker Symbol	Headquarters City, State	Website Address
American Tower Corp. (REIT)	AMT.REIT	Boston, MA	www.americantower.com
CorEnergy Infrastructure Trust	CORR	Kansas City, MO	corenergy.reit
Crown Castle Intl. (REIT)	CCI.REIT	Houston, TX	www.crowncastle.com
Power REIT	PW	Old Bethpage, NY	www.pwreit.com
SBA Communications Corp (REIT)	SBAC.REIT	Boca Raton, FL	www.sbasite.com
Uniti Group Inc.	UNIT	Little Rock, AR	www.uniti.com

Sources: Nareit, S&P Global Market Intelligence.

TABLE C.5 Timber REITs

Company Name	Ticker Symbol	Headquarters City, State	Website Address
CatchMark Timber Trust Inc.	CTT	Atlanta, GA	www.catchmark.com
PotlatchDeltic Corp.	PCH	Spokane, WA	www.potlatchdeltic.com
Rayonier Inc.	RYN	Yulee, FL	www.rayonier.com
Weyerhaeuser Co.	WY	Seattle, WA	www.weyerhaeuser.com

Sources: Nareit, S&P Global Market Intelligence.

TABLE C.6 Health Care REITs

Company Name	Ticker Symbol	Headquarters City, State	Website Address
CareTrust REIT Inc.	CTRE	San Clemente, CA	www.caretrustreit.com
Community Healthcare Trust Inc	CHCT	Franklin, TN	www.chct.reit
Diversified Healthcare[a]	DHC	Newton, MA	www.dhcreit.com
Global Medical REIT	GMRE	Bethesda, MD	www.globalmedicalreit.com
Healthcare Realty Trust Inc.	HR	Nashville, TN	www.healthcarerealty.com
Healthcare Trust of America	HTA	Scottsdale, AZ	www.htareit.com
Healthpeak Properties [b]	PEAK	Irvine, CA	www.healthpeak.com
LTC Properties Inc.	LTC	Westlake Village, CA	www.LTCreit.com
Medical Properties Trust Inc.	MPW	Birmingham, AL	www.medicalpropertiestrust.com
National Health Investors Inc.	NHI	Murfreesboro, TN	www.nhireit.com
New Senior Investment Group	SNR	New York, NY	www.newseniorinv.com
Omega Healthcare Investors	OHI	Hunt Valley, MD	www.omegahealthcare.com
Physicians Realty Trust	DOC	Milwaukee, WI	www.docreit.com
Sabra Health Care REIT	SBRA	Irvine, CA	www.sabrahealth.com
Universal Health Realty Trust	UHT	King of Prussia, PA	www.uhrit.com
Ventas Inc.	VTR	Chicago, IL	www.ventasreit.com
Welltower Inc.	WELL	Toledo, OH	www.welltower.com

[a]During 2019, Diversidied Healthcare Trust (NASDAQ: DHC) changed its name and ticker symbol from Senior Housing Properties Trust (NASDAQ: SNH).

[b]During 2019, Healthpeak Properties (NYSE: PEAK) changed its name and ticker symbol from HCP, Inc. (NYSE: HCP).

Sources: Nareit, S&P Global Market Intelligence.

TABLE C.7 Industrial REITs

Company Name	Ticker Symbol	Headquarters City, State	Website Address
Americold Realty Trust	COLD	Atlanta, GA	www.americold.com
Duke Realty Corp.	DRE	Indianapolis, IN	www.dukerealty.com
EastGroup Properties Inc.	EGP	Ridgeland, MS	www.eastgroup.net
First Industrial Realty Trust	FR	Chicago, IL	www.firstindustrial.com
Industrial Logistics Ppts	ILPT	Newton, MA	www.ilptreit.com
Innovative Industrial Ppts Inc.	IIPR	Park City, UT	www.innovativeindustrialproperties.com
Liberty Property Trust[a]	LPT	Wayne, PA	www.libertyproperty.com
Monmouth Real Estate	MNR	Holmdel, NJ	www.mreic.reit
Plymouth Industrial REIT Inc.	PLYM	Boston, MA	www.plymouthreit.com
Prologis Inc.[a]	PLD	San Francisco, CA	www.prologis.com
PS Business Parks Inc.	PSB	Glendale, CA	www.psbusinessparks.com
Rexford Industrial Realty Inc.	REXR	Los Angeles, CA	www.rexfordindustrial.com
STAG Industrial Inc.	STAG	Boston, MA	www.stagindustrial.com
Terreno Realty Corp.	TRNO	San Francisco, CA	www.terreno.com

[a]In the first quarter of 2020, Prologis, Inc. acquired Liberty Property Trust.
Sources: Nareit, S&P Global Market Intelligence.

TABLE C.8 Lodging/Resort REITs

Company Name	Ticker Symbol	Nareit Sub-Property Type	Headquarters City, State	Website Address
Apple Hospitality REIT	APLE	Hotel	Richmond, VA	www.applehospitalityreit.com
Ashford Hospitality Trust	AHT	Full-Service	Dallas, TX	www.ahtreit.com
Braemar Hotels & Resorts	BHR	Hotel	Dallas, TX	www.bhrreit.com
Chatham Lodging Trust	CLDT	Hotel	West Palm Beach, FL	www.chathamlodgingtrust.com
Condor Hospitality Trust	CDOR	Limited-Service	Bethesda, MD	www.condorhospitality.com
CorePoint Lodging Inc.	CPLG	Limited-Service	Irving, TX	www.corepoint.com
DiamondRock Hospitality Co.	DRH	Hotel	Bethesda, MD	www.drhc.com
Hersha Hospitality Trust	HT	Limited-Service	Harrisburg, PA	www.hersha.com
Host Hotels & Resorts	HST	Full-Service	Bethesda, MD	www.hosthotels.com
InnSuites Hospitality Trust	IHT	Full-Service	Phoenix, AZ	www.innsuitestrust.com
Park Hotels & Resorts Inc.	PK	Hotel	Tysons, VA	www.pkhotelsandresorts.com
Pebblebrook Hotel Trust	PEB	Hotel	Bethesda, MD	www.pebblebrookhotels.com
RLJ Lodging Trust	RLJ	Full-Service	Bethesda, MD	www.rljlodgingtrust.com
Ryman Hospitality Properties	RHP	Full-Service	Nashville, TN	www.rymanhp.com
Service Properties Trust[a]	SVC	Limited-Service	Newton, MA	www.svcreit.com
Sotherly Hotels Inc.	SOHO	Full-Service	Williamsburg, VA	www.sotherlyhotels.com
Summit Hotel Properties Inc.	INN	Limited-Service	Austin, TX	www.shpreit.com
Sunstone Hotel Investors Inc.	SHO	Full-Service	Irvine, CA	www.sunstonehotels.com
Xenia Hotels & Resorts Inc.	XHR	Hotel	Orlando, FL	www.xeniareit.com

[a]During 2019, Service Properties Trust (NASDAQ: SVC) changed its name and ticker symbol from Hospitalities Properties Trust (NASDAQ: HPT).

Sources: Nareit, S&P Global Market Intelligence.

TABLE C.9 Residential mREITs

Company Name	Ticker Symbol	Headquarters City, State	Website Address
AG Mortgage Investment Trust	MITT	New York, NY	www.agmortgageinvestmenttrust.com
AGNC Investment Corp.	AGNC	Bethesda, MA	agnc.com
Annaly Capital Management	NLY	New York, NY	www.annaly.com
Anworth Mortgage Asset Corporation	ANH	Santa Monica, CA	www.anworth.com
Arlington Asset Investment-Class A	AI	McLean, VA	www.arlingtonasset.com
ARMOUR Residential REIT	ARR	Vero Beach, FL	www.armourreit.com
Capstead Mortgage	CMO	Dallas, TX	www.capstead.com
Cherry Hill Mortgage Investment Corp.	CHMI	Farmingdale, NJ	www.chmireit.com
Chimera Investment Corp.	CIM	New York, NY	www.chimerareit.com
Dynex Capital, Inc.	DX	Glen Allen, VA	www.dynexcapital.com
Ellington Financial	EFC	Old Greenwich, CT	www.ellingtonfinancial.com
Ellington Residential Mortgage REIT	EARN	Old Greenwich, CT	www.earnreit.com
Great Ajax Corp.	AJX	Beaverton, OR	www.greatajax.com
Hunt Companies Finance Trust	HCFT	New York, NY	huntcompaniesfinancetrust.com
Invesco Mortgage Capital	IVR	Atlanta, GA	www.invescomortgagecapital.com
MFA Financial, Inc.	MFA	New York, NY	www.mfafinancial.com
New Residential Investment Corp.	NRZ	New York, NY	www.newresi.com
New York Mortgage Trust	NYMT	New York, NY	www.nymtrust.com
Orchid Island Capital	ORC	Vero Beach, FL	www.orchidislandcapital.com
PennyMac Mortgage Investment Tr	PMT	Westlake Village, CA	www.pennymacmortgage investmenttrust.com
Ready Capital Corp.	RC	New York, NY	www.sutherlandam.com
Redwood Trust	RWT	Mill Valley, CA	www.redwoodtrust.com
Two Harbors Investment Corp.	TWO	New York, NY	twoharborsinvestment.com
Western Asset Mortage Cap'l Corp.	WMC	Los Angeles, CA	www.westernassetmcc.com

Sources: Nareit, S&P Global Market Intelligence.

TABLE C.10 Commercial mREITs

Company Name	Ticker Symbol	Headquarters City, State	Website Address
Apollo Commercial Real Estate Finance	ARI	New York, NY	www.apolloreit.com
Arbor Realty Trust Inc.	ABR	Uniondale, NY	arbor.com
Ares Commercial Real Estate Corp.	ACRE	New York, NY	www.arescre.com
Blackstone Mortgage Trust Inc - Class A	BXMT	New York, NY	www.blackstonemortgagetrust.com
Colony Credit Real Estate, Inc. - Class A	CLNC	Los Angeles, CA	www.clncredit.com
Exantas Capital Corp.	XAN	New York, NY	www.exantas.com
Granite Point Mortgage Trust	GPMT	New York, NY	www.gpmtreit.com
Hannon Armstrong Sustainable Infra. Cap'l	HASI	Annapolis, MD	www.hannonarmstrong.com
iStar Inc.	STAR	New York, NY	www.istar.com
Jernigan Capital Inc.	JCAP	Memphis, TN	jernigancapital.com
KKR Real Estate Finance Trust	KREF	New York, NY	www.kkrreit.com
Ladder Capital Corp. - Class A	LADR	New York, NY	www.laddercapital.com
Sachem Capital Corp.	SACH	Branford, CT	www.sachemcapitalcorp.com
Starwood Property Trust	STWD	Greenwich, CT	www.starwoodpropertytrust.com
TPG RE Finance Trust	TRTX	New York, NY	www.tpgrefinance.com
Tremont Mortgage Trust	TRMT	Newton, MA	www.trmtreit.com

Sources: Nareit, S&P Global Market Intelligence.

TABLE C.11 Office REITs

Company Name	Ticker Symbol	Headquarters City, State	Website Address
Alexandria Real Estate	ARE	Pasadena, CA	www.are.com
Boston Properties Inc.	BXP	Boston, MA	www.bostonproperties.com
Brandywine Realty Trust	BDN	Philadelphia, PA	www.brandywinerealty.com
CIM Commercial Trust Corp.	CMCT	Dallas, TX	www.cimcommercial.com
City Office REIT Inc.	CIO	Dallas, TX	www.cityofficereit.com
Columbia Property Trust	CXP	Brooklyn, NY	www.columbia.reit
Corporate Office Properties Trust	OFC	Columbia, MD	www.copt.com
Cousins Properties Inc.	CUZ	Atlanta, GA	www.cousins.com
Douglas Emmett Inc.	DEI	Santa Monica, CA	www.douglasemmett.com
Easterly Government Ppts Inc.	DEA	Washington, DC	www.easterlyreit.com
Empire State Realty Trust Inc.	ESRT	New York, NY	www.empirestaterealtytrust.com
Equity Commonwealth	EQC	Chicago, IL	www.eqcre.com
Franklin Street Properties	FSP	Wakefield, MA	www.fspreit.com
Highwoods Properties	HIW	Raleigh, NC	www.highwoods.com
Hudson Pacific Properties Inc.	HPP	Los Angeles, CA	www.HudsonPacificProperties.com
Kilroy Realty Corp.	KRC	Los Angeles, CA	www.kilroyrealty.com
Office Properties Income Trust	OPI	Newton, MA	www.opireit.com
Paramount Group Inc.	PGRE	New York, NY	www.paramount-group.com
Piedmont Office Realty Trust	PDM	Atlanta, GA	www.piedmontreit.com
SL Green Realty Corp.	SLG	New York, NY	www.slgreen.com

Sources: Nareit, S&P Global Market Intelligence.

TABLE C.12 Multifamily/Apartment REITs

Company Name	Ticker Symbol	Headquarters City, State	Website Address
Aimco	AIV	Denver, CO	www.aimco.com
American Campus Communities	ACC	Austin, TX	www.americancampus.com
AvalonBay Communities Inc.	AVB	Arlington, VA	www.avalonbay.com
Bluerock Residential Growth	BRG	New York, NY	www.bluerockresidential.com
BRT Apartments Corp.	BRT	Great Neck, NY	www.brtapartments.com
Camden Property Trust	CPT	Houston, TX	www.camdenliving.com
Clipper Realty Inc.	CLPR	Brooklyn, NY	www.clipperrealty.com
Equity Residential	EQR	Chicago, IL	www.equityapartments.com
Essex Property Trust	ESS	San Mateo, CA	www.essex.com
Independence Realty Trust Inc.	IRT	Philadelphia, PA	www.irtliving.com
Investors Real Estate Trust	IRET	Minot, ND	www.iretapartments.com
MAA	MAA	Germantown, TN	www.maac.com
NexPoint Residential Trust Inc.	NXRT	Dallas, TX	www.nexpointliving.com
Preferred Apartment Communities	APTS	Atlanta, GA	www.pacapts.com
UDR Inc.	UDR	Highlands Ranch, CO	www.udr.com

Sources: Nareit, S&P Global Market Intelligence.

TABLE C.13 Manufactured Housing REITs

Company Name	Ticker Symbol	Headquarters City, State	Website Address
Equity LifeStyle Properties	ELS	Chicago, IL	www.equitylifestyleproperties.com
Sun Communities Inc.	SUI	Southfield, MI	www.suncommunities.com
UMH Properties Inc.	UMH	Freehold, NJ	www.umh.reit

Sources: Nareit, S&P Global Market Intelligence.

TABLE C.14 Single-Family Home REITs

Company Name	Ticker Symbol	Headquarters City, State	Website Address
American Homes 4 Rent	AMH	Agoura Hills, CA	www.americanhomes4rent.com
Front Yard Residential Corp.	RESI	Christiansted, VI	www.FrontYardResidential.com
Invitation Homes Inc.	INVH	Dallas, TX	www.invitationhomes.com

Sources: Nareit, S&P Global Market Intelligence.

TABLE C.15 Shopping Center REITs.

Company Name	Ticker Symbol	Headquarters City, State	Website Address
Acadia Realty Trust	AKR	Rye, NY	www.acadiarealty.com
American Finance Trust	AFIN	New York, NY	www.americanfinancetrust.com
Brixmor Property Group Inc.	BRX	New York, NY	www.brixmor.com
Cedar Realty Trust Inc.	CDR	Port Washington, NY	www.cedarrealtytrust.com
Federal Realty Investment	FRT	Rockville, MD	www.federalrealty.com
Kimco Realty Corp.	KIM	Jericho, NY	www.kimcorealty.com
Kite Realty Group Trust	KRG	Indianapolis, IN	www.kiterealty.com
Regency Centers Corp.	REG	Jacksonville, FL	www.regencycenters.com
Retail Opportunity Investments	ROIC	San Diego, CA	www.roireit.net
Retail Properties of America	RPAI	Oak Brook, IL	www.rpai.com
Retail Value Inc.	RVI	Beachwood, OH	www.retailvalueinc.com
RPT Realty	RPT	New York, NY	rptrealty.com
Saul Centers Inc.	BFS	Bethesda, MD	www.saulcenters.com
SITE Centers Corp.	SITC	Beachwood, OH	www.sitecenters.com
Tanger Factory Outlet Centers	SKT	Greensboro, NC	www.tangeroutlet.com
Urban Edge Properties	UE	New York, NY	www.uedge.com
Urstadt Biddle Properties Inc.[a]	UBA	Greenwich, CT	www.ubproperties.com
Weingarten Realty Investors	WRI	Houston, TX	www.weingarten.com
Wheeler REIT Inc.	WHLR	Virginia Beach, VA	www.whlr.us

[a]Nareit also lists Urstadt Biddle Properties, Inc. - Class A shares.
Sources: Nareit, S&P Global Market Intelligence.

TABLE C.16 Mall REITs

Company Name	Ticker Symbol	Headquarters City, State	Website Address
Brookfield Property REIT Inc.	BPYU	New York, NY	www.bpy.brookfield.com/en/bpr
CBL & Associates Properties	CBL	Chattanooga, TN	www.cblproperties.com
Macerich Co.	MAC	Santa Monica, CA	www.macerich.com
Pennsylvania REIT	PEI	Philadelphia, PA	www.preit.com
Simon Property Group	SPG	Indianapolis, IN	www.simon.com
Taubman Centers Inc.	TCO	Bloomfield Hills, MI	www.taubman.com
Washington Prime Group Inc.	WPG	Columbus, OH	www.washingtonprime.com

Sources: Nareit, S&P Global Market Intelligence

TABLE C.17 Freestanding Retail REITs

Company Name	Ticker Symbol	Headquarters City, State	Website Address
Agree Realty Corp.	ADC	Bloomfield Hills, MI	www.agreerealty.com
Alpine Income Property Trust	PINE	Daytona Beach, FL	www.alpinereit.com
Essential Properties Realty Trust	EPRT	Princeton, NJ	www.essentialproperties.com
Four Corners Property Trust	FCPT	Mill Valley, CA	www.fcpt.com
Getty Realty Corp.	GTY	Jericho, NY	www.gettyrealty.com
National Retail Properties	NNN	Orlando, FL	www.nnnreit.com
Postal Realty Trust	PSTL	Cedarhurst, NY	www.postalrealtytrust.com
Realty Income Corp.	O	San Diego, CA	www.realtyincome.com
Seritage Growth Properties	SRG	New York, NY	www.seritage.com
Spirit Realty Capital Inc.	SRC	Dallas, TX	www.spiritrealty.com
STORE Capital Corp.	STOR	Scottsdale, AZ	www.storecapital.com

Sources: Nareit, S&P Global Market Intelligence.

TABLE C.18 Self-Storage REITs

Company Name	Ticker Symbol	Headquarters City, State	Website Address
CubeSmart	CUBE	Malvern, PA	www.cubesmart.com
Extra Space Storage	EXR	Salt Lake City, UT	www.extraspace.com
Global Self Storage	SELF	New York, NY	www.globalselfstorage.us
Life Storage Inc.	LSI	Williamsville, NY	www.lifestorage.com
National Storage Affiliates Trust	NSA	Greenwood Village, CO	www.nationalstorageaffiliates.com
Public Storage	PSA	Glendale, CA	www.publicstorage.com

Sources: Nareit, S&P Global Market Intelligence.

Glossary

The following is a glossary of terms referenced in the REIT industry and throughout this book. Some definitions are based on information provided by Nareit and company-specific documents filed with the SEC; others were sourced from Barron's *Dictionary of Real Estate Terms* and from online resources such as Investopedia.com and Leasing Professionals.com.

adjusted funds from operations (AFFO) As explained more fully in Chapter 11, because it incorporates adjustments for non-cash items and deducts recurring capital expenditures (defined later in this Glossary), AFFO represents a more normalized, recurring measurement of a REITS's FFO (i.e., "earnings"). Please also refer to Chapter 11.

basis points (bps) The daily, often tiny, percentage changes in financial instruments in a portfolio, such as the yield on a fixed-income security, are expressed in basis points. A basis point is equal to 1/100 of a percentage point, so 1% equals 100 basis points.

base rent The minimum rent due to a landlord, as defined in a lease. Please refer to the discussion of rent in Chapter 5.

base (expense) year As explained in Chapter 5, a base year typically is the first year of a lease, during which time the landlord determines the actual taxes and operating expenses associated with a tenant's occupying their space. After the base year, the landlord agrees to pay an expense amount based on base year expenses, and the tenant pays any increases in expenses over the base amount.

C-Corporations A C-corporation is a legal entity that is separate and distinct from its owners. Corporations enjoy most of the rights and responsibilities that individuals possess, such as the right to enter into contracts, loan and borrow money, hire employees, own assets, and pay taxes. The most important aspect of a corporation is limited liability; that is, shareholders of a corporation have the right to participate in the profits, through dividends and/or the appreciation of stock, but are not held personally liable for the company's debts.

capital expenses GAAP requires that certain expenditures be capitalized rather than included in current period operating expenses. There are two primary classifications of capital expenses, or "capex":

1. **Recurring (or replacement) capex** is money spent on improvements to a property that facilitate its leasing and on replacing non-structural elements, such as mechanical systems and HVAC units. Examples of such expenditures include leasing commissions and tenant improvement paid to lease a space, both of which are capitalized into the property's basis and then amortized over the life of the lease.
2. **Non-recurring capex** is money spent on structural elements that increase the economic capacity of the asset (such as expanding the square footage), adding new revenue streams (e.g., adding a parking deck), and also the replacement of major elements after the expiration of its original useful life. Like recurring capex, non-recurring capex dollars are capitalized into the basis of a property. For example, if a property was worth $25 million and the landlord builds a $5 million parking deck, all else being equal the new basis of the property would be $30 million.

As discussed in Table 11.2 in Chapter 11, *only recurring capital expenditures are deducted in calculating AFFO.*

capitalization rate A capitalization rate (or "cap rate") measures the expected unleveraged return of an asset. The cap rate for a property is determined by dividing the property's cash net operating income (NOI, defined later in the Glossary) by the purchase price. Thought of another way, cap rates are the inverse of a price/earnings ratio, where earnings are measured by property-level cash NOI. High cap rates generally indicate higher expected returns and/or greater perceived risks. Please refer to Chapter 11 for additional information.

cash available for distribution (CAD) Also referred to as Funds Available for Distribution (FAD), cash available for distribution better approximates a REIT's free cash flow than AFFO and, therefore, is a more meaningful denominator for determining a REIT's dividend safety. CAD is calculated by subtracting the following items from AFFO: capitalized interest expense and monthly principal and interest payments due on secured debt (excluding maturities). Please see Chapter 11 for more information.

cash NOI Cash NOI adjusts the NOI calculated from a REIT's statement of operations (its income statement) to exclude the effects of straight-lined rent (discussed in Chapter 5). Please see Chapter 11 for more information on cash NOI.

common area maintenance (CAM) "Common areas" are areas within a property that are used by all tenants, such as an office building's lobby, sidewalks, landscaping, parking lot lighting, and snow removal services. As explained in Chapter 5, certain lease structures allow a landlord to charge tenants for their proportionate shares of the additional cost to maintain a property's common areas. CAM charges therefore are additional rent charged for maintenance that benefits all tenants.

cost of capital Cost of capital is the cost a company bears to have a form of equity and debt capital issued and outstanding. The cost of common stock generally is considered to include the dividend rate paid to shareholders plus investors' expected equity growth rate, the two of which typically total between 8% and 12% annually. The cost of preferred equity equals the dividend or "coupon" payment associated with each preferred share and/or unit. The cost of debt capital is the interest rate associated with each type of debt (e.g., mortgage loan or senior note) issued by a company. Please see Chapters 1, 10, and 11 for additional information.

DIVERSIFICATION SEE PORTFOLIO DIVERSIFICATION.

EBITDA Earnings before interest, taxes, depreciation, and amortization.

economic cycle The natural fluctuation of an economy between periods of expansion (growth) and contraction (recession).

economic indicator According to Investopedia.com, an economic indicator is a piece of economic data, such as the weekly employment report, used by investors to interpret the overall health of the economy.

equity market capitalization (EMC) A company's equity market capitalization is calculated by multiplying the stock price times the number of common shares outstanding. If the REIT is an UPREIT or has a DownREIT structure, the number of operating partnership (OP) units outstanding should be added to the common share count before multiplying by the stock price. Please refer to Chapter 11 for additional information.

escalation clauses Provisions in a lease that allow a landlord to pass through increases in operating expenses subject to the first- or "base"-year expense levels. Rent escalations usually occur on an annual basis and tend to be tied to increases in the Consumer Price Index or are expressed as fixed periodic increases. Please refer to Chapter 5 for additional information.

exchange-traded fund (ETF) According to Investopedia.com, an exchange-traded fund (ETF) is a marketable security designed to track the performance of an index, a commodity, bonds, or a basket of assets. Unlike mutual funds, an ETF trades like a common stock on a stock exchange and experiences price changes throughout the day as they are bought and sold. Please also refer to Chapter 1 and 10 for more information.

Fannie Mae The Federal National Mortgage Association (commonly known as Fannie Mae) was established as a federal agency in 1938. In 1968, Congress chartered Fannie Mae as a private shareholder-owned company. Fannie Mae is a government-sponsored enterprise (GSE) that operates in the US secondary mortgage market, rather than making home loans directly to consumers.

fee simple interest Also referred to as "fee simple absolute" and "fee simple estate," fee simple interest in a property indicates the owner has absolute ownership of a property and the unconditional right to dispose of it. For example, most homeowners have a fee simple interest in their homes and can sell the property at their convenience or transfer ownership to an heir upon their deaths.

Freddie Mac Created in 1970, the Federal Home Loan Mortgage Corporation (commonly known as Freddie Mac) is similar to Fannie Mae in that it is a government-sponsored enterprise (GSE) whose mission is to provide liquidity to the secondary mortgage market.

FTSE Nareit indexes Indexes published by Nareit to track the performance of REITs. The FTSE Nareit indexes are not publicly traded; they simply aggregate performance data on the component REITs.

full-service lease A lease in which the tenant pays the landlord a fixed monthly rent that includes an expense stop calculated off the base year. The landlord pays all the monthly expenses associated with operating the property, including utilities, water, taxes, janitorial, trash collection, and landscaping and charges the tenant in subsequent years to the extent operating expenses exceed the expense stop. The tenant gets full service in exchange for the monthly rent and does not have to contract with service providers directly. Please refer to Chapter 5 for additional information.

funds from operations (FFO) A supplemental though more broadly used measurement of REIT earnings, created by Nareit in 1991 and recognized by the SEC in 2003. FFO is the REIT equivalent of earnings. Please refer to Chapter 11 for more detail.

Garn–St. Germain Act of 1982 The federal law that deregulated the savings and loan industry.

generally accepted accounting principles (GAAP) The set of rules considered standard and acceptable by Certified Public Accountants.

Global Industry Classification Standard (GICS) According to the website www.msci.com/gics, MSCI and Standard & Poor's developed the GICS in 1999 to create an efficient investment tool that would capture the breadth, depth, and evolution of industry sectors. GICS is a four-tiered industry classification system that originally consisted of 10 investment sectors, 24 industry groups, 67 industries, and 156 subindustries. In 2016, Real Estate became the 11th GICS sector.

gross absorption According to CBRE (www.cbre.us), the absorption rate is the rate at which rentable space is filled. Gross absorption is a measure of the total square feet leased over a specified period with no consideration given to space vacated in the same geographic area during the same time period. (See also **net absorption**.)

gross lease A lease wherein the tenant pays a fixed monthly rent to the landlord; the landlord pays the property expenses, which includes insurance, utilities, and repairs, and usually property taxes. Please refer to Chapter 5 for additional information.

hedging According to Investopedia.com, a hedge is an investment to reduce the risk of adverse price movements in an asset. Hedging is analogous to taking out an insurance policy. If you own a home in a flood-prone area, you will want to protect yourself financially from the risk of flood damage – to hedge, in other words – by taking out flood insurance.

Internal Revenue Service (IRS) The US government agency responsible for the collection and enforcement of taxes. Established in 1862 by President Lincoln, the IRS operates under the authority of the US Department of the Treasury.

lease A lease is a legal agreement between a landlord (the *lessor*) and a tenant (the *lessee*) whereby the tenant agrees to pay a monthly sum for a defined period of time (*rent*) in exchange for the right to occupy the landlord's space. Please refer to Chapter 5 for additional information.

limited partnership (LP) interests A partnership between at least two partners, one of whom is passive and whose liability in the venture is limited to his amount invested, and the active partner, whose liability in the venture extends beyond his monetary investment. Please refer to Chapter 8 for additional information.

market rent The rate a landlord could charge a tenant to occupy space, based on the competing spaces and current market conditions. Please refer to Chapter 5 for additional information.

modified gross lease A lease in which the tenant pays rent plus the property taxes and insurance, and any increases in these items over the base year. Please refer to Chapter 5 for additional information.

MSCI® US REIT Index (RMZ and RMS) A real-time, price-only index, the ticker symbol for which is RMZ. At December 31, 2019, the RMZ tracked the price movements of 151 equity REITs. Mortgage and hybrid REITs are not included in this index. MSCI® also publishes the RMS, a daily total return version of the RMZ, which encompasses the companies' dividend yields. The RMS is not a real-time index; total returns for the constituent REITs are published at the end of the day.

Nareit Formerly the National Association of Real Estate Investment Trusts, Nareit is the worldwide representative voice for REITs and publicly traded real estate companies with an interest in US real estate and capital markets. Please see www.reit.com for more information.

net absorption Calculated as the amount of occupied square feet at the end of a period, less the amount of square feet leased at the beginning of a period, net absorption measures the square feet leased in a specific geographic area over a fixed period of time, after taking into account any space vacated in the same area during the same period. (See also **gross absorption**.)

net asset value (NAV) An estimate of the current market value of a REIT's tangible assets, including but not limited to its properties, less the sum of all liabilities and obligations. Please refer to Chapter 11 for additional information.

net, double-net, and triple-net lease As described in Chapter 5, there are three levels of "net" when referencing lease structures wherein expenses are paid by the tenant as part of total rent:

1. maintenance, which includes items like utilities, water, janitorial, trash collection, and landscaping;
2. insurance; and
3. taxes.
   - A net lease generally implies that the tenant pays rent and the costs of maintaining the property; the landlord pays the insurance and taxes.

- In a double-net lease, the tenant pays rent, including the taxes and insurance; the landlord pays the maintenance costs.
- In a triple-net lease, the tenant pays rent to the landlord and pays all costs associated with maintenance, insurance, and taxes. The landlord essentially collects monthly "coupon" payments, as if he owned a bond.

net operating income (NOI) The owner's rental revenues from property less all property operating expenses, including taxes and insurance. The term ignores depreciation and amortization expenses as well as interest on loans incurred to finance the property. Please also refer to Chapter 11.

NON-RECURRING CAPEX SEE CAPITAL EXPENSES.

operating partnership unit (OP unit) Units of ownership in a REIT that generally can be exchanged on a one-for-one basis into common stock of the REIT but that are not publicly traded. Please refer to Chapter 8 for more detail.

percentage rents Additional rent payable to the landlord, based on a percentage of the volume of tenant sales generated on a property. The percentage is usually based on base year sales volume. For example, a retailer's lease may require contractual rent plus percentage rents equal to 1% of sales revenue that exceed sales revenue achieved in the first year of operations. Please refer to Chapter 5 for additional information.

portfolio diversification The act of investing in different asset classes and securities (i.e., stocks and bonds) in order to reduce investment risk and to enhance the expected return from an invested amount.

positive spread investing The ability to raise capital at a cost significantly less than the initial returns that can be obtained on real estate investments.

property cycle According to Wikipedia.com, the property cycle is a sequence of recurrent and predictable events reflected in demographic, economic, and emotional factors that affect supply and demand for property.

R&D property Industrial buildings in which research and development (R&D) processes are performed, including any assembly, manufacturing, or office space required to support them. R&D buildings typically have a parking ratio of at least three parking spaces per 1,000 square feet, are one to two stories high, and feature interior clear heights of less than 18 feet.

Real Estate Investment Trust Act of 1960 The federal law that authorized REITs. Its purpose was to allow small investors to pool their investments in real estate to get the same benefits as might be obtained by direct ownership while also diversifying their risks and obtaining professional management.

real estate investment trust (REIT) A corporation or business trust that operates and qualifies to be taxed as a REIT (for federal income tax purposes), and that combines the capital of many investors to own or provide financing for all forms of investment real estate. A REIT is generally not required to pay corporate income tax if it distributes at least 90% of its taxable income to shareholders each year.

REIT Modernization Act of 1999 (RMA) The federal law that further increased REITs' abilities to operate as fully integrated operating companies, primarily by allowing REITs to provide tenant services through taxable REIT subsidiaries (TRSs). The RMA became effective in 2001.

RECURRING CAPEX SEE CAPITAL EXPENSES.

REIT Simplification Act of 1994 Predecessor to the REIT Modernization Act, the REIT Simplification Act was the federal law that streamlined the REIT structure, enabling management teams to operate their companies as more fully integrated businesses.

revenue per available room (RevPAR) The product of a hotel's average daily room rate (ADR) and its daily occupancy rate.

RMZ AND RMS SEE MSCI® US REIT INDEX.

Securities and Exchange Commission (SEC) A government commission created in 1934 by Congress to regulate the securities markets and protect investors. In addition to regulation and protection, it also monitors the corporate takeovers in the United States. The SEC is composed of five commissioners appointed by the US President and approved by the Senate.

straight-lined rent In compliance with GAAP, REITs "straight-line" the rental income they receive by reporting the average annual rent to be received over the life of a lease instead of the actual cash received. The straight-lined rent adjustment REITs report is the amount to be added to or subtracted from GAAP rents to arrive at cash rents received or to be collected. Please refer to Chapter 5.

taxable REIT subsidiary (TRS) Taxable REIT subsidiaries are stand-alone corporations for tax purposes that are owned directly or indirectly by a REIT.

Created as part of the REIT Modernization Act of 1999, TRSs allow REITs to compete more effectively with other landlords by enabling REITs to provide nontraditional services to tenants or provide traditional real estate management services to third parties. TRSs also allow REITs the (limited) ability to invest in and derive income from nonrental real estate assets.

Tax Reform Act of 1986 The federal law that substantially altered the real estate investment landscape by permitting REITs not only to own but also to operate and manage most types of income-producing commercial properties. It also eliminated real estate tax shelters that had attracted capital from investors based on the amount of losses that could be created.

total market capitalization The sum of a REIT's equity market capitalization, plus the liquidation value of any preferred equity outstanding, and the principal amounts of debt outstanding.

total return A stock's dividend income plus capital appreciation, before taxes and commissions.

transparency Corporate transparency describes the extent to which a corporation's actions are observable by outsiders.

Treasury Inflation-Protected Securities (TIPS) First issued by the US government in 1997, TIPS are a Treasury security that is indexed to inflation. According to Vanguard Investment Counseling & Research, TIPS are like most other bonds in that they are issued with a fixed coupon interest rate and a fixed maturity date. Unlike traditional bonds, TIPS have a principal value that the Treasury raises (or lowers) each month to keep pace with inflation. As a result, the semiannual coupon payments to investors also change, because they are derived by applying the fixed coupon rate to an inflation-adjusted principal amount.

triple-net lease See **net, double-net, and triple-net lease**, as well as Chapter 5.

UPREIT Umbrella partnership real estate investment trust. Please refer to Chapter 8 for information.

Index

Note: Page references in *italics* refer to figures and tables.